Finding God in the Devil's Music

T0041070

Finding God in the Devil's Music

Critical Essays on Rock and Religion

Edited by
ALEX DiBLASI *and*
ROBERT McPARLAND

McFarland & Company, Inc., Publishers
Jefferson, North Carolina

ALSO OF INTEREST FROM ROBERT MCPARLAND

Crosby, Stills, Nash and Young: Music to Change the World (McFarland, 2019)

Myth and Magic in Heavy Metal Music (McFarland, 2018)

Science Fiction in Classic Rock: Musical Explorations of Space, Technology and the Imagination, 1967–1982 (McFarland, 2017)

LIBRARY OF CONGRESS CATALOGUING-IN-PUBLICATION DATA

Names: DiBlasi, Alex, 1987– | McParland, Robert.
Title: Finding god in the devil's music : critical essays on rock and religion / edited by Alex DiBlasi and Robert McParland.
Description: Jefferson, North Carolina : McFarland & Company, 2019 | Includes bibliographical references and index.
Identifiers: LCCN 2018048482 | ISBN 9781476671505 (paperback : acid free paper) ∞
Subjects: LCSH: Rock music—Religious aspects.
Classification: LCC ML3921.8.R63 F56 2019 | DDC 781.66/112—dc23
LC record available at https://lccn.loc.gov/2018048482

BRITISH LIBRARY CATALOGUING DATA ARE AVAILABLE

ISBN 978-1-4766-7150-5 (softcover : acid free paper)
ISBN 978-1-4766-3394-7 (ebook)

Front cover images © 2019 iStock

Printed in the United States of America

McFarland & Company, Inc., Publishers
  Box 611, Jefferson, North Carolina 28640
  www.mcfarlandpub.com

Dedicated to the loving memory
of Eric J. DiBlasi, Sr. (1956–2019)
without whom this book never would
have happened.—Sai Ram, Alex and Bob

Table of Contents

Preface

During the past sixty years rock music has been filled with a spirit that might be considered "religious." This spirit has animated hope, vision, and quests for cultural alternatives. Rock has been energized by the spiritual quests of some of its performers. Audiences have made claims that music has prompted experiences of transcendence. There has also been an ongoing tension between rock and aspects of religious life. In this collection, ten contributors — musicologists, scholars of theology and religious studies, and cultural studies theorists — examine this phenomenon from a variety of viewpoints. This book, with its strong emphasis on rock music makers and personalities, is designed to appeal to both secular and religiously oriented readers. We define rock music as a popular music emerging from the early rock and roll of the mid- to late 1950s, based in the blues/rhythm and blues and country western roots, evolving through 1960s British invasion bands and American pop groups into the variety of genres that appeared in the 1970s and 1980s and have persisted since. We have taken a broadly comparative approach to religion that corresponds well with the ecumenical tendencies of baby boomers, Generation X, and later cohorts of American and British rock music listeners described by sociologists of religion. This collection of essays investigates the relationship of rock music with religious experience from sociological, theological, and musicological perspectives. Contributors have made use of artist biographies, record and concert reviews, videos, published interviews, rock music forums, fan testimonials, social media interaction, personal experience, and analytical tools from the practices of musicology, sociology, theology, and cultural studies.

This book began when Alex DiBlasi organized the panels on rock and religion at the American Popular Culture Conference in Chicago in 2014. Readers may contact Alex at alexcharlesdiblasi@gmail.com or contact Robert McParland at mcparlandr@felician.edu.

Introduction

Rock music has throughout the years been in a dance with religion. For some listeners, rock itself has been like a spiritual experience: a path to transcendence. The blues, father of rock, is laden with a spiritual tug of war between good and evil. Consider the case of Rev. Robert Wilkins, a bluesman who rerecorded his 1929 blues tune "That's No Way to Get Along" some 35 years later as a retelling of Jesus' parable of the prodigal son. Suggestive of their newfound left-hand spiritual path, The Rolling Stones would cover "Prodigal Son" on the same album featuring Mick and Keith's own hymn to Lucifer, "Sympathy for the Devil." Alongside the blues, spirituals and gospel alike inform the musical backgrounds of Elvis and Little Richard. A spiritual experience Little Richard had in 1957, when he caught an earlier flight and avoided a fatal crash, inspired him to pursue a career in the ministry. The following year, he was touring the United States as a big-tent revival preacher.

A decade later, English rock artists like Pete Townshend and George Harrison turned toward the East, with both making their first forays into charity through causes connected with their respective spiritual masters, Meher Baba and Bhaktivedanta Swami Prabhupada. From The Rolling Stones' "Sympathy for the Devil" and The Beatles' "Magical Mystery Tour" to the spiritual quests of the Woodstock generation, the search for authenticity has extended to rock's successors: grunge, heavy metal, and punk. There is a spiritual flavor to the quest through music for the heart and soul, for heightened consciousness, and the embrace of new experience and new sounds.

These essays offer a look at rock music across categories of hard rock, punk, reggae, and heavy metal. Whereas these genres, aside from reggae, frequently have been considered resistant or even strongly opposed to religious belief, contributors to this book describe how much of the work in these genres is involved with spiritual interests. The writers provide examples of the appropriation of religious resources such as biblical imagery and religious language. They explore public fascination with religion as a platform for expression and social critique. Candace Ursala Grissom explores the religious dialogue of Black Sabbath. Gavin F. Hurley, considering heavy metal, and James E. Willis III, studying Nine Inch Nails, show how negation and critique of institutional arrangements correlates with a dialectics of belief in a significant movement beyond the profane. Karen Fournier examines Christian hardcore punk. This meeting of rock music forms that may at first seem antagonistic to religion is complemented by Sabatino DiBernardo's deconstructive reading of binary oppositions such as secular/religious and sacred/profane.

Rock artists have drawn upon religious topics and imagery within their song lyrics and their performances. The religious sensibilities of rock music artists are discussed in Alex DiBlasi's study of Pete Townshend and in Erin E. Bauer's inquiry into the religious transformations of Matisyahu. DiBlasi probes Pete Townshend's musical art and his relationship with the teachings of God-claimant Meher Baba. Bauer observes Matisyahu's movement from Reconstructionist Judaism to Hasidism and then his shedding of this persona. Erika M. Nelson Mukherjee explores Duncan Sheik, Buddhism and the theater. Morgan Shipley points out that rock music creativity has, at times, included a fascination with mystical experience and alternative consciousness. Shipley investigates the interior journey of The Beatles' "Tomorrow Never Knows." Robert McParland makes use of psychology and theological resources to inquire about the mysteries in songwriting, improvisational music making, and how participation in music may convey a sense of the ineffable. McParland reflects upon the work of Van Morrison, George Harrison, Bob Dylan, in an essay on rock music and inspiration.

The aim of this book is to explore the relationship between religion/spirituality and rock music. Much has been written on the history of religious music itself, but not much exists on the role religion and spirituality have played in popular song. Music itself has long been considered a spiritual and even meditative practice; this book seeks to investigate rock music as an expression of religious inquiry, religious devotion, and even as a religious experience itself. From the rise of the American evangelical movement to the widespread introduction of Eastern philosophies in the West, the past century has seen a radical change in the religious makeup of Western culture. Rock artists across the world have incorporated both "new" and old religious beliefs into their work. (The word "new" is placed in quotation marks, with respect to ideas that predate Western civilization.) It is our aim to take a similarly ecumenical approach with the essays in this book, covering a range of philosophies and belief systems. In gathering these essays, we welcomed perspectives from a variety of backgrounds—music, religious studies, cultural studies, anthropology. There are also many subjects that could be explored in a book on rock and religion. Further studies might include inquiries into:

- Comparative religion/world religions
- The appearance of religion or spirituality in the work of major rock artists and their spiritual journeys—conversion, life changes, etc.
- Wonder and a sense of the Divine
- Seeking transcendence
- Relationships between music/rock music and religion (i.e., the "God rock" movement of the 1970s, the Hare Krishna movement, etc.)
- Heavy metal and organized religion
- Seeking and spiritual exploration
- Millenialism, apocalypticism
- The quiet, meditation, contemplation and music
- Mythology
- Mystery
- Salvation
- Values of respect, diversity, charity, love, compassion, hope, faith, justice, wisdom, kindness, care
- Parables
- Community
- Prayer
- Prophecy

- The afterlife (heaven and hell, reincarnation)
- Celebration
- Ecstasy
- Rock and ritual
- Charism
- Rock drawing upon black gospel spirituals
- Psalms
- Peace/shanti/shalom
- Rock music and religious dialogue
- Theodicy (that is, explaining suffering in a world designed by a good God)
- Soul
- Karma
- Musical pilgrimages (Liverpool, Memphis/Graceland, Haight-Ashbury)
- The Divine/Holy Spirit/Great Spirit
- Angels/angelic visions
- Atonement
- Haggadah: religious storytelling
- Songs that quote religious scripture (the Bible, the Tao, Bhagavad Gita, Koran, etc.)
- Lamentations (songs for a broken world, modern chants of misery like those in the Hebrew Bible)
- Miracles

The plan for this book is principally to address the relationship between religion/spirituality and rock music. It was the aim of both editors to include essays addressing all major world religions. As such, we asked that the contributors write as objectively as possible, avoiding dogmatic statements, agendas, or arguments with specific religious paths.

In our investigation of rock music we have sought discursive categories:

origin myths, narratives, rules of conduct and prohibitions, saints and martyrs, prophets. To locate these elements our contributors have investigated commentary from journalists, scholars, rock musicians, and rock music listeners. We investigate rock music *as* religion, investigate the "religious" character of rock concert audiences, and we ask how spiritual practices may affect creativity. Our central argument is that religion is conspicuously present in rock music, including in unexpected ways. Religious expression in rock music must be looked at beyond the sectarian categories of obvious market categories like contemporary Christian or gospel music. We have followed a broadly ecumenical approach that includes Judeo-Christian traditions, Eastern religious perspectives, and bands (like Black Sabbath) that at first glance may not appear to express any religious commitments but are clearly fascinated by religious phenomena and symbols. Such bands stimulate the interest of rock fans in the sacred and spirituality, although this awakening to religious wonder is often accompanied by resistance to institutional religious forms.

Our goal in selecting these essays has been to offer diversity and balance. We explore rock's rhetoric and imagery alongside religious images and speech. Contributors examine rock as religion and how rock and religion mirror each other. Overall, we subscribe to Ninian Smart's model of the discourses of religion (ethical, ritual, experiential, institutional, material). We are particularly interested in comparing rock rituals with religious ritual, evaluating purported experiences of transcendence and the experience of community, and recognizing the impact the material culture of recordings, videos, concert merchandise, items exchanged by fan communities which may be compared with an exchange of relics. This volume explores the work of rock music artists, their commitments to religious paths or their interpretations of spirituality, and the enthusiasms of fan cultures as a meaningful engagement with religion in a modern context.

The Religious Rock Meditations of Black Sabbath

Candace Ursala Grissom

A middle-aged businessman stands in the middle of a black and white, dystopic vision of Times Square as an electric guitar plays contemplatively in the background. In both his mind's eye and surrounding him on multiple Jumbotrons, images of the heavy metal band Black Sabbath play—a retrospective intended to prompt introspection. The man lets his briefcase fall from his hand as he drops to his knees in a worshipful, supplicant pose. He gazes upward, as if looking to the heavens for guidance, while the images of the band fade into a montage of boardroom scenes and headlines, suggestive of the casually menacing powers that be who are the thinly veiled masterminds behind the evils of modern society. Wars, economic crises, and human rights disasters scream out across the headlines, while the members of the board meeting nonchalantly smoke cigars and snooze. The image returns to the businessman, who looks up from his prayerful meditation, now more alert to the problems of society that surround him. His eyes have been opened to the fact that he is living in and working to support the big lie of the machine that, according to the lyric has either killed God or called His existence and involvement in the human cause into serious question. But what has caused this revelation? Once again, through the mind's eye of the businessman, the audience sees the answer.

For over 45 years, the religious rock mediations of Black Sabbath have caused fans to question the mechanisms of modern existence and to ponder the origins of humanity's greatest evils. As this video from their most recent album, *13*, demonstrates, Black Sabbath has always been a controversial band: one that is not afraid to question reality in hopes of mastering it, even if such questioning results in accusations of devil-worship and blasphemy. As a result, Sabbath's members have become legends in the rock community, regarded as not just icons but modern-day prophets, preaching the gospel of rock and roll resistance and rebellion against the decidedly sinister status quo. Yet, what exactly is that gospel? What does it advocate, and what does it admonish?

The aforementioned video for Black Sabbath's 2013 hit, "God Is Dead," suggests the answers to these questions by offering images of a full-circle retrospective, showing that Sabbath has always been more than a heavy metal freak show, demonstrating that they have been concerned with the direction of society since their origins during the Vietnam era, and implying that they have been offering guidance through their music and lyrics since that time. Yet, the true origin of the answers lies in another question that is the first line from the first song, also called "Black Sabbath," recorded by the band in 1970. In the song, Ozzy Osbourne sings over guitarist Tony Iommi's plodding and deliberate diminished fifth riffs for God to help save him from a mysterious, robed and fiery-eyed figure in black, who tells him that he has been chosen as the One to help fulfill the secret desires of others. These evil longings that Geezer Butler's lyrics describe so vividly are clear and ancient. Pride and vanity; greed, gluttony, and sloth; envy and the wrath used to carry out these devil's desires: such a mediation on the seven deadly sins could only have been written by a practicing Catholic, whom Butler has been since childhood, but who also has watched the world with eyes that couldn't forget the kind of paradoxical society that Butler and his bandmates grew up in in post–World War II Birmingham, England. As the serpentine rhythm of Bill Ward's drumline suggests in the song, Satan can take his time, because modern men and women will flock to him willingly, begging to have their desires fulfilled. Further, Satan is so strong in the latter half of the 20th century that he can even point out and select the completely unready and terrified man whom he chooses to toy with as an opponent in his struggle for the soul of humanity: the laughably mad Ozzy Osbourne. And yet, almost a half-century later, perhaps we see that the Devil should not have been so smug in his dismissal of four working-class Brummie boys. Clearly, there was more to them than he, or anyone else, realized. Therefore, the answer to Ozzy's spiritual question about the devilish figure must begin with a story about the origins of Black Sabbath's members.

Growing up in bombed-out, post-industrial Birmingham, Ozzy and crew would have found little to relate to in the peace, love, and happiness rhetoric of the 1960s. By 1968, when he placed an ad in a local music store as a vocalist looking for a band, Ozzy had dropped out of high school (after being severely bullied by both teachers and other students for his dyslexia and general different-ness) as well as working turns in both an auto factory tuning car horns and as a puke-remover in a Digbeth slaughterhouse, before turning to burglary as a means of making a living. As Ozzy stated in his 2009 autobiography, no one in run-down Aston, England, could relate to the music coming out of the counterculture movement from Haight-Ashbury:

> Who gave a dog's arse about what people were doing in San Francisco, anyway? The only flowers anyone saw in Aston were the ones they threw in the hole after you when you croaked it at the age of fifty-three 'cos you worked yourself to death. I hated those hippy-dippy songs, man. *Really* hated them [46].

Thus, the natural reaction for a frustrated young singer who was disillusioned by the discrepancies he saw between the drudgery of blue-collar English life and the Mother Earth aesthetics that popular culture was desperate to dump on him, was to find a lyricist who had a similarly damaged, yet still inquisitive spirit, and who could help him give voice to these concerns.

Enter one Terence "Geezer" Butler, a vegetarian, Catholic bass player, also from Aston, who was working a day job as an accountant but who was well-read in metaphysical philosophy and popular occult mythologies that were circulating at the time. In numerous interviews given over the years, Geezer claims to have gained inspiration for the idea of the original "Black Sabbath" song's lyrics from several sources, which included the following: the 1963 film *Black Sabbath*, starring Boris Karloff, the novel (1934) and subsequent film adaptation (1968) of Dennis Wheatley's *The Devil Rides Out* (a clear indictment of the evils of modern excess among the rich), a then-popular occult magazine series called *Man, Myth, and Magic*, and a 16th century grimoire that Ozzy found in a used bookshop and gave to Geezer, who read it, had a nightmare about it, woke up to find it mysteriously missing, and then wrote a song about the menacing, robed figure whom he had seen. Still, despite these various literary and cinematic inspirations, Ozzy and Geezer felt that there were still pieces missing to complete their musical meditations.

As fate would have it, these missing members turned out to be guitarist/astral projection practitioner Tony Iommi and jazz drummer Bill Ward, who answered the music shop ad titled, "Ozzy Zig Needs a Gig." When the group first got together, they played blues-influenced rock covers, while working through a series of unsatisfactory name and image changes, from The Polka Tulk Blues Band (so named after Ozzy's mom's brand of talcum powder) to Earth (which everyone liked, except that it was already being used by another band). Ultimately, the four knew that they had to find some way to stand out from the crowd of other talented bands then forming in their social circles, including Led Zeppelin. Always the most practical member of the group, it was through Tony that Geezer and Ozzy came to the conclusion that the best way to reach musical audiences was to give them what they wanted, namely horror-themed music to match the rising popularity of horror films and fiction. As Tony put it, "Isn't it strange how people pay money to frighten themselves? Maybe we should stop doing blues and write scary music instead" (Osbourne 82). From this inspiration, Tony began experimenting with tritones, or "Devil's intervals," in constructing his guitar riffs (Iommi 54). After telling his bandmates the origins of tritone religious symbolism, namely that the chords were banned by the medieval Catholic Church for being frightening and powerful enough to summon the Devil, the four decided that they had found a signature sound. Geezer and Tony finished out the lyrics and after playing a few gigs, the band was signed to a record deal and went into the studio to record their first album in January 1970. According to Ozzy, Tony had judged the pop culture audience of that moment in time perfectly. As Ozzy stated in his autobiography, they gained attention from the new name, sound, and image:

> The name Black Sabbath made a big difference, I think. At the time there was an occult author called Dennis Wheatley, whose books were all over the best-seller list, Hammer Horror films were doing massive business at the cinemas, and the Manson murders were all over the telly, so anything with a dark edge was in big demand. Don't get me wrong, I'm sure we could've done it on the strength of the music alone. But sometimes, when it comes to getting a deal, all these little things have to come together at the right time. You need a bit of luck, basically [91].

In all likelihood, Ozzy's assessment of the cultural climate that allowed Black Sabbath to find a market early on correctly gave credit to "luck." However, Bill Ward thought that the source of this luck was anything but random. In a memorable and often reprinted interview with author Steven Rosen, Bill discussed many spooky coincidences that happened to the band during their early years, including several occasions in which all four members recalled having the same dream that translated upon waking into songs for their first few albums. Bill also claimed that at rehearsals, he often felt the presence of a "fifth member" in the group, explaining it thusly: "The fifth member of Black Sabbath was whatever the phenomenon was. A lot of times, we didn't write the fucking songs at all. We showed up and something else wrote them for us. We were conduits" (Clerk 21). Apparently, Ozzy's father agreed. Happy for his son's newfound success, but still wanting to offer him some sort of spiritual protection from what he also saw as supernatural forces guiding the band, Mr. Osbourne handmade in his metal shop an aluminum cross for each member, with his name etched on the front. To this day, the members still wear these crosses or their replicas, recast in gold, onstage every night.

Thus began Black Sabbath's rise to musical fame on the oddly mismatched wings of supposed occultism coupled with social commentary. Their second album, *Paranoid*, also released in 1970, contains two particularly notable examples of this phenomenon. In "War Pigs," one of the album's more memorable tracks, Ozzy sings about military generals gathered in a manner similar to witches at black masses, which is a clear reference to what Sabbath biographer Carol Clerk has called "a protest song, condemning the war in Vietnam and the hypocrisies of the politicians and the propagandists who sent young men off to die in the jungles" (25). The song culminates after the so-called war pigs have been reduced to crawling on their knees toward an apocalyptic Judgment Day, while Satan, the true power behind their work, laughs and flies away to wreak destruction through some other power-hungry governmental pawns. In contrast, with "Iron Man," another iconic song from *Paranoid*, audiences are treated to a different kind of metaphorical warning, this time against the nefariously transformative power of industry and big business instead of governmental war machines. Considering that all four members of the band grew up in the post-industrial, bombed-out and never-repaired wasteland of 1960s Birmingham, it is not surprising that they would choose to speak out in song against the ravages left behind by technological advancement as well. As Geezer Butler stated in an interview with Carol Clerk about his mindset when writing the lyrics for "Iron Man," "I wrote it about a guy who's blasted off into space and sees the future of the world, which isn't very good. Then he goes through a magnetic storm and is turned into iron. He's trying to warn everyone about the future, but he can't speak, so everyone is taking the mickey out of him all the time, and he just doesn't care in the end" (28). Ozzy adds further, "He goes a bit barmy and starts killing people. He tries to do good, but in the end, it turns to bad" (Clerk 28). Touching a cultural nerve about fear of the decline of Western industrial power and its odd juxtaposition with the rising age of space exploration, all taking place during a decade of sociopolitical upheaval and war back on Earth, the song was Sabbath's greatest hit for 45 years, coming in as a single at #2 on the Billboard charts, and cementing Black Sabbath's place in rock iconography as prophets of pop culture.

Regardless of their rising status as harbingers of the apocalypse cleverly disguised as rock gods, the original members of Black Sabbath were curiously unable to predict the cause of the first cycle of their demise. Although the band had always drunk excessively, smoked pot, and dabbled in other substances, it was not until their tour of the United States in support of their third album, *Master of Reality*, that the members of Black Sabbath began using cocaine. Although Sabbath extolled the virtues of using marijuana in the song "Sweet Leaf," listeners can hear a distinct change in their attitude with their move toward harder drug use, cocaine in particular, with the track "Snowblind" from their uncharacteristically, unimaginatively titled fourth album, *Vol. 4*. In "Sweet Leaf," Geezer wrote that smoking pot was a "cure-all," a way to "fill empty lives, lift depression, and help its users feel free and clear" (Clerk 34). In contrast, the lyrics of "Snowblind" demonstrate a knowledge not only of the pleasures of cocaine use, but also an awareness of its destructiveness, as well as the drug's tendency to leave users emotionally cold, alone, and without capacity for human empathy (*Vol. 4*). Perhaps this is why Ozzy has claimed that completing the *Master of Reality* album ended the first cycle of Black Sabbath's existence. As he has stated, "*Master of Reality* was a turning point. That was the last real Sabbath album, as far as I am concerned" (Clerk 33). Once again, Ozzy's self-evaluation appears accurate, in retrospect. When one considers Sabbath's original creative direction, namely using spiritual and horrific images to call the values of modern society into question, then it is easy to see those motivations still behind the *Master of Reality* album, in tracks such as the pro–Christian "After Forever," the battle cry to fight for young people to fight for peace in the face of a nuclear war generated by their parents that is "Children of the Grave," and even in their one self-proclaimedly Satanic song, "Lord of this World," in which Ozzy sings about how the modern world is so possessed with Satan, that he has replaced all natural tendencies for self-healing and redemption through religious confession. Further, the band preaches urgently to their fans in the song, "Into the Void," to reject the evils of war, racial prejudice, and industrial destruction of the environment for profit, saying to instead to seek out peace, love, and happiness in an idealistic future, while leaving the Earth to Satan and his materialistic followers. However, this gospel of rock, although present in *Vol. 4*, is somewhat overshadowed by the "Changes," to use a track from the album as a reference point, to their overall worldview.

By 1972, the band's primary mindset was all about drugs, not metaphysical meditations on the state of humanity and its indulgences. Although they continued to point out the dangers of the rich and their excesses as the source of the Devil's power in society, such warnings begin to seem hollow when coming from the mouths of wealthy, cocaine-addicted, hedonistic rock stars, with the entire world at their feet, instead of from four down-and-out kids from Birmingham. In short, by the time they produced *Vol. 4*, Black Sabbath's members had sold their souls, not for rock and roll, but for bags of coke, symbolic of the hypnotic allure of Satan's tendencies to push successful people into endless, ouroboric cycles of self-indulgence followed by self-destruction.

One might wonder then, how did Black Sabbath continue to soldier on, even through the loss of all its original members, save Tony Iommi, only to reunite in a new century and produce *13*, the only number one album of their career, albeit 45 years in the making? Why did they feel it was time once again to preach the gospel of rock and roll rebellion for a new generation of fans and haters in the 21st century? The answer lies in the cyclic thought processes of two of the band's original members, Geezer Butler and Ozzy Osbourne. To lead into this examination of the possible motivating factors behind *13*, I must engage in a bit of autobiographical digression…

Growing up as I did in a small town in north Alabama, there was a water tower with one name spray-painted on it: Ozzy. I wondered who this person was, who was so bold as to climb a five-story ladder, just to display his name for the world to see. At the time, I had no idea that fans painted graffiti also. So, I did the natural thing for a third-grader to do. I asked my Mom about the name. "Oh, him," she replied, dismissively waving her hand. "He's just some guy who bites the heads off of bats and sings about the Devil. Don't pay any attention to him. He's been around forever." If her response had been, "Oh, him … he's the guy who stands on the street corner handing out thousand dollar bills," I could not have been more intrigued. I sought out and listened to Black Sabbath's albums, as many as I could find. Flash forward to about twenty-five years later … and there I was, listening to their latest album, *13*, one Sunday morning. As I flipped through the channels, I stumbled upon EWTN, the Catholic network. They were showing an old rerun of a sermon by a man considered by many today to be the first international televangelist, Bishop Fulton Sheen. The topic of Sheen's sermon was "The Death of God." As I listened to the words of Sheen's sermon while the second track of *13*, "God Is Dead," played softly in the background, my jaw dropped. The question being raised and answered by the rock star and the televangelist were both word-for-word the same, "Is God dead?" and "I don't believe that God is dead." Immediately, my mind began to wander. Had the members of Black Sabbath seen this sermon? And had it influenced them, almost 45 years later, to write the most popular album of their career by returning to the deepest thematic roots of their music? What in 21st century society had awakened the sleeping lion of Sabbath's creativity? I had to know the answers to these questions, so I began researching Fulton Sheen in hopes of comparing him to Sabbath.

I found more than I could have ever hoped to connect the two spiritual guides with polar opposite lifestyles, but who nevertheless preached the same gospel. Most obviously, Sheen references the work of atheist philosopher Friedrich Nietzsche, and his "Parable of a Madman," written as part of his 1882 volume, *The Gay Science*. In the "Parable," a madman, running the streets with a lantern, proclaims the truth as he sees it, "God is dead … and we have killed Him" (Nietzsche). Contrast this with the song, "Diary of a Madman," on Ozzy's second solo album after the initial breakup of Black Sabbath, in which he opines whether he can ask the voices that he hears in the darkness a question in hopes of preserving his mental health. The question that Ozzy seems to want to ask, so that he can save himself, might be interpreted as an indictment, that surely Nietzsche must be wrong. There must be a God, or fate, or something controlling the world, right? Otherwise, how might a petty thief from Birmingham become one of the most successful singers of all time? Thus, when Ozzy asks whether God is dead, he fears the worst, that as Nietzsche said, God and the potential for eternal peace that he brings to the world is dead, and modern capitalist society has killed him. Yet, Ozzy, like Bishop

Sheen but unlike Nietzsche, still hopes for the best, singing in "God Is Dead" about his awareness of man's current state of suspension in the struggle between spiritual darkness and light. From the songs on Black Sabbath's latest album, *13*, it is easy to see how Ozzy seems to view himself and the rest of the band as sort of a group of latter-day Nietzsche's, albeit ones being pulled away from the more sinister German's philosophy on their left shoulders while simultaneously being pushed by the angel of Catholicism, as voiced by Bishop Sheen, on their right. In short, Black Sabbath, with Ozzy as its leading madman, gives voice to the sacred cause of hope for the future, whether on Earth or in some yet-to-be-determined location of Paradise outside of this world. After all, as Ozzy sings in "You Can't Kill Rock and Roll," religion and law are both superseded by an even more powerful, perpetually regenerative force: rock and roll. Thus, if the excesses of modern life can't kill rock and roll, then they can't kill God. This entanglement of the sacred and profane has made Black Sabbath the subject of controversy, praise, and ridicule for 45 years and counting. But as his the title of his 2011 documentary states, *God Bless Ozzy Osbourne* for trying.

All that remains is to connect the dots of influence, to show how Ozzy and Geezer, the band's primary lyricists, might have had access to various television programs and books that were circulating just prior to the first Black Sabbath album, and which the two might have chosen to recall now, in the twilight of their careers, when the Final Tour was looming in 2016.

Geezer Butler was raised a Catholic. He would have been seventeen and still living at home during the year that Sheen's sermons on the Death of God were making their way across the Atlantic to British television stations. Sheen had a considerable following in the Catholic communities of England, and by 1969 had become an Archbishop in Wales, so it is possible that he and a young Geezer Butler may have crossed paths, if only on opposite sides of a television screen. In fact, it is more highly probable than merely possible that Geezer watched a significant number of Sheen's sermons with his strict Catholic parents, and from that point, held onto his subconscious considerations about the Death of God until the proper time to use them, 45 years later.

Further, in numerous interviews regarding the release of *13*, Ozzy said that he was inspired to assist in the writing of songs for the latest album, *13*, by a *Time* magazine cover article, published in April 1966, that he claimed to have seen recently, entitled, "Is God Dead?" The only problem with this assertion is that Ozzy's recollection might be a bit hazy. After all, that article was published 47 years before Ozzy helped write the songs for *13*. Of course, it is entirely possible that Ozzy is telling the truth as he sees it, given his unique mental state after years of drug use. That for Ozzy, time has come full circle once again. Things that were once the concerns of Americans and Englishmen, such as national involvement in unwinnable wars for monetary gain, excessive drug use leading to decomposition of society by rendering its youth unable or unwilling to think critically, racial profiling and discrimination, and even the fight to preserve the natural environment in the face of ever-expanding industrialism, are once again at the forefront of the world's conscience. Therefore, the answer to why audiences around the world have been receptive to Black Sabbath's spiritual messages now more than ever is simple. In 1970, Sabbath was a prophetic band, way ahead of its time in predicting what would become of our socioeconomic culture. Today, Sabbath merely shines light from the proverbial Lamp of Diogenes into the darkest corners of our collective cultural memory, in hopes of causing us to remember the state world culture was in during the late '60s and early '70s, and as a result, to not stumble blindly through the same mistakes along such pathways again.

And so, to use the name of the title track from *13*, here we are once again at the "End of the Beginning." During the Age of Aquarius, peace, love and understanding comprised the countercultural rhetoric, but foreign wars, hedonistic consumerism, futility of drug law enforcement, vast economic decline, and massive distrust and disengagement with governmental authority were the issues that truly maintained their grip on youth culture. Amidst this downward spiral, cultural demons were conjured and given some degree of venting through horror films. Yet Black Sabbath performed the first rock and roll cultural exorcisms, and they continue to perform them in today's strangely similar world. Audiences need only look at Sabbath's video for "End of the Beginning" in comparison to their one for "God Is Dead" from the same album. In the former video, the band is shown as they currently look now, not in their youth, as they are shown in the latter video. "End of the Beginning" is basically a concert film, showing Sabbath evangelizing the gospel of rock and roll to the masses. Preaching his latest gospel, Ozzy cautions his listeners about the perils of becoming what he calls robot ghosts, or automated shells of their true selves, merely shuffling through the drudgery of daily life. Through the song, "End of the Beginning," audiences see at last the true identity of the black-robed figure whom Ozzy referred to in Black Sabbath's very first song. This specter is their own image—but changed: A hollow, robotic ghost of themselves, left over from when they were young, hopeful, and foolish, after decades of relentless analysis and endless coping mechanisms employed in futile attempts to prove to themselves that they have not strayed from the rock and roll gospel of individuality and rebellion. Hearing these songs again in retrospect, the original generation of Black Sabbath fans at last must realize that they have become the very demons that they feared in the 1970s.

What is this Devil that stands before us then, threatening the world with its greed and its rage? It is ourselves, only come full-circle, in a burnt-out, sold-out, dystopic future, so obvious as to be unidentifiable by anyone except madmen. Fortunately for now, we still have Black Sabbath, those madmen who exorcise society's demons through the illuminating power of rock and roll. Are we at the end of the beginning, or the beginning of the end in our cultural struggle for spiritual freedom? For now, that question remains unanswered. After Black Sabbath is no more, who will draw the next magic circle of musical protection? And perhaps more importantly, who among us will step inside?

WORKS CITED

Clerk, Carol. *Diary of a Madman: Ozzy Osbourne, the Stories Behind the Songs*. Thunder's Mouth, 2002.

Elson, John T. "Is God Dead?" Cover of *Time Magazine*. 8 Apr. 1966.

Iommi, Tony. *Iron Man*. Da Capo, 2011.

Nietzsche, Friedrich. *The Complete Works of Friedrich Nietzsche: The First Complete and Authorized English Translation. Vol. 10: The Joyful Wisdom (La Gaya Scienza)*, 1882. Translated by Thomas Common. Macmillan, 1924.

Osbourne, Ozzy. "Diary of a Madman." *Diary of a Madman*, Jet, 1981.

_____. *I Am Ozzy*. Grand Central, 2009.

Venerable Bishop Fulton John Sheen. "The Death of God." *YouTube*. Uploaded by Sensus Fidelium, 25 Jan. 2013, https://www.youtube.com/watch?v=gPa-EtQS0ls. Originally broadcast 1966. Accessed 26 Feb. 2017.

Faith in Something Bigger

Pete Townshend, Meher Baba and Tommy

ALEX DIBLASI

The Who's creative trajectory took its share of twists during the 1960s. The group started out as a squad of angry young men, mean-mugging on their record sleeves like the gang of hoodlums they probably would have been had it not been for music. Following the more artsy whims of their chief songwriter Pete Townshend, as well as producer/creative director Kit Lambert, The Who took a turn as a Pop Art group. Townshend became obsessed with the group's image. Discussions of the band's "look" in the 1960s and their sex appeal feature prominently in Jeff Stein's unintentional funeral pyre for the band's classic lineup, *The Kids Are Alright*. Their onstage destruction had its roots in the theories of artist Gustav Metzger, a notion that took such wanton acts beyond mere hooliganism and into the political.

Through both Townshend's art school tendencies and bassist John Entwistle's twisted comic sensibilities, The Who became among the first progressive rock groups in 1960s, with the experimentalism that inspired "A Quick One, While He's Away" (wherein Lambert commissioned Townshend to fill the remaining ten minutes on the group's sophomore release with a single, linear story comprised of several two-minute segments) and the mock-radio experience, ads and all, of *The Who Sell Out*. The adverts were more the efforts of Entwistle and madman drummer Keith Moon, but Townshend's songwriting had reached a new level of maturity, understandable as he was all of twenty-two years of age.

This stunning array of singles and LPs from 1966 to 1968 by The Who is part of the same time that saw a collective coming of age among Britain's finest songwriters, the ones who made the cut so to speak in the wake of *Rubber Soul*, England's answer to *Bringing It All Back Home*: The Beatles' creative zenith was under way, taking the world to Pepperland with them; Ray Davies and The Kinks had a series of masterful, albeit decidedly British, records; The Rolling Stones dropped their acid at the crossroads and created some of the best white-boy blues ever; The Small Faces served up some of the catchiest pop songs ever about sex and drugs; Syd Barrett's version of Pink Floyd came not from outer space but the London underground scene; and, despite being American, it was from English recording studios that Jimi Hendrix launched his career and recorded his most focused, daring work.

It is sometimes hard to believe, while watching D.A. Pennebaker's spooky neon footage of The Who tearing it up at Monterey, that these destructive imps dressed like punk bards from some neo-Renaissance faire would go on to produce a work of such spiritual depth as *Tommy* just two years later. For those who look beyond The Who's hyper-masculine facade, one will find a calculated mixture of genius, madness, and mysticism. The stage antics that made them famous across London, inspired by Metzger's writings on auto-destructive art, often cloaked the sagely wisdom found in even their earliest releases.

Pete Townshend himself is a man of startling contradictions. The young Union Jack–clad mod, a dapper proto-punk of the highest order, just five years later would become a spiritual journeyman relaying his beliefs through the same outlet that had once vented his anger, his sexual frustration, and his attachment to his material self. Rock and roll is steeped in *maya*, the material world, where one's attainment of romantic affection, of a fast car, or of wealth is celebrated through song. Dylan broke the songwriting mold, and his own spiritual leanings have merited its share of study over the years, but Townshend stands alone with only George Harrison, a "plainclothes devotee" of A.C. Bhaktivedanta Swami Prabhupada, as such a strong proponent for God consciousness in the rock scene during what the author calls the classic rock era, defined as beginning with *Bringing It All Back Home*'s release in 1965 and ending sometime between Neil Young's *Rust Never Sleeps* in 1979 and the murder of John Lennon in 1980.

Although Townshend was no stranger to the worldly attachments typical to rock songs at the start of his career, even his earliest efforts as a songwriter reveal a deep mind that would only expand in the coming years. The Who's debut release, "I Can't Explain," is marked by its choppy, insistent riff, admittedly cribbed from The Kinks, but its lyrics show remarkable depth for a man barely twenty years of age. Although Roger Daltrey provided the voice, the words are very much Townshend's. His inner world is in turmoil. He's having sleep disturbances. He doesn't quite feel like himself. The words of an unnamed "you" dominate his thoughts. In the song, he concludes these manifestations to be the side effect of love. While assumed to be a romantic love, the emotions and thoughts expressed in "I Can't Explain" seem right in step with the language of spiritual yearning. After all, the feelings in this song are emanating not from his heart, like in so many other pop songs, but rather from his soul.

Often remembered as a gravity-defying, guitar-smashing lunatic, Pete Townshend's search for meaning represents his equally important other half: his inner self. Beyond the stage antics, the witty interviews, and those many poor, unsuspecting guitars he abused is a spiritually aware soul. He used his position as a rock star to share far and wide the universal philosophy of Meher Baba. A Persian-born mystic who lived within a cultural confluence of world faith traditions (Zoroastrianism, Christianity, Vedism, Buddhism, and Islam), Baba told the world that he was the Avatar (God-Incarnation) of his time, bearing a worldwide message of love for all mankind.

This essay seeks to explore Townshend's relationship with Meher Baba and his teachings, how Townshend integrated Baba's philosophy into his own works—*Tommy* specifically—but certainly throughout The Who's work in the 1970s, and how his successes and failures in achieving the balance of rock star life with spiritual life also impacted his work. Although this chapter will discuss some of Townshend's more human aspects, the author writes from a place of admiration, empathy, and respect.

Behold the God-Man: Meher Baba

Drug use may be forbidden by both Baba and Prabhupada, but both Townshend and Harrison have mentioned cannabis and LSD playing a role in the early stages of their spiritual journeys. (It bears to mention both also credit the crushing weight of stardom as a cause for their more meaningful pursuits.) Marijuana tends to drive one's thoughts inwards, whereas psychedelic experiences are guided (with some cautions) by Ram Dass as a means of addressing the divine. His trippy spiritual memoir *Be Here Now* inspired Harrison to write a song bearing the same name. In his autobiography, *Who I Am*, Townshend recounts his art-school discovery of pot, which he felt enhanced his abilities as a listener of music. His later experiments with psychedelics, specifically LSD, offered a similar awakening on a multi-sensory level:

> [In early 1967] the couple of acid trips I'd done had definitely changed the way I perceived things. Trees bare of their leaves in winter, for example, began to look like those medical student mock-ups of the vein and artery network inside the human lung; in effect I suddenly saw trees for what they really are: planetary breathing machines. I wasn't a tripped-out freak, but the way I looked at things was evolving [109].

That final phrase, "the way I looked at things was evolving," is an apt summary of the many radical changes that took place in Western society during this period. It was a time of new ideas, imageries, aspirations, and points of view. The limitations of materialism, capitalism, and indeed Western thought in general had begun to show in the Occident, and a generation of youth sought answers from sources beyond their own culture. Though immigrants from India in the UK—regardless of their religious background—have a history dating back to the early 19th century, the Johnson Administration's passage of the Immigration and Nationality Services Act (INS) in 1965 led to a massive influx of Indians onto American soil, bringing ancient Eastern philosophies to the materialist Western masses.

In tandem with the birth of America's counterculture came a series of swamis, gurus, and mystics, typically clad in robes either of white or the more traditional saffron orange, offering teachings on life, death, suffering, and the meaning of existence, all of which were in sharp contrast to the average American's Judeo-Christian upbringing. Among these teachers were Maharishi Mahesh Yogi, who introduced meditation to The Beatles, Donovan, and a Beach Boy, albeit for a nominal fee; Swami Satchidananda, who ended up giving the opening lecture at Woodstock; and Swami Prabhupada, who in 1966 began chanting a Vedic mantra under an elm tree at Tompkins Square in New York City, leading to the foundation of the International Society for Krishna Consciousness, or ISKCON, also known as the Hare Krishna/Krsna movement. Prabhupada would later form a relationship with George Harrison. These three men, while hardly the only leading figures in Indian thought at the time, provide examples of the direct influence of Vedic, once widely known as Hindu, religious ideals in the world of rock music during the 1960's.

Along with these newcomers came a revival of sorts for a previous generation of philosophers, reformers, and gurus from India; all of whom had found themselves courted by the intelligentsia of their time, but it was during the cultural revolution of the 1960s in the West that these mystics and thinkers found their largest audiences. The most notable of these included Swami Vivekananda, founder of the Vedanta Society and whose 1893 speech to the World Parliament of Religions presented a nutshell encapsulation of Vedic philosophy; Paramahansa Yogananda, author of *Autobiography of a Yogi*, a miracle worker in his time, and who can be seen just below Bob Dylan, to the right of H.G. Wells, and above Lawrence of Arabia on the *Sgt. Pepper* cover; Jiddu Krishnamurti, who refused to be Madame Blavatsky's token Indian and broke away from sectarianism to become the greatest *jnana* yogi of the 20th century; and finally Meher Baba, who had first come to the West in the early 1930s and was known as "the Silent Master," due to his lifelong vow of silence, taken in 1925.

Meher Baba was born Merwan Sheriar Irani in India, raised in a Zoroastrian family, receiving his education at a Christian school, and studying under mystics from both Vedic and Sufi Islamic backgrounds. Sufism is perhaps the largest single influence on Baba. The most theologically liberal sect of Islam, Sufism encourages mysticism from its followers, and it is from this tradition that the world has been graced with dervishes, the ascetic followers of Islam often seen dancing in circular trance-like states. During these years, Merwan approached five spiritual masters, a practice dictated in the *Bhagavad Gita*.

Although they only met once, Baba called meeting the famed Sai Baba of Shirdi one of the most important experiences of his life. Sai Baba was revered as both a Muslim *faqir* and Vedic *satguru* during his life, beloved to this day by both communities as a saint. Baba's primary spiritual tutelage came from two sources. The first was a *faqir* named Hazrat Babajan, who blessed young Merwan with a kiss on the forehead; the second was a disciple of Sai Baba named Upasni Maharaj. Upasni greeted young Merwan by throwing a stone at him, which according to a number of sources struck the young aspirant in the same spot where he had received Babajan's kiss. Despite this rather unorthodox greeting, Merwan became his disciple. After five years together, Upasni declared "Merwanji" (the "ji" suffix is an honorific in India) to be the Avatar in 1922.

As Avatar, Merwanji was considered the latest in a lineage of God-Men that included Zoroaster, Rama, Krishna, Jesus, Buddha, and Mohammed (Peace Be Upon Him). The Baha'i belief in "progressive revelation" echoes this idea; many Baha'i ideas come from Sufi theology. After leaving Upasni with his blessing to go change the world, Merwanji cultivated a legion of followers and disciples. These followers renamed him Meher Baba, which means "compassionate father." As for his vow of silence, which he began in 1925, Baba explained: "Because man has been deaf to the principles and precepts laid down by God in the past, in this present Avataric Form I observe silence. You have asked for and been given enough words—it is now time to live them" (Baba, "The Universal Message").

Taking Baba as who he said he was, an avatar of God, a glance at history and the evolution of religious thought would suggest that the people of Earth needed only to return to already-existing sources of wisdom for answers. Within nearly every religious system is the belief of loving others as oneself, known as the Golden Rule in Western thought. For Meher Baba, who studied at least six different faith traditions in his lifetime—while also coexisting in a land that is also the point of origin for Jainism and Sikhism—he encountered the same answer: God is love, we emanate from God, and therefore we must love each other. Similar conclusions came from Sai Baba of Shirdi and Sri Ramakrishna, spiritual master of Swami Vivekananda.

As for the great mystery of how a man who never spoke can be quoted,

Baba communicated first with a letter board, then later in life with a series of hand gestures and facial expressions, not unlike sign language, with an ever-ready interpreter at his side to either take dictation or say Baba's words aloud. It was through this process that Baba conducted all correspondences, including sermons and books.

Though modern claims of God-hood can understandably summon up images of Charles Manson, Jim Jones, David Koresh, or the Heaven's Gate suicide cult, Baba used his status as Avatar—whether one agrees with his claims or not—for the greater good. He founded free schools in India that admitted all students, regardless of religion and even caste. He loved children and he loved animals. He spearheaded charity efforts for and commiserated with lepers, seen in pictures washing their feet at a time where India's caste system had deemed them *dalits*, untouchable by law. Baba also spent time with people that he called *masts*, individuals he believed to be intoxicated by God, echoing the Sufi concept of God-intoxication. His travels through Iran, India, and Pakistan to visit with *masts* were documented by a British doctor named William Donkin in the book *The Wayfarers: Meher Baba with the God-Intoxicated*.

A humanitarian and lover of all mankind in his actions, Baba authored several books. The most notable of these are *God Speaks* and his *Discourses*. *God Speaks* is a dense exploration of metaphysics, both earthly and ethereal. Textually, his work in *God Speaks* expands on the origin stories of the universe found in the Upanishads, tracing the soul's existence in countless non-human forms (including stone, metal, and plant-matter before moving on to invertebrate life), buttressing J.C. Bose's experiments which proved life-force can be found in seemingly inanimate objects, and bringing together the core beliefs of religious thought.

The esoteric discussions of *God Speaks* are fleshed out through numerous diagrams and charts depicting the hierarchy of existence. Baba uses syncretism to see the unity in the mystical practices of what he calls Vedantic, Mystic, and Sufi traditions. A diagram in *God Speaks* includes a table of varying terms related to God, discipleship, and existence. Though the terms vary in origin, Sanskrit, English, and Arabic, respectively, Baba saw the similarities in each spiritual path. He expressed in *God Speaks* a comprehensive unifying vision that emphasized parallels rather than quibbling over doctrinal minutiae.

A complete and comprehensive statement from beyond the beyond, to use Baba's own phrasing, *God Speaks* is also a difficult read. The *Discourses* delve less into terminologies and metaphysics and instead cover more practical applications of Baba's teachings into daily life. The lessons cover meditation, the nature of love, more bite-sized discussions of themes explored in great depth within *God Speaks*. This author's experience with devotees of

Baba and his own reading of the material has resulted in a nearly universal conclusion: that *God Speaks* is undoubtedly the most important document of Baba's teachings, and yet all agree that *Discourses* is the so-called "desert island" book of the two.

I have spoken of Baba having devotees, followers, and disciples, but he was emphatic about his purpose not to be the creation of a new religion. His own followers that I've encountered said so as well. Anecdotally, though, one did add, "But I'm sure Jesus and Buddha said the same thing." Regardless, Baba's focus in his work was to emphasize similarities over differences. Baba wanted to see unity and understanding over sectarianism, and he did not wish to create yet another theological "ism" for what he considered an already confused and troubled world: "I have not come to establish any cult, society, or organization; nor even to establish a new religion. The religion I will give teaches the knowledge of the One behind the many" ("Public Message Upon Arrival on His Second Visit to America").

The key points of Baba's teachings are that God is love, that love is the greatest force in the universe, and that we are to recognize our own inner soul and love one another. Later in his life, however, Baba explicitly spoke out against drug use, specifically the use of drugs to attain God-consciousness. At a time of consciousness-expansion and a lysergic explosion helped along by Project MKUltra and the Edgewood Arsenal experiments, Baba and a few of his peers were boldly instructing hippies to stay drug free. He corresponded with several Westerners who held differing views, including Richard Alpert (later Ram Dass), and these letters were compiled to form Baba's essay "God in a Pill?," which contains his observations:

"To a few sincere seekers, LSD may have served as a means to arouse that spiritual longing which has brought them into my contact, but once that purpose is served further ingestion would not only be harmful but have no point or purpose. The longing for Reality cannot be sustained by further use of drugs but only by the love for the Perfect Master which is a reflection of his love for the seeker.

An individual may feel LSD has made a "better" man of him socially and personally. But one will be a better man through Love than one can ever be through drugs or any other artificial aid. And the best man is he who has surrendered himself to the Perfect Master irrespective of his personal or social standing.

As for possible use of the drug by an enlightened society for spiritual purposes— an enlightened society would never dream of using it!" ["Excerpts from 'God in a Pill?'"].

Baba was hardly alone. Swami Prabhupada of ISKCON, for example, demanded that initiated devotees abstain from meat, gambling, illicit sex, and intoxication. These regulations and austerities seemed radical in the decadent West during the Age of Aquarius. Frankly, they still are. However, from the Vedic perspective, society is viewed as having entered *Kali Yuga*, the era of darkness. The *Srimad Bhagavatam*, known also as the Krishna Purana or the Bhagavad Purana, describes Kali Yuga as a time where "the path of the Vedas will be completely forgotten in human society, and so-called religion will be mostly atheistic. The kings will mostly be thieves" (*Srimad Bhagavatam* 12:2:17). It should be noted that during this same time, atheist activist Madalyn Murray O'Hair led efforts to outlaw prayer and scriptural reading in schools, as well as filing a case against NASA regarding the Apollo 8 astronauts' reading from the Book of Genesis while documenting the earth rise over the moon's surface.

In short, Baba's message seemed more needed than ever. As Baba approached the twilight of his earthly life in India, in England, Townshend and The Who were toiling away in the studio on an album that would immortalize Baba's teachings for the flower power generation: *Tommy*. It was through *Tommy* that the world at large would hear many of Baba's ideas, including spiritual evolution, God-intoxication, achieving self-realization, the failures of the psychedelic experience, and all forms of love.

From Pothead to Godhead:
A Disciple Awakens

Pete Townshend first encountered Meher Baba's teachings in the spring of 1967 through Mike McInnerney, an artist friend of his in London who gave him a copy of Charles Purdom's biography of Baba, *The God-Man*. Townshend recalled years later, "I read a few lines, and found that everything Meher Baba said fitted perfectly with my view of the cosmos." What struck Townshend first, as recounted in his autobiography, was Baba's distinct countenance. Townshend described him as "a strange-looking, charismatic fellow with a large, rather flattened nose, flowing dark hair and a generous moustache" (110). Many photographs of Baba portray his piercing gaze directed at the viewer, in a manner akin to depictions of Vedic entities or of Jesus Christ. Portraits of Baba in his later years show Baba with a more bulbous and smushed nose, the aftermath of facial injuries he sustained in one of two car accidents; the first occurred in 1952 outside Prague, Oklahoma, resulting in Baba breaking his leg and nose. Four years later, the second accident in Udtare, Maharashtra, severely impacted Baba's ability to walk and put him in chronic pain for the remainder of his life.

The Who first came to the United States on the heels of the "Happy Jack" single, their highest charting in the States at that time. Though it was only a brief stint in New York City as part of Murray the K's package shows, the band made an impression. Predating Townshend's first encounter with Meher Baba, the young songwriter's worldly ambitions dictated his every move.

Townshend said, "We worked hard on propaganda for the first three days before we played [the shows] ... I think I was doing about twenty or thirty interviews per day, and each one had to be a little different or important than the last" (106). Keith Moon and John Entwistle ordered vintage champagne and an abundance of liquor through room service. The band's stage presence matched their real-life antics. Townshend sported a jacket bedecked with lights that connected to his guitar. Despite only having two songs in the showcase, Moon shared in an interview that the band was told, as they had become notorious for across the UK and Europe, to smash up their gear at the end of each set.

Inspired by performance artist Gustav Metzger, Townshend incorporated auto-destructive art into The Who's stage show, which would end with Pete smashing his guitar to splinters (he quipped that Stratocasters are the most durable, recounting one occasion where his Strat destroyed the amplifier and remained perfectly in tune), Roger Daltrey swinging his microphone like a lasso, and Keith Moon kicking over his drum kit while stage hands deployed smoke bombs. Bassist John Entwistle would never engage in the action, often leaning against his amp nonchalantly while the makeshift Aghori ritual played out around him. Although Jimi Hendrix would later turn guitar-smashing into a true *yajna* (Vedic offering) in that it involved fire, Townshend's axe abuse can also be seen as a kind of sacrifice, even if it became a gimmick used to attract audiences.

During the same time Townshend first encountered Meher Baba, which followed The Who's American debut, Pete began to experience life as one of the beautiful people. He immersed himself in the booming underground arts scene in London, being a regular at various happenings of the London Underground like the opening of the Indica Gallery and the 14-Hour Technicolor Dream. Townshend and The Who were also fixtures at the Bag O'Nails in Soho, a club that served as a hangout for all the hip musicians of the time.

After a short stint in Germany that April, where audiences would smash up the theaters whether or not The Who would destroy their gear (respectively, out of enthusiasm or out of protest), the band returned to their homeland with a show at the Brighton Dome. Featuring Cream in one of their earliest appearances, the concert's light show was orchestrated by Townshend's artistic idol, Gustav Metzger. Such worldly success in Townshend's life—his new friends, his new lifestyle, having the thrill of playing for one of his inspirations—was counterbalanced that night by his growing inner dissatisfaction. In his autobiography, Townshend reflects pensively on the evening, saying "I wanted something more from myself than silly pop songs and stage destruction" (115). Those feelings were crystallized at the end of the night when he talked with Metzger, who had never seen The Who perform.

"Though he was pleased to have been such a powerful influence," Townshend recalls humbly, "he tried to explain that according to his thesis I faced a dilemma; I was supposed to boycott the new commercial pop form itself, attack the very process that allowed me such creative expression, not contribute to it." This evening marked the beginning of Townshend's disenchantment with his original Pop Art aspirations for The Who. Pete received the admonishment from Metzger as a wake-up call. Having heard Metzger's observation, Townshend wrote years later, "I agreed. The gimmicks had overtaken me" (115).

With that evening in his memory, Townshend and The Who returned to America in a big way, gimmicks and all, in June. They gave a charged performance at the Monterey Pop Festival, where a coin toss placed them ahead of Hendrix. Contrary to some legends, the scene backstage was in fact fueled by Hendrix and Townshend loving each other's music so much that they neither one wanted to follow the other. That said, given the "boy's club" nature of so much rockist lore, the idea of them fiercely competing for that favored closing spot does make for better press. Monterey Pop gave both Hendrix and The Who, plus Janis Joplin, Otis Redding, and Ravi Shankar, widespread exposure. Culturally, the event, just days short of the summer solstice, is credited with kicking off the Summer of Love in 1967.

During the band's return flight to London, Pete had a powerful psychic episode. Just before take-off, Pete ingested a hit of a drug called STP, its name an acronym for "serenity, tranquility, and peace." Despite its flower power nickname, the hallucinogen STP, technically called 2,5-Dimethoxy-4-methylamphetamine (DOM), is notorious for its slow onset, extreme potency, and long duration. Townshend's trip led to hallucinations of the flight attendant turning into a pig and auditory hallucinations of multiple songs playing at once, before going into an out-of-body experience, where he saw himself passed out in his girlfriend Karen Astley's arms. During these moments, he reported no longer feeling the effects of the drug. "I could see clearly now, my eyes focused, my senses realigned," Townshend wrote in *Who I Am*, "yet I was completely disembodied" (122). As he saw himself, Karen, and his bandmates, Pete then claims hearing a female voice urging him to go back, and that he could not stay where he was. Townshend then descended back into his human form, where the rest of his trip was "saturated by wonderful color and sound" (122).

During The Who's tour of the United States a few months later, Townshend had another supernatural experience, this time at a Holiday Inn in Rolling Meadows, Illinois. Though he is uncharacteristically withholding in his memoirs about just what occurred, Townshend claims he heard the voice of God. He writes about spending his time offstage pondering the role of music in the lives of his listeners. The concert experience was one he hoped to become more than just a backdrop for "the acid trips of an audience that no longer cared when a song began or ended" (126)

With his two favorite albums in steady rotation, *Pet Sounds* and *Sgt. Pepper's Lonely Hearts Club Band*, Townshend would toke up and immerse himself in the music. He found the experience yielded many musical discoveries, but that in terms of substance, "these two great albums ... passed on no tools, codes or obvious processes that would lead to a door. I ached for more than just a signpost to the future, which is what these albums were to me" (Townshend 127).

Townshend's cognizance of a greater need for himself and his generation as a whole was a further step in his journey. His motel room conversation with God was "a call to the heart," the beginning of his spiritual search. In Vedic language, Townshend's epiphany showed him his *dharma*, his divine will. After losing a staring contest with the afterlife on an airplane and chatting with the Almighty in Illinois, Townshend's life took a clear step towards a search for a greater connection with his spirituality. He experienced all of this at the age of 22.

Taking inspiration from Metzger's goading, The Who's next record, *The Who Sell Out*, showcases Townshend making the transition from pop songster to spiritual journeyman. Being a few years younger than the likes of Dylan and John Lennon, *Sell Out* serves as Townshend's *Rubber Soul*, his "Subterranean Homesick Blues," where he shed his Mod skin for the life of a spiritual aspirant. Amidst the mockeries of pop banality and Western consumerism served up by the band's rhythm section in the fake ads, Townshend also delivered several songs that abstractly dealt with his new musings. Having just discovered mysticism, the omniscient "I Can See for Miles" is the great hit The Who never quite had, and supposedly inspired McCartney to write "Helter Skelter." *Sell Out* saw Townshend drift into Romantic territory on songs like "Relax," "Sunrise," and "I Can't Reach You."

"I Can't Reach You" is a delicate slice of pop, with its narrator again longing for the "you" of its title. Though dressed up as a traditional love song, Townshend's vivid imagery and use of hyperbole with relation to time, where millions of ages pass between meetings and the distance between the two entities number in the thousands of miles, suggests a more eternal yearning. The song's language seems more in step with the Tanakh/Old Testament or the Upanishads; similar echoes in search of lost youth can be found in Lennon's work during this time and in Barrett's acid-dipped nursery rhymes. Only Harrison's heavily raga-influenced *Sgt. Pepper* showstopper "Within You Without You," released a few months earlier, shares a similar level of spiritual depth.

The seductive acoustic ballad "Sunrise," which showed that Townshend owes just as much to Django Reinhardt as he did to Gustav Metzger and Link

Wray, once again has the narrator addressing "you." This time, the object of the narrator's affection is capable of taking his breath away, their presence guiding him to avoid temptations. In solitude, Townshend reveals that their smile brings him solace; he spends his day pondering them. Viewed one way as lovesickness for an amorous relationship, viewed another way the song is a *bhakti yoga* devotional hymn. Viewed through that lens, the amorous daydreams become pious meditations on a beloved deity, those meditations bringing the narrator closer to salvation.

Townshend began to spend more time with Mike McInnerney, the artist who initially introduced him to Meher Baba, around the time The Who were finishing *Sell Out*. Pete and Karen began attending *satsang* gatherings with McInnerney and his wife Katie at their home with other Baba devotees. During this time, Townshend stopped taking acid and eventually gave up pot. Writing in *Rolling Stone* in 1970, Townshend was frank in addressing why he had gotten into marijuana in the first place: "It gave me confidence, it gave me beautiful girls, it gave me R&B" ("In Love with Meher Baba").

His feeling that it was only through pot that he was able to have these experiences created a cycle of depression and continued use. "If I hadn't been stoned," Townshend wrote with disarming candor, "the sun wouldn't have come up." In quitting pot, Townshend found relief that the acutely sensitive musical response he attributed to getting high remained intact. In the same *Rolling Stone* piece, Pete quipped that he could still risk running his car off of the road any time "Green Onions" came on the radio.

"Assemble the musicians"—Tommy's Inception

This newfound appreciation for spirituality and sobriety, although he still drank during this time, was an opportunity for Townshend to connect with people outside the music world. Of the other Baba devotees he met through McInerney, Townshend said, "Everyone I met in connection with Meher Baba seemed to have been someone I knew from some other lifetime, from some mysterious other place directly connected with my own inner life" (139). Townshend certainly didn't have the same level of metaphysical harmony with his bandmates. Andy Neill writes that among Daltrey the working-class tough guy, Entwistle the strong but silent *bon vivant*, and Moon the resident court jester, their attitude towards Townshend's new interest "could best be described as tolerant" (100).

Harrison experienced a similar feeling with his fellow Beatles towards first the Maharishi's Transcendental Meditation retreat in Rishikesh and then with John and Yoko's interest in, and then documented rejection of, ISKCON and its philosophy. Though Harrison and Townshend, to this author's knowledge, never shared a recorded conversation over spiritual matters, Townshend found a spiritual comrade in fellow musician Ronnie Lane from The Small Faces, crediting him as "the first friend who listened to my interest in Meher Baba without sniggering" (138).

The following year, Townshend penned two of his first overtly spiritual songs, "Faith in Something Bigger" and "Glow Girl." Shedding the Romantic tone for one of lamentation, "Faith in Something Bigger" warns of the impending change of seasons; the approaching winter is an allegory for hardships, the call being for everyone to remain steadfast through faith. Its attachment to the impending change of seasons suggests a time and even a culture that is more inclined towards God-consciousness. In its bridge, "Faith in Something Bigger" touches on the Vedic concept of worldly knowledge displacing spiritual strength. George Harrison would make a similar contention the same year on both "It's All Too Much" and the *Tao Te Ching*-inspired "The Inner Light." The lyrics on "Faith in Something Bigger" are somewhat sparse, but the message is clear: faith is the greatest sustainer.

"Glow Girl" chronicles a young woman on an ill-fated flight (no doubt inspired in part by Townshend's brush with STP), rummaging through her bag as the plane heads towards the inevitable. In her final moments, she realizes the purpose of life: that all of her worldly possessions and desires are nothing compared to what lies ahead. The band turns in a spirited performance, complete with a musical plane crash. At its coda, the girl is reincarnated, born again literally as an obstetrician declares the birth of a baby girl. This heady ending would later resurface as "It's a Boy" on *Tommy*, with "Glow Girl" acting as its spiritual predecessor. (One could even argue the Glow Girl is Tommy's immediate past life.) Though neither song saw official release at the time, they were both deemed important enough for inclusion on The Who's 1974 rarities collection, *Odds and Sods*.

While 1967 was a year of struggle met with matching success, by the time The Who returned to the studio in spring 1968 to being work on their new album, the group was in peril. They toured relentlessly through the first part year, visiting Australia and New Zealand with The Small Faces, where they partied like rock stars and paid dearly for it, two runs through the United States, and scattered gigs in England and Scotland. After playing arenas and festivals in the United States, the band were somewhat dismayed at the low-paying university gigs in their homeland. Life went on for the band as well, with all four members settling into some semblance of domesticity with their partners; Pete and Karen Astley married in May of that year.

As the newlyweds settled into their new home, Townshend built a home studio where, with Meher Baba's *The Everything and the Nothing* (a collection of shorter devotional readings) on the shelf, Townshend began recording demos for his new project. From the demo stage until its release, the whole process to create *Tommy* took nearly a year. Its production is storied and well-documented in various sources. The album could just as easily have been The Who's final release, and were it not for a few key moments during its production, it could very well have gone unfinished.

During the band's stint in the U.S. that summer, as "Magic Bus" performed coolly in the charts, Townshend gave a lengthy interview with *Rolling Stone* where he shared his plans for the next Who album. It would focus on a boy named Tommy, who is unable to see, hear, or speak. As per Townshend, Tommy "exists in a world of vibrations. This allows the listener to become profoundly aware of the boy and what he is all about" (149). It would be a story told through rock opera, complete with musical themes, or leitmotifs, for its main character and various sentiments through the album. Much of what Townshend described was made up on the spot, but these ideas would remain intact throughout the album's lengthy process. Its working title was *The Amazing Journey*.

Townshend had made similar attempts at narrative storytelling in pop music before, but to varying degrees of success. Their 1966 single "I'm a Boy," a song that deserves re-examination during the current cultural discussion of queer sexuality and gender identity, was intended to be part of a larger project called *Quads*. Nothing else ever came of it. The band's earlier song "A Quick One, While He's Away" was a series of mini-songs bundled into a cohesive tale, meant to help eat up the remaining ten minutes set aside for the album. The nearly 10-minute "mini-opera," as Townshend called it, would be pared down into a leaner, louder version for its live performances. Their rendition of "A Quick One" recorded for *The Rolling Stones Rock & Roll Circus* was so powerful that The Rolling Stones, who felt their own performance was tired and suffered from a particularly strung-out Brian Jones, shelved the project. Who fans were luckily treated to the performance when it was included in Jeff Stein's *cinema verite* celebration of The Who's years with Keith Moon, *The Kids Are Alright*. In a case of Zappaesque conceptual continuity, "A Quick One" would later be introduced in concert as being about Tommy's parents.

The Who Sell Out closes with "Rael," a story-song set in a futuristic dystopia where overpopulation has become a problem. A global war is on, and a fleet of ships awaits orders to attack China on Christmas. The commander gives instructions for his successors to look for either a red flag, signaling to invade, or a yellow one, indicating he plans to stay, but the fleet should return home. Its wartime imagery harkened back to World War II while also touching on the antiwar movement during the conflict in Vietnam. Musically, the band delivers a Pop Art glance at World War III, from the marching triplets of the song's front to the musical bombing run in the song's back half. A year and a half later, this same melody occurs twice on *Tommy*, first as "Sparks" and again as the "Underture." Other portions of the song were excised and discarded, notably heard in Townshend's demos from this time and the track "Rael #2" included on reissues of *Sell Out*.

The inspirations for *Tommy* come from a variety of sources. Kit Lambert, The Who's manager and producer, introduced the idea of rock opera to Townshend. Pete credits Lambert for encouraging him to defy songwriting traditions as early as The Who's second album, *A Quick One* (released with a slightly altered track order in the U.S. as *Happy Jack*), including the development of "A Quick One, While He's Away" as a mini-opera. Lambert provided similar encouragement for *Tommy*, especially in encouraging Townshend to tap into his own life story, but the project was Townshend's brainchild. Townshend's secular inspirations include sci-fi author Robert Heinlein. He said in his autobiography, "As the Sixties dripped by I felt like the messenger from Mars in Robert Heinlein's *Stranger in a Strange Land*, who promises that the secret of all existence is simply to learn to wait" (127).

Content warning: details of child abuse, sexual abuse.

Townshend's experiences with cannabis and LSD allowed him some introspection, as well as providing an entheogenic means of spiritual enlightenment. Cannabis and psychedelics both have been lauded for their ability to help survivors of abuse unpack their trauma, especially for those suffering from post-traumatic stress. It is no mystery that John Lennon, himself a survivor of a traumatic childhood and adolescence, would produce his most honest and most introspective work with The Beatles while experimenting with cannabis and psychedelics.

Townshend writes frankly in *Who I Am* some of the abstract details of living with his grandmother as a small boy. He recalls witnessing questionable late-night exchanges involving strange men coming and going during the night (it is possible his grandmother was a sex worker) as well as experiencing physical abuse, of his grandmother "slapping me, brutally scrubbing my body in the bath or ducking my head under the water to wash off the soap" (Townshend 18). On a trip with the Sea Scouts at age 11, Townshend experienced sexual abuse at the hands of two Scoutmasters. He describes being stripped, sprayed naked with a hose, and humiliated while the men masturbated (Townshend 31). Acute childhood trauma, physical abuse, and sexual abuse all occur on *Tommy*, no doubt the end result of Townshend beginning to do some of his own unpacking.

It wasn't just the painful experiences of his childhood that Townshend used to inspire *Tommy*. He describes several powerful encounters with music as a boy. In one instance, while playing his harmonica on a rainy fishing trip, Townshend "had the most extraordinary, life-changing experience. Suddenly I was hearing music within the music—rich, complex harmonic beauty that had been locked in the sounds I'd been making" (Townshend 30). He writes with passion about how the sounds of a river sent him into a trance.

His most profound experience of hearing music within his surroundings came on the same fateful Sea Scouts trip, when he heard music coming from an outboard motor. "I heard violins, cellos, horns, harps and voices, which increased in number until I could hear countless threads of an angelic choir," he wrote, chronicling what can be viewed as an early spiritual awakening. "It was a sublime experience. I have never heard such music since, and my personal ambition has always been to rediscover that sound and relive its effect on me" (Townshend 31).

This statement provides an explanation for many facets of Townshend's six decades as a musician: his sonic feedback-drenched assaults, his adoration of synthesizers and biofeedback, his use of various electronics to modify his guitar's tone, the themes of interconnectedness on a religious level within music as explored within *Lifehouse* (the rock opera that became *Who's Next* after some whittling), and the internalized ruminations of young Tommy Walker. His quest, both to reconnect to the sound as well as the effect it had on him, can be heard in nearly every song he created from "I Can't Explain" through "Who Are You" and beyond.

Musically, The Who took some interesting steps forward on *Tommy*. Townshend had used the acoustic guitar as the lead on several Who tracks, namely "Substitute" and "Magic Bus," but its usage on *Tommy* is distinct. Originally intended as guide tracks to be erased after production, the acoustic rhythm guitar throughout the album is paired with Townshend redoing the parts on electric. Although Townshend didn't get the extra overdubs he wanted, which would have had "a killer combination of full-bodied acoustic guitar and driving electric rhythm guitar," the result is a unique study in rhythm, harmony, and texture (157). Townshend's original wish for the guitar sound on *Tommy* would be granted on The Who's next studio offering, *Who's Next*.

Townshend seemed to have taken a few notes from the past year's musical excursions: complex, overproduced music didn't translate well onstage at the time. It wouldn't for another 25 years. Unlike many of the big records that had helped set off the psychedelic revolt, *Tommy* does not feature the studio trickery, the intense overdubs, or ethnomusicological explorations of *Pet Sounds*, *Sgt. Pepper*, or *Their Satanic Majesties Request*. There are no violins, cellos, violas, harps, big brass sections, saxophones, Theremins, dilrubas, sitars, or tablas.

Instead, the recording is the four-man Who, plus some extra keyboards and French horn parts overdubbed by Townshend and Entwistle, as well as some backing vocalists. Its full-bodied sound comes from the vocal harmonies, which The Who certainly deserve some praise in their ability to replicate this on stage, as well as the dual rhythm guitar tracks and Moon's bombastically *maestoso* drumming. Entwistle's background in classical and jazz certainly helped hone their sound in the studio as well. His wide-ranged voice is frequently heard amid their more intricate harmonies.

Roger Daltrey embodies Tommy throughout the opera, though he originally was only going to perform the character from "I'm Free" onward—which is on side four of the original LP! Daltrey recalls the sessions in a less than positive light, with even Townshend noting Daltrey's initial boredom given the reduced role he almost had on the album. After what must have been a struggle, Daltrey took over the narrator role on "Amazing Journey" and "Christmas," both originally to be sung by Townshend. Roger also worked hard to develop the falsetto needed for Tommy's inner monologues during the first part of the opera, allowing him to take over all of the vocal duties for the main character. Townshend sings the narration in the "Overture" and plays the Acid Queen, a drug-dealing prostitute who comes later in the story.

Townshend delegated songwriting duties to Entwistle for two of the more difficult episodes in the story. Entwistle delivered two darkly twisted tales of abuse, both imbued with its author's signature dark humor, giving the rock opera a sinister edge in contrast to Townshend's introspective songwriting. Tommy suffers bullying at the hands of his cousin Kevin. Bullying was a tough subject for Townshend to revisit, having both suffered from it and having inflicted his own share of suffering. He credited John for a job well done, calling "Cousin Kevin" "brutally comedic." On "Fiddle About," Tommy is molested by a character named Uncle Ernie, voiced by Entwistle. "I liked it very much," Townshend wrote, "it was disturbing, relentless and powerful [...] it did the job nicely, and I was relieved not to have to battle with the subject myself" (159). Keith Moon received songwriting credit for "Tommy's Holiday Camp"; although the song was composed by Townshend, it was Moon who suggested Tommy's home, first presented in the sluggish, slightly stoned "Welcome" near the album's end, be turned from a hippie collective-style home into a holiday camp for his followers to attend.

The most dramatic development during the *Tommy* sessions was when news came from Baba devotee Delia DeLeon, who called Townshend to share that Meher Baba had dropped the body on January 31, 1969. He was unable to attend the London gathering of devotees that night, but Townshend had made plans to visit Meher Baba for March. Accompanying him would have been Mike and Katie McInnerney as well as Ronnie Lane and his wife Susie. They decided to cancel their tickets. Saddened by Baba's passing, Townshend recalls "a long journey and there was an eerie silence throughout" the return drive from Redcar to London following a Who show (160–161).

Meher Baba dropping the body profoundly impacted Townshend. His ponderings since his last psychedelic experience, about his art's relevancy and the role pop music could play for the masses, seemed to merge into a resounding sense of purpose with *Tommy*. The death of Meher Baba coincided with Townshend's work on a musical project that sought to answer many of the questions he raised to himself during his spiritual quest, of finding the "door" not pointed to by *Pet Sounds* and *Sgt. Pepper*, at least according to Townshend.

It was time to bring elements of Baba's teachings to the material world. The cosmic significance of Baba dropping the body was not lost on Townshend. A final development in Townshend's personal life, the birth of his daughter Emma on March 28 of that year, cemented his resolve. "It was as though I had a caveman's primitive drive to hunt and kill to provide food for his family" (165). That renewed sense of purpose can be likened to *dharma*. Though this occurred as *Tommy* was in its final stages of mastering, this intense urge to provide for his family fueled the passion behind *Tommy*'s initial public performances. With *Tommy*, Townshend sought to present a higher message using the medium of *maya*, the pop album, as a means to awaken listeners to an existence beyond the acid trips for which his music, he felt, had become a backdrop. It was time for the music to get more serious.

Vibration-Land: The Gospel According to Tommy

Kit Lambert directly inspired Townshend to compose the "Overture" for the album, citing the importance of creating a piece of music that incorporates the various leitmotifs to be heard throughout the opera. It was the last song written for *Tommy*, and accordingly it incorporates the main themes from the album: the opening chords are from "See Me, Feel Me," at the 30 second mark Entwistle's French horn ushers in the main theme from "We're Not Gonna Take It," then the band goes into "Go to the Mirror!" with Entwistle playing the melody on the horn. Each section is roughly 30 seconds. At 1:34 the music stops and a wordless choir brings the listener back to "See Me, Feel Me." As the music crescendos, the band drifts into "Go to the Mirror" again before a spirited preview of "Listening to You," the album's closing song. "Overture" returns to the main theme from "We're Not Gonna Take It" before the signature riff from "Pinball Wizard" comes in, played on acoustic guitar, met with more French horn heraldry from Entwistle. The inclusion of the French horn gives the "Overture" a regal air, coupled with Moon's rolling march patterns on the snare drum. An almighty gong summons Townshend's solo acoustic guitar. He sings with the curtness of a liaison of the British Army that Captain Walker won't be returning from the front, that his baby will be born not knowing his father. Townshend fingerpicks through a solo that includes some themes from "Sparks" before segueing into the next track, "It's a Boy."

The birth of Tommy shares lyrics, after a gender change, with the coda of their earlier, then-unreleased song "Glow Girl." "It's a Boy" is the first of several short tracks that help link together the narrative. "1921," credited in other releases as "You Didn't Hear It," is a pivotal moment in the story. Tommy's mother is celebrating that 1921 is going to be a good year as she has taken on a new lover; in that moment, Tommy's father returns and gets rid of the lover, presumably in a violent manner. Admittedly, the language is vague. (As a child, I heard the opening verse as Tommy's mother singing to her baby.) The lyrics are intentionally vague, meant for the listener to fill in the blank in their mind's eye as to what exactly happened. Ken Russell's film adaptation further convolutes the narrative, as it is the lover who instead disposes of Tommy's father.

Although the specifics were spelled out by Townshend in his 1968 *Rolling Stone* interview, as well as the liner notes for various incarnations of *Tommy* in the digital era, and his autobiography, it is important to maintain focus on context rather than content during these moments of narrative abstraction. The episode is played out from the point of view of a traumatized child, rendered literally senseless psychologically as a result. His parents ask about the boy, as he saw the whole thing. They gaslight him into believing he saw and heard nothing, and that he'll never say a word to anybody. As the parents do this, Roger, voicing Tommy, provides a counter-chorus directly defying his parents' commands. It's subtle, but present, indicating Tommy's strong will, and hinting that his senses of vision, hearing, and speech are both acute and intact.

On "Amazing Journey," we are given a portrait of ten-year-old Tommy Walker. He presents as deaf, mute, and blind; this lack of ability suggests a child who needs support for the most basic of tasks, but the lyrics describe Tommy's internal world as a rich land of vibrations. Inside his head is a constellation of music. The dramatic, open-air chords of Townshend's guitar is met with an explosive drum cadence that sets the song into motion. Tommy is only ten, but capable of deep thought. Despite his state, and the hardships he is to endure, the lyrics describe him as content with his lot, with wisdom arising from his seemingly austere life; this idea touches on the religious notion of asceticism, that simple living can arouse higher thinking. Reference is made to Tommy being ill, perhaps from a high-temperature fever, as it is said his mind will go to some unusual places.

As the delirium sets in, Tommy has a divine vision. He sees a tall man in a glittering robe, with a lengthy beard that flows to the floor. This could be Meher Baba, especially when one sees pictures of Baba from the 1920s, during which time he sported a gaunt figure, long, stringy hair, and a shaggy beard. His visage during that time is consistent with accurate depictions of Jesus Christ. In the second verse, Tommy absorbs sensory input—sensations—with the intention of collecting them in the creation of his own masterwork, described as a symphony. This relationship of music and sense perception seems to come from Townshend's early experiences hearing music in non-musical settings. During the second bridge, the narrator hails the wisdom within Tommy's eyes. His eyes are capable of passing along knowledge, even from just a glance.

This reference to Tommy's eyes conveying wisdom is the first overt connection to Meher Baba presented on *Tommy*, aside from the veiled reference to reincarnation in "It's a Boy." Being drawn to the physical presentation of a deity is central to mystical worship: Ramakrishna had his moment of awakening before a likeness of Kali, Catholics cite a miracle when the face of Jesus or Mother Mary appears in rock formations or slices of toast, and Townshend himself admits being drawn into Baba by his eyes. The author can provide direct anecdotal evidence of Baba followers who all describe their "moment" of being struck by his image, and it was always his eyes that drew them in. In an article discussing Baba's Avataric Features, author David Fenster quotes at length one of Baba's dearest disciples, Mehera J. Irani, with her account of Baba's appearance. She describes how, despite having a full head of hair and facial hair, his body was largely hairless, the shape of his feet are described as "lotus feet" with the reverent language found in so much *bhakti*, or devotional, literature in the Vedic tradition, and the apparently infantile softness of his skin.

Mehera gives a full description of Baba's appearance, and it is his eyes she speaks about the most: "Baba's eyes were so expressive, as if he spoke with his eyes. His expression was so eloquent. With a look he could ask, 'What are you saying?' You felt what he was trying to say. His eyes were warm and brown[....] There was a gold spark in them. They had a beautiful shape. When Baba talked, when he was happy, his eyes would shine. They were lovely. I loved his eyes, because they were so beautiful, the most beautiful eyes in the world" ("Avataric Features"). The author wishes to note that such descriptions are not meant to be read in a sexualized light. The simplest distillation of Baba's teachings is the conclusion that God is love. As such, this universal force—love—comes in many varied forms.

Bhakti devotion seeks to sublimate all forms of love into a divine nature, where aspirants seek to love the Lord as a parent, friend, sibling, child, and lover. Regarding the approach towards the Lord as a Divine Lover, accounts of Krishna's exploits with *gopi* maidens in the *Srimad Bhagavatam* are not meant to just titillate or arouse the reader, and no doubt is it part of the intended effect, but the ultimate message is one of Divine Love. This and other depictions of sex and sexuality in Vedic literature are frequently exoticized wrongly and either denigrated or abused in the West, especially in the work of Wendy Doniger. Presented as neoliberal cultural examination from an armchair, Doniger's work is simply an updated form of racist Orientalism.

As "Amazing Journey" concludes, the narrator shares that Tommy, with his wise eyes, is going to one day be a spiritual leader. The word is not used, but he is likened to a guru, guiding people on their own amazing journeys. This echoes the story in the Gospel of St. Luke, where Mary presents baby Jesus at the temple in Jerusalem, in keeping with the requirements of Torah. The attending priest, Simeon, had pledged he would not die before seeing the Messiah of the prophecies in the Tanakh. Upon seeing Jesus, Simeon praises the Lord and celebrates that he may die in peace, "For my eyes have seen your salvation, which you have prepared in the sight of all nations: a light of revelation to the Gentiles, and the glory of your people Israel" (Luke 2:30–32, NIV). Simeon offers a similar blessing for Mary, that her child's destiny will include deliverance for all people.

The song's use of exposition rather than storytelling allows "Amazing Journey" to stand on its own separately from the narrative; even an abbreviated reading of the song in that context leaves the listener with the tale of a spiritually aware child with a future of great religious significance. A dynamic performance in the studio, "Amazing Journey" proved to be an impressive part of their live act, evidenced by the full *Tommy* performance on the *Live at Leeds* reissue. Live and in the studio, "Amazing Journey" segues into the instrumental "Sparks."

It is a jarring shift. The acoustic guitar takes on a funky, percussive rhythm amid a sea of unearthly screeches and backwards electric guitars. About 50 seconds into "Sparks," Entwistle's bass takes over the lead while Moon provides a heavy tom-driven beat and Townshend's acoustic filigrees in place of a percussion arrangement. At the ninety-second mark, the band settles into the main theme, a melancholy meditation on E with Townshend doing his signature suspended seconds and fourths as variation. The three instrumentalists create tension: Entwistle's staccato bass, Moon's drums awash with cymbals and sixteenth-note runs, and Townshend's choppy riffs; this all climaxes with returns to the main "Sparks" theme.

Its gentle ending is much like the awakening that occurs after emerging from a trance or meditation. Within the framework of *Tommy*, "Sparks" is as crucial to the narrative as the previous track. On its own and out of context, "Sparks" is still a dramatic exercise in suspense and catharsis, a compact and expertly delivered instrumental. The 2003 CD reissue bears a manufacturing error, in that "Amazing Journey" goes an extra minute and a half into the next song, "Sparks," before changing tracks. The 2013 reissue from Geffen Records corrects this mistake.

"Eyesight to the Blind (The Hawker)" closes out side A of the original record and is the only song not written by a member of The Who included on *Tommy*. Townshend was familiar with Mose Allison's cover of this Sonny Boy Williamson number, in which the narrator—the "Hawker" of the title—is extolling the virtues of his partner. Williamson's original includes a bridge that serves as the instrumental in The Who's version, along with a harmonica solo. At the end of each verse, the narrator declares his woman can cure blindness and muteness. The sexual implication is obvious: a woman so beautiful she brings back people's eyesight. Allison's version is as jazzy as Williamson's is steeped in the blues, with upright bass, tinkling pianos, and a brushed drum kit.

Townshend incorporated this song into *Tommy*, performed in typical Who fashion, adding an extra reference to this woman's prowess as also being capable of curing deafness. With this, each verse then speaks to a different sensory deprivation. Significantly, during the second verse, the millionaire daddy of the earlier versions becomes a magician. The final verse, written by Townshend, includes direct reference to this woman being a healer. In the *Tommy* story, the woman being hawked here will appear after some scenes with Tommy's family.

"Christmas" begins side B, starting with Roger's lead vocal; the effect on the listener can be jarring. The immediacy is intentional, as the song places the audience in the middle of a bustling Christmas morning with the Walker family. Roger urgently asks if the listener has seen the look on the children's faces as they open their gifts, waking up before dawn to indulge in the parcels of the holiday. By contrast, Tommy, in his state, is unable to comprehend Christmas or its meaning. The family pompously asks what will save his soul, before observing Tommy sitting by himself playing pinball. This can be likened to a child playing mindlessly with a fidget, frequently used with students on the autism spectrum and with attention issues. The family ponders Tommy's spiritual future, speculating that if he is never cured of his condition, he'll never achieve salvation.

This song skewers the hypocrisy of Christmas as it is celebrated in the West, a day—now a whole season—centered less around the birth of Jesus and more focused on materialism. The family senses that due to Tommy being unable to experience the joy of opening presents, due to his state of blindness, muteness, and deafness, his soul is Hell-bound. What Tommy's family doesn't observe is his own inner dialog, just as much a plea for human comfort as it is a hymn, where he longs to be seen, felt, touched, and healed. That this is juxtaposed with Pete's frantically voiced shout to Tommy if he can hear him further illustrates the lack of his family's awareness of his own, and even their, spirituality. The song ends with a reprise of the first verse, and the listener can practically hear the Walker family panting as they rip open the wrapping paper.

Content warning: child abuse, torture.

Tommy suffers his first misfortune—though pins instead of arrows—at the hands of his Cousin Kevin, the subject of the following track. Townshend handed over songwriting duties on this one to John Entwistle, and it is a very cruel ordeal indeed. Kevin mocks Tommy's condition, saying a game of hide and seek would take a week. He ties Tommy to a chair and subjects him to straight up torture: dunking his head under water, locking him outside in the rain, putting a cigarette out on his arm and observing his facial expressions, dragging him around by his hair, and pushing him down the stairs. This is not for the faint-hearted. Musically, the band delivers a raucous performance. The parallels of mockery and abuse between Tommy and Christ during his trial can be observed in both its cruelty and in its violence.

On "The Acid Queen," Tommy is given LSD as an attempted cure for his condition. The Acid Queen, a self-professed Gypsy (the term was not considered a racial slur at the time), is presumably the subject of "The Hawker." She promises to help the boy achieve his potential all from a single night in her company; the sexual overtones are obvious when she states the boy will be losing his childhood as well. As she prepares him for the journey, she foresees a time where Tommy will be cured of his condition, traveling in a manner similar to her itinerant life on the road.

With Tommy's mystical qualities already outlined in "The Amazing Journey," the Acid Queen's vision can be seen as a prophecy of Tommy's role as a spiritual figurehead. Despite the potency of her insight, the Acid Queen's acid proves more potent, as the experience only leaves Tommy with convulsions. Musically, on an album full of wondrous performances, the band is in top form here. Townshend opens the song with a dreamy guitar riff, Moon maintains the suspense of the Acid Queen's flirty sales pitch with his cymbals and toms. Pete sings lead, voicing the Acid Queen in a way that is both seductive and sinister. This is an excellent standalone Who single; it tells a complete story, one addressing youth angst (albeit in a twisted way), with a signature Pop Art musical "statement" in the middle. On "Glow Girl," it had been a plane crash, this time around, it is the onslaught of an acid trip.

The "Underture" is the musical representation of Tommy's acid trip. He hears the same musical theme that dominated his fever dream in the past. The same theme variates, extending beyond the cycle heard on "Sparks" to incorporate haunting vocal harmonies, new melodies, and changes on already-familiar chord patterns. With its constant shifts in pace and rhythm, the "Underture" is a hallucinogenic dream sequence that is meditative and yet busy. It goes on for over 10 minutes, like a trippy carpet ride. Each musical theme is casually presented to the listener, some bright, others dark, but approached without much engagement or attachment, a sensation akin to a psychedelic experience.

Moon's oceanic drums are accented by blasts from Entwistle's French horn and, near the song's end, a gong. The "Underture" takes the main theme of "Sparks" down multiple musical avenues each time before returning to the same conclusion; the meditation here is akin to the observation made by many illumined sages before that the paths are many, but truth is one. The same theme returns at the end of each passage, no matter how dramatic the musical variation may be. This musical exploration is intended to mimic the syncretic experience not just of Meher Baba, but one also shared by Sai Baba of Shirdi, Ramakrishna, and Ram Dass. The "Underture" concludes the first LP of the original album.

Content warning: sexual abuse.

Before Tommy's journey towards self-discovery can continue, his parents once again seek to leave him in the care of another questionable family member. On "Do You Think It's Alright," the parents debate whether Uncle Ernie is fit to watch over Tommy. Roger, singing as the father, mentions Ernie drinks to excess. Tommy's experience with Uncle Ernie, "Fiddle About," defies his parents' wildest expectations in that Ernie is a sexual predator and pedophile who molests his nephew. This is not an easy song to listen to, especially when Entwistle, as Ernie, cajoles Tommy out of his pajamas. He relishes the opportunity to have a victim unable to speak, see, and hear him. The musical performance builds in intensity before its climactic release.

The inspiration for this trauma came from Townshend's real-life experience with the Sea Scouts, and for similar reasons as "Cousin Kevin," Pete had John Entwistle write this song. As reporting of sexual violence has become more commonplace, helping to empower survivors of such abuse, a song like "Fiddle About" has aged poorly. In some circles, the song should come with a content or trigger warning. However, Townshend's efforts to address his traumatic childhood experience—with some help from his friends—deserves commendation. As for the song's relevance or even necessity within the narrative, this is a value judgment best left to the individual.

Strangely enough, where the tale of Uncle Ernie remains attached to the story by a tether, "Pinball Wizard," the most famous song on the album, was not part of the original vision Townshend had for *Tommy*. The song almost didn't happen. Kit Lambert invited Townshend's friend, music critic Nik Cohn, to visit IBC studios to hear the work in progress. Cohn enjoyed it, but remarked to Lambert and Townshend that he found the work a bit too serious. Townshend recalls that as he explained to Cohn that Tommy was meant to be a "divine musician, [who] felt vibrations as music," he became further dismayed. We can forgive his short-sightedness.

Knowing Cohn to be an immense fan of pinball, Townshend proposed that what if, instead of being this divine musician, Tommy was renowned as a pinball champion? Cohn at that point promised a stellar review: "Of course it would get five stars," he said to Townshend, "and an extra ball" (162). This one evening in conversation altered the narrative; a line in "Christmas" was changed to mention pinball and Townshend hurriedly composed "Pinball Wizard." He mentions in his memoir that "I made a huge leap into the absurd when I decided that the hero would play pinball while still deaf, dumb and blind. It was daft, flawed, and muddled, but also insolent, liberated and adventurous" (162). This author contends that the song emphasizes Townshend's original point made to Cohn rather than detracts from it. Tommy's interaction with the world comes through his perception of vibrations. His tactile senses are strongly intact and this guides his skills as a pinball player.

Townshend is being humble. "Pinball Wizard" is a beautiful composition, with its acoustic intro slowly picking up into the main riff, the vocal harmonies, and the dynamic shift into hard rock at the song's first chorus. The band's energy matches that of the song's narrator, a local pinball player who is observing Tommy playing the game effortlessly. Onlookers at the arcade come to form a fan base around Tommy, and they are even called disciples by the final verse, as they usher him up to the latest challenger.

"Pinball Wizard" also echoes Meher Baba's life story. He was an avid player of marbles, as noted by several of his devotees. He mentioned playing marbles as an expression of his capacity for joy ("When I Am in My Divine State"). Baba's childlike humor, such as his occasional preference to eschew writing duties for a game of marbles, is well-documented and is often present in his teachings. Baba writes that words relating to God ultimately "mean nothing" ("If You Love God You Become One With Him"). He describes that written and spoken explanations are an "insult" and that the only answer is Love.

When applied to the story of *Tommy*, his inability to see or hear does not impact his ability to love. In this same passage, speaking as the Lord, Baba writes, "There will be no more explanations. I will play marbles with you! I am so full of humor and so human that it is difficult even for *rishis* [advanced souls] and Saints to know Me as I am. I am at every level and act according to that level. With a child I am a child; with the highest saints I am one with them" (162).

Tommy's ascent to fame as a child, and his widespread adoration, has its roots in religious narratives. This devotional love of the Lord as a child can be seen in the Christian scene of the Nativity, where baby Jesus and Mary are worshipped by Joseph, visiting shepherds, barnyard animals—including by cattle, a sacred animal in Vedic teaching—and Zoroastrian astronomers known as the Magi or "wise men." Similarly, Vaisnavites venerate Bala Krishna, depictions of Lord Krishna as a baby and (often mischievous) toddler. Shaivites have similar images of Shiva, Ganesh, Karthikeya, and Devi in their iconography.

Tommy's newfound fame as a pinball legend grants him a degree of celebrity, and his parents are relieved in "There's a Doctor" that they are able to pay for advanced medical treatment for their child. This introduces "Go to the Mirror," where Tommy undergoes an examination by a medical expert. Sung by the doctor (Roger), he reports to the family that he finds Tommy's condition to be psychological. His testing shows eyes that are responsive to light and the capacity to hear but an inability to answer. Tommy again voices his inner monologue from Christmas: desiring to be seen, felt, touched, and healed.

The doctor states that Tommy is able to see, hear, and speak, but that some external stimuli is needed to remove his internal block. At this point in the song, the doctor commands Tommy to the mirror. As Tommy sits in front of the mirror, his parents and the doctor observe his trancelike state. While they ponder his thoughts, the audience is treated to them: a prayer of devotion, "Listening to You," which offers praises to an unnamed figure. This powerful anthem comes abruptly, rich with vocal harmonies and simple, but powerful, imagery. With cinematic vision that rivals Ray Davies of The Kinks, the song shifts back to Tommy's parents and the doctor, still engaged in conjecture over what is happening inside the boy's mind. This speculation leads to a more active plea on the next track.

"Tommy Can You Hear Me?" is a simple, repetitive mantra. Sung by Tommy's parents, the audience empathizes with their pleas to lend aid to their son. As the acoustic, drum-less song ends, Roger is left repeating Tommy's name, echoing as it fades away. (The version included on the *Kids Are Alright* soundtrack, recorded after *Tommy*'s release, ends with Roger shouting "HELLO!" in a pronounced Cockney accent.) Tommy's world of vibrations and the material plane are about to converge. Roger delivers his arena-ready macho-man shout for the first time on "Smash the Mirror." Tommy's parents have shifted in tone from forlorn to frustrated; in noting Tommy is staring into the mirror, Tommy's father suggests he truly has sight.

Parental frustration escalates into a rising falsetto that suggests a looming temper tantrum for a cartoon character before Townshend dive-bombs down the neck of his guitar, a musical signature in The Who's most raucous performances that is as iconic as his windmill and his ability to fly. The song is a strange inversion of "My Generation," where it is the parents screaming at the nonresponsive youth and engaging in destruction. Tommy's father accuses Tommy of being capable of hearing as well, offering the ultimatum of speaking up or he will smash the mirror. The sound of glass breaking is met with an angelic chorus.

Tommy emerges on "Sensation," noting his overwhelming presence after breaking out of his catatonic state. Sung in the first person, Tommy witnesses himself being worshipped by people stunned by the miraculous nature of his cure. The lyrics are flimsy. Tommy describes himself as a sensation, proclaiming himself to know the answer and to be the light. While the lyrics to "Sensation" would be perfectly at home within the pages of Meher Baba's *The Everything and the Nothing*, from a storytelling perspective it creates an image of Tommy having an inflated ego. (One cannot help but wonder if this was one of the "too serious" songs that led to Cohn's originally tepid response.) Musically, the song disappoints in its verses with a confusing melody before settling into a more steady chorus. "Sensation" was rarely included in The Who's live performances of *Tommy*.

The story behind "Sensation" is more interesting than the song itself. During The Who's visit to Australia in January 1968, Townshend met a fan named Rosie who was also a follower of Meher Baba. "Unsurprisingly," he writes, "we ended up sleeping together." He wrote the first verse of what would become "Sensation" about Rosie. With its haughty language of her approach being capable of breaking lovers' caresses, in its original form the song is an objectifying ode to lust. Townshend does not shy away from talking about this unflattering episode and his thoughts at the time about his relationship with then future wife Karen Astley.

Citing jet lag, plus commitment issues, Townshend found himself concluding that he "had made the right choice in Meher Baba and the wrong choice in Karen," adding rather cheekily, "for here before me was a very sexy girl who shared my new spiritual enthusiasm precisely" (141). He was also a 22-year-old man visiting the other side of the planet as a rock star. Rosie became Townshend's groupie for the course of their tour. On the return flight from New Zealand, Townshend decided he had to confess his infidelity to Karen.

Pete's account of his confession is karmic. Townshend remembers after saying he needed to talk about "something very important," that Karen positioned herself in a specific piece of furniture. He recalls the chair by name, where they got it, and that it was "one of the very first bits of furniture we had purchased together." Karen sat in the chair "with legs crossed, looking very regal indeed." As he struggled to produce words, Karen presented a letter that had come from Rosie. Their discussion resulted in deciding to ultimately marry, with Townshend calling himself a fool who was "damned lucky" to have Karen as a partner (Townshend 143).

A year later, at a garden party hosted by the sister of Baba devotee Delia DeLeon, Pete ran into Rosie again, with Karen and their baby in tow. "I felt that life was conspiring to teach me a lesson," he wrote. He was wise enough to recognize he had been wrong. In characteristic fashion, Townshend seals his tale with humor: "I had no doubt the girl was uneasy in this moment, and I sympathized, but the heartless artist in me rejoiced that from our liaison I had produced a good song" (Townshend 175).

Side D of *Tommy* opens with an urgent news bulletin: "Miracle Cure" for the famed Pinball Wizard. Lasting all of twelve seconds, we are aware that Tommy has become an international star. The mini-song ushers in the honky-tonk piano that starts "Sally Simpson," a much more nuanced depiction of Tommy's celebrity by making him a bit player in his own story. Sally Simpson is a young girl stuck in a bourgeois home environment. Her dad bluntly tells her she can't see Tommy while hand-washing his Rolls Royce. The chorus states that Sally knew from the outset that her attempt to find romance with Tommy would prove fruitless, but her mother nevertheless encourages her to follow her heart, urging her to follow *dharma*, regardless of the outcome.

Sally decides to sneak out when she sees the title of Tommy's sermon, which asks followers to join him, ending with the common-parlance adage "love will find a way," perhaps a nod to The Beatles' "You've Got to Hide Your Love Away" which includes the same line. She arrives at six and the music gets started at nine, suggesting a big program for the evening. As she waits, biting her nails and crying, one can picture fans in the throes of Beatlemania doing the same thing in *A Hard Day's Night* or their Shea Stadium concert.

The Who deliver another Pop Art experience, this time capturing the audience fanfare as Tommy comes onto stage. Moon fills in for the applause during this fun, cacophonous bridge. The song settles down as the narrator comments that the atmosphere had calmed down; Sally decides in that moment to rush Tommy. Barely able to touch his cheek, a man in a uniform—the impending threat warned about in the bridge—grabs Sally and throws her off the stage. As she lies on the ground with a gashed cheek, she tries in vain to catch Tommy's attention, but he goes on speaking, unable to see her from the stage lights.

The big, loud bridge comes again as Tommy exits the stage; in the song's coda, Roger does some more arena-ready shouting as he delivers the fallout from Sally's actions. She had to get stitches, her father arrogantly rebukes her, and she still ends up running away to marry a rock star in California. The entire episode came from Townshend witnessing the security at a Doors concert do the same thing to a young fan, who was brought backstage and met Townshend and presumably the members of The Doors (148). While Tommy still recalls the day his followers got out of hand, Sally by contrast thinks the scar on her cheek looks like Tommy's smile. This is yet another great standalone Who performance, a compact story-song much like "Tattoo" from *The Who Sell Out*.

After the softer "Sensation" and the piano-driven "Sally Simpson," "I'm Free" gives the audience a heavy electric guitar riff. The accented drum pattern was difficult for Moon to perform, so Entwistle and Townshend recorded the drums on the song. Tommy declares his freedom and his embracement of reality. In the song's only verse, he tantalizes the listener by promising to hold a different answer than what other Messianic claimants have offered. After a lush acoustic guitar solo, the song reprises the riff of "Pinball Wizard" as a falsetto chorus asks how they can follow him. Sequentially, this song was placed in what this author considers its proper place in the 1975 film adaptation, occurring right after "Smash the Mirror." (Along with casting Tina Turner as the Acid Queen, that is one of two things Ken Russell's movie got right.)

The song "Welcome" portrays a tranquil, albeit cultish, scene at Tommy's home. It's a party, with plenty of drinking, and all are welcome. "Welcome" plods along as a turgid folksy waltz severely lacking in energy before its samba-esque bridge, a burst that fizzles out and returns to the main slog. Townshend wrote the song before *Tommy* was fully realized; unlike "Sally Simpson," which was inspired sometime in 1967, the adaptation of "Welcome" into the story is rickety at best.

Unsurprisingly, the song was not included in live performances of *Tommy* and its inclusion on the finished album remains an unforced error. Townshend expressed some disappointment with the song as well, citing that it "lacked edge" and that this could confuse listeners as to the nature of Tommy's abode (Townshend 159). The lyrics depict a haven for people to gather and commiserate, but the sleepy musical performance suggests a less than lively atmosphere. A last-minute suggestion from Moon helped correct the mistake.

For reasons unknown, Townshend's demo for "Tommy's Holiday Camp" is on the finished album. Featuring a cheesy carnival organ, a banjo, and Townshend's double-tracked vocals, it works, lending the ditty a homespun feel. A wordless band version can be found on the CD reissue. Sung by Uncle Ernie, the jingle offers the somewhat menacing promise that the holiday goes on forever at Tommy's.

Writing within a theocracy that includes a Creationist Museum in the Commonwealth of Kentucky and a biblical theme park in Florida that recreates the Crucifixion for paying spectators, the satire of "Tommy's Holiday Camp" is lost in a now-commonplace, but still frightening, reality. At the time of *Tommy*'s inception, however, it was a joke to suggest a commercialized religious retreat center disguised as a holiday camp. All of this sets up for the rock opera's finale.

"We're Not Gonna Take It" begins with Tommy welcoming his followers to the camp. He tells them that if they are to follow him, if they are to achieve self-realization as he did, they must do it the way he did it. They must cover their eyes, ears, and mouths and play pinball. It is an obvious, heavy-handed statement about the oppressive nature of not just organized religion, but of the various personality cults that surround false prophets, fake gurus, and phony yogis. Such a specified prescription for the attainment of salvation disregards the individual experience; Vedic teaching describes four *yogic* paths towards enlightenment: meditation (*raja*), philosophical speculation (*jnana*), devotion (*bhakti*), and charitable action (*karma*). Each approach appeals to different personality types and can be further developed into specific practices, while still sharing a goal and philosophical grounding.

Tommy's domineering leadership inspires a revolt that starts with the whispered chorus of the song's title. As he watches over his disciples—with eyeshades, earplugs, and corks in their mouths—the reformed Uncle Ernie is on standby to usher them to their pinball machines. This time, the chorus is loud and proud as the followers declare their rejection. They not only don't want Tommy, they are rejecting religion as a whole. As they revolt, their language becomes violent, pledging to forsake their leader. The usage of the ugly trigger word "rape" in this song is not meant to be taken literally; rather, it should be interpreted as meaning the theft of something that cannot be easily taken back. Tommy's best ideas will be stolen, plundered by a fickle public just as ready to forget him.

This segues into "See Me, Feel Me," where Tommy, broken and destitute, finally recites aloud his internal lamentation. Rather than expressing his longing of being seen, felt, touched, and healed to his family, an acid-peddling seductress, or a doctor, Tommy is speaking to a higher power. Held aloft by a thin guitar arrangement, organ, and vocal harmonies, this is one of Roger Daltrey's finest moments as a vocalist. As the band joins in on "Listening to You," Tommy reaches a state of *samadhi*, full consciousness; in the Buddhist tradition it is called *nirvana*. Meher Baba would call it "God-intoxication." It is only at this point, humbled by the shortcomings of his grandiosity, a true ego death, that Tommy achieves true enlightenment and self-awareness. Whether he returns to his previous catatonic state, newly established as a *mast*, remains up for debate.

With a simple, ascending major chord structure of A-B-C, "Listening to You" is a majestic closer. The chorus that greets Tommy may as well be voices from the heavens. Tommy's divine vision includes seeing behind the Lord an assembly of millions—presumably saints and sages—and praises the Lord for the delivery of a blessing and of divine truth. The lyrics are laden with imagery framed by his sensory input, all from the "You" of the title, without a doubt taken to mean God. It is from listening to God that Tommy can hear music. It is from gazing upon God (*darshan*) that he feels warmth. He likens his journey to climbing a mountain, reflecting the tumultuous path he has treaded.

The reference to feet is straight from Vedic practice, specifically *charanasparsha*, where one makes salutation to a venerated individual (deity, spiritual teacher, or elder) by touching their feet. Similarly, references to the "lotus feet" of the deities permeates *bhakti* literature throughout the Vedic tradition. Feet are considered dirty and taboo in many cultures, including Vedic society; in performing *charanasparsha*, one is showing a sign of immense reverence. Jesus washes his disciples' feet in the book of John, while foot-washing is later mentioned as common practice in the early Christian church in Paul's first epistle to Timothy. On the original record, the song fades into oblivion.

The band's extended performance of "See Me, Feel Me/Listening to You" from the Woodstock Festival is of note. Besides the raw sound of four musicians playing live, the second half continues to speed up to a faster tempo than what is on the record. Daltrey, and allegedly other members of The Who, had been dosed unknowingly with LSD prior to their performance. Roger, clearly overpowered by the music, can be seen stepping away from the microphone several times, allowing Townshend to play several guitar solos. By the time of Woodstock, the band had been playing *Tommy* for several months, and the beauty of spontaneity charges the performance with a vitality that suggests the band is playing as though their very souls depend on it. It is a truly sublime moment, and a blessing that it was captured on film and audio. The clip is in the *Woodstock* movie as well as in *The Kids Are Alright*. The performance helped cement The Who's reputation as one of the foremost acts of their time.

No Easy Way to Be Free: A Glance Further Down the Amazing Journey

By 1970, Townshend and The Who were rock royalty. His cover story for the November 26 issue of *Rolling Stone*, "In Love with Meher Baba," is a heady piece that recounts Townshend's initial contact with Baba's teachings, a breakdown of his philosophy, and an honest account of his drug use prior to becoming a devotee himself. When he first smoked pot, he didn't get into it so much as he fell in love with it. However, he realized, much like John Sinclair wrote during the same period, that the high didn't last. The article is all written in Townshend's style, which is witty, at times self-aggrandizing, but an enjoyable read in its own right. He truly was alone among his peers, save for Frank Zappa, as a critic of even marijuana during this time of indulgence and the occasional death by misadventure.

Baba's ideas would further inspire The Who's 1970 single "The Seeker." In it, Townshend rejects Bob Dylan, The Beatles, and Timothy Leary, representing turning on, tuning in, and dropping out, respectively, as sources for the answer to life's most important questions. He pledges to look for the answer until his death, concluding in the final verse, in a manner similar to a Zen Buddhist *koan*, that he and his companion are looking at one another whilst looking for themselves. Musically and lyrically, "The Seeker" is a transition into what I call Townshend's God-rock phase, lasting until about 1972. He is seen on stage around this time looking like Heaven's janitor, in an all-white boiler suit with black boots. Eventually, Townshend tie-dyed one suit, adding a hippie element to his appearance (198–199). He kept his beard just unkempt enough as to look like a shaman. This phase of scraggly asceticism was a benefit of Townshend's worldly success, which also allowed him more time to engage in his creative pursuits.

His rock opera *Lifehouse* borrowed from some of the more intricate elements of Baba's philosophy, namely that the vibrations of the universe we know as music double as a way of channeling the Almighty—an idea held to by ISKCON and Science of the Soul as well—though struggles within both the band and the record label yielded a different result. With a resequenced, pared-down track lineup, shortened from 2 LPs to just one, *Lifehouse* became The Who's next album, *Who's Next*. As with *Tommy* and the spiritually inspired songs that preceded it, songs from the *Who's Next* album like "Bargain," "Baba O'Riley," and "The Song Is Over" take on new meanings when read through a theological lens. Conversely, "Love Ain't for Keeping" celebrates the life of a householder (*grihastha* in Vedic terms) with a wife and children, enjoying a moment of domesticated romance, while "Won't Get Fooled Again" is an objectively blunt meditation on political violence.

Other *Lifehouse* songs would turn up on Townshend's 1972 full-length solo debut, *Who Came First*. Compiling a few earlier EP's Townshend had put together with Ronnie Lane and some other Baba devotee musician friends, plus a few new songs, *Who Came First* is a stunning listen. On his tracks, Townshend plays all of the instruments, showing off his skills as a bass player and as a competent drummer whose style is closer to that of Stones' beat keeper Charlie Watts than the maniacal stylings of Keith Moon. Townshend shares space for Ronnie Lane's "Evolution" and Billy Nicholls' "Forever's No Time at All." Lane's contribution is a Dylanesque folk ode about the process of reincarnation in various states of life, first heard in a longer version titled "Stone" on The Faces' 1970 debut *First Step*. (The group had formed out of a merger of sorts between Rod Stewart and Ronnie Wood of the Jeff Beck Group and several Small Faces, including Lane and drummer Kenney Jones.) Nicholls' contribution is a luscious hippie drone, a #1 hit from that summer in a perfect world. The album ends with "Parvardigar," a Universal Prayer penned by Meher Baba with music by Pete Townshend. Most of the *Lifehouse* project can be reassembled using Townshend's demos along with the tracks from *Who's Next* (get the deluxe edition) and *Who Came First*.

Townshend's writing over the next few years on *Quadrophenia* and *The Who by Numbers* avoids spiritual teachings like what is present on *Tommy* or *Who's Next*; indeed, *Quadrophenia* is Townshend attempting to present a secular, parochial version of *Lifehouse* by making it a tale of a young Mod in search of himself. On *The Who by Numbers*, Townshend is openly singing about his drinking, wondering aloud how many true friends he has, and confesses that he is feeling adrift. At this point, George Harrison was in a similar struggle; his friend Chris O'Dell said of this time, "Pattie [Harrison] and I used to joke that we didn't know if his hand was in the prayer bag or the coke bag" (188). It was during this time Harrison produced *Dark Horse* and *Extra Texture (Read All About It)*, albums laden with songs expressing his own shortcomings and battles with depression as the result of what he perceived as earthly failures.

The title track from *Who Are You* takes its chorus from one of Baba's prayers, and while The Who's 1978 album showed a revisiting of themes first presented on *Lifehouse*, *Who's Next*, and *Who Came First*, the ideas remained unexplored on subsequent records. Townshend, impacted greatly by the loss of Keith Moon in September of that year, eventually broke his vow to avoid chemical intoxicants when he began using cocaine. Though relapses are common and his twelve-year streak of sobriety is commendable, Townshend is his harshest critic. He publicly distanced himself from Meher Baba–related organizations, citing his own human shortcomings as reason for him to not be considered the best representative of Baba. Despite this, it was during that time that he composed perhaps the finest and most succinct summary of Baba's teachings, "(Let My Love) Open the Door," in 1980.

Townshend's spiritual awakening first met the public through *Tommy*, a parable disguised as a rock opera. The lesson imparted is for the aspirant to find their own path to bliss, not to force any single one method or practice as being superior or supreme. So long as one's efforts stem from a place of love, executed without attachment to self, it will not be in vain. A musically groundbreaking record on its own merits, *Tommy*'s spiritual message and linkage to Meher Baba, who bears credit in the record's sleeve as "Avatar," lends a timeless importance to the work. May it continue to lead people towards Baba's life-affirming, God-positive message of love.

WORKS CITED

Baba, Meher. *Discourses*. Sheriar Foundation, 2011.
Baba, Meher. *The Everything and the Nothing*. Sheriar Foundation, 2003.
Baba, Meher. "Excerpts from *God in a Pill*." http://www.avatarmeherbaba.org/erics/godpill. html. Accessed 1 May 2017.
Baba, Meher. *God Speaks*, 2nd ed. Sufism Reoriented, 2010.
Baba, Meher. *If You Love God You Become One with Him*. http://www.avatarmeherbaba.org/ erics/honesty2.html. Accessed 1 May 2017.
Baba, Meher. "Public Message upon Arrival on His Second Visit to America." http://www. avatarmeherbaba.org/erics/prusa.html. Accessed 1 May 2017.
Baba, Meher. "The Universal Message." http://www.avatarmeherbaba.org/erics/univmsg.html. Accessed 1 May 2017.

Baba, Meher. "When I Am in My Divine State." http://www.avatarmeherbaba.org/erics/mydivinestate.html. Accessed 1 May 2017.

Bible quotations are sourced from New International Version, https://www.biblestudytools.com/niv/. Accessed 1 May 2017.

Dass, Ram. *Be Here Now*. Lama Foundation, 1971.

Donkin, William. *The Wayfarers: An Account of the Work of Meher Baba with the God-Intoxicated, and also with Advanced Souls, Sadhus, and the Poor*. https://www.ambppct.org/Book_Files/Wayfarers_1.pdf. Originally published in 1948, posted online in 2011, accessed 1 May 2017.

Fenster, David. "Avataric Features." http://www.avatarmeherbaba.org/erics/avataricbody.html. Accessed 1 May 2017.

Greene, Joshua M. *Here Comes the Sun: The Spiritual and Musical Journey of George Harrison*. Wiley, 2006

Gupta, Mahendranath. *The Gospel of Sri Ramakrishna*. http://www.belurmath.org/gospel/. Originally published in 1942, accessed online 1 May 2017.

Neill, Andrew, and Matt Kent. *Anyway, Anyhow, Anywhere: The Complete Chronicle of the Who, 1958–1978*. Friedman/Fairfax, 2009.

O'Dell, Chris. *Miss O'Dell: Hard Days and Long Nights with the Beatles, the Stones, Bob Dylan and Eric Clapton*. Touchstone, 2010.

Prabhupada, A.C. Bhaktivedanta Swami. *Bhagavad-Gita as It Is*. Macmillan, 1972.

Prabhupada, A.C. Bhaktivedanta Swami. *Srimad Bhagavatam*. http://www.vedabase.com/en/sb/. Accessed 1 May 2017.

Purdom, Charles. *The God-Man*. https://www.ambppct.org/Book_Files/godMan-1.pdf. Originally published in 1964, posted online in 2011. Accessed 1 May 2017.

Stein, Jeff, director. *The Kids Are Alright*, 1979.

Townshend, Pete. "In Love with Meher Baba." *Rolling Stone*, 26 November 1970. www.rollingstone.com/music/news/in-love-with-meher-baba-by-pete-townshend-19701126, accessed 1 May 2017.

Townshend, Pete. *Who I Am*. HarperCollins, 2013.

Heavy Metal as Religion

Rhetorically Repurposing Catholic Motifs Within Power Metal

GAVIN F. HURLEY

Conservative critics of heavy metal may assume that the music diametrically opposes virtue, traditional beauty, and religious faith. Hair metal bands in the 1980s, such as Poison and Skid Row, may call to mind hedonistic excess and partying. Death metal bands, like Cannibal Corpse, contradict traditional conceptions of orderly harmonic music. Black metal bands, like Mayhem and Gorgoroth, actively undermine religious faith through blasphemous or satanic spectacle. Metal often embraces transgression, veering away from traditional norms. Heavy metal and the various subgenres of heavy metal often rebel against the mainstream "world." However, if channeled in a different direction than the aforementioned examples, heavy metal can also identify as a religious discourse. Through musical and cultural solidarity, metalheads find hope by resisting against mainstream culture and searching for a more peaceable world.

In this essay, I show that some metal subgenres fight against the world's material program to announce "heavy metal as religion" itself, equipped with its own (albeit vague) metaphysics and quest for Truth. It is important to recognize that these bands are not Christian metal bands like Stryper or Trouble. Rather, they appropriate existing Christian traditions for their own productive purposes, sharing similar goals as Christianity. Specifically, this essay examines one strand of this appropriation, the Catholic tradition within the subgenre of power metal. The examination concludes with a celebration of such rhetorical strategy: for both heavy metal and Christianity.

Manowar and Fighting the World

Power metal fully blossomed in the early 1990s but evolved from influences from the 1980s with American bands like Dio and Manowar, British bands like Iron Maiden and Judas Priest, and fantasy-driven power metal bands like Helloween from Germany. The subgenre evolved from the speedy guitar riffing and vocal stylizing of 1980s metal bands (especially Iron Maiden and Judas Priest); power metal supplemented this musical stylizing with epic imagery, storytelling, and mythological elements. Fully embracing the fantasy genre, German metal bands such as Helloween led the way for the international success of power metal in the 1990s, a trend which still continues today (Sharpe-Young 262).

As an influential American power metal band who began in the early 1980s, Manowar (1980–present) began to appropriate religion into heavy metal. Specifically, Manowar evoked the spirit of pagan traditions in their music and lyrics. For instance, their 1983 *Into Glory Ride* album includes a song entitled "Gates of Valhalla"; their 1984 *Sign of the Hammer* EP includes songs such as "Thor (The Powerhead)," "Sign of the Hammer," and "The Oath." All songs recount pagan myth in an expository manner. However, later in their discography they complicate this pagan approach. On the 1996 *Louder than Hell* album, Manowar offers a heavy metal anthem entitled "The Gods made Heavy Metal." In the song, Manowar claims that the gods created heavy metal and these deities want metalheads to play and listen to metal "louder than hell." Do listeners literally believe creation myths about heavy metal music? Of course not. Manowar's process of combining pagan myth with statements about metal becomes the message. Their message is that metal transports its listeners beyond the mundane using artistic equipment: musical arts, poetic arts, and narrative arts.

Ultimately a Platonic framework is applied; the world is mundane and metal becomes a vehicle to transport listeners beyond the material and toward the ideal. This move is similarly illustrated in the song "Fighting the World" on their 1987 album *Fighting the World*. In this song, Manowar explicitly proclaim that both the band and fans fight the world for the opportunity to play "true" heavy metal. Based on this logic, one can assume that the "world"—that is, contemporary mainstream civilization—does not allow heavy metal to be played. Additionally, as Manowar repeatedly mentions in various songs: the world is filled with "false metal" as well. Thusly, metal bands must fight the world as a means to manage this communal resistance as they quest toward a truthful ideal.

The cover artwork of *Fighting the World* by fantasy artist Ken Kelly displays a subtle religious representation of this reverence for the ideal. On the album cover, the band stands on a large pile of rocks. Their swords and hammers are on the ground. It is assumed that the band has just fought an enemy—presumably "the world"—and they stand victorious. Behind the band, upon a backdrop of sky, a beam of light shines down. This nuance indicates a gesture to a transcendent ideal, appropriating a classic Christian allusion to God or heaven.

This gesture to transcendence more fully connects to religion in the Manowar song "Holy War" from the *Fighting the World* album. Here, holiness—specifically Christian holiness—is associated with the heavy metal experience and heavy metal membership. In "Holy War," Manowar proclaims metalheads are "*baptized*" ("in fire and steel") and alludes to an apocalyptic "last battle," two Christian references. But more compellingly, Manowar directly asserts that "metal's our religion" in the second verse. Although in previous albums Manowar primarily relies on pagan myth and legend, "Holy War" marks Manowar's first song to *directly* associate heavy metal to religion as well as to the Christian religion.

Nevertheless, the line "metal's our religion" is complicated in Manowar's *Louder Than Hell* song "The Gods Made Heavy Metal" which also indicates "true" metal's relationship with religion. Unlike "Holy War," "The Gods Made Heavy Metal" mentions that metal is *more* than religion, rather "it's the only way to live." What is the meaning of this contradictory phrase? Manowar seems to be pointing out that religion is not merely a club or a hobby.

A metalhead cannot "be metal" selectively; rather a metalhead must be "metal" at all moments, in all areas of life. Therefore, Manowar gestures to the full understanding of a religious lifestyle, not the secular misunderstanding of religion as a club or organization. Albeit a bit misstated, Manowar seems to be evoking the true spirit of a church—one that is encompassing and counter-cultural. This is a similar perspective to Evangelical Christian leader Charles W. Colson's famous remark, "Biblically the church is an organism not an organization—a movement not a monument. It is not part of the community; it is a whole new community. It is not an orderly gathering; it is a new order with new values, often in sharp contrast with the values of the surrounding society" (Manser 42). Similarly, Manowar fosters a self-directed community in sharp contrast with the world—and persuades their fans to be of a similar idealistic attitude in all areas of their life.

In short, Manowar uses references to religion and the concept of religion itself to attract a following. And in doing so, they indirectly harness the power of transcendence to help sweep listeners away from the everyday and unite behind a greater cause: the heavy metal religion, an autonomous community opposed to mainstream culture.

Freedom Call and the Heavenly Kingdom on Earth

German power metal band, Freedom Call (1998–present) offers a "metal as religion" iteration that fully distances itself from pagan religions and aligns with Christianity. Unlike Manowar who has songs like "Hail and Kill," "Kill with Power" and "Die for Metal" Freedom Call offers brighter songs like "Stairway to Fairyland," "Heart of the Rainbow" and "Land of Light." Freedom Call's lyrics are less focused on war; additionally, the music sounds more mirthful and melodic, featuring the vocalist Chris Bay who provides a lighter charm than the Manowar's occasionally raspy vocalist Eric Adams. Freedom Call does not embrace the metal-as-"Holy-War" *agon* as much as Manowar; instead, they stress positive end results: an eventual metal utopia unfolding on Earth. Their songs illustrate the war with an enemy; however, the negative aspects of the war are not fronted. For example, on the 2002 *Eternity* album, Freedom Call has a song titled "Warriors" which describe angelic soldiers who are born from light and "return from darkness" to fight and reclaim heaven. The album also features the song "Land of Light" which also refers to emergence from the darkness into the light, ushering mass euphoria and a heavenly kingdom. However, their most religiously revealing moment in this *Eternity* concept album is the first song: "Metal Invasion." Despite the militant sounding title, the song differs from Manowar's more aggressive approach. Freedom Call's song opens with several chanted lines in Latin; the song proceeds to discuss the battle and the bravery of a Crusade; it references a quest for eternal life; then it essentially remarks that a "heavenly kingdom" will unfold on earth from this "metal invasion."

"Metal Invasion" indirectly evokes several dimensions of religion, but specifically, they evoke the Roman Catholic religion. They integrate Catholic references—but more importantly, they imprint heavy metal with similar religious goals as Catholicism. What are the Catholic references and goals? First, the song begins with Latin, which is the universal language of the Catholic Church. Secondly, the crusades were Roman Catholic holy wars, which sought to rescue Christian places from non–Christian populations. Finally, apart from the Crusades, the wider Catholic goal is to set human beings in right praise of God—and thusly, usher heaven onto Earth. This is a dimension seen revealed in the pivotal Christian "Lord's Prayer": "Thy kingdom come, thy will be done on Earth as it is in heaven."

Although they never refer to metal as a religion, Freedom Call has an imaginative narrative in place—one by which metal warriors of light usher heaven on Earth via commitment to heavy metal. This universal aim is similar to the Catholic universal aim. However, Freedom Call is careful not to be too heavy-handed with the Catholic motif. Therefore, they subtly undercut the Catholic motif with polytheist references to be more accommodating and inclusive. Freedom Call hits their inclusive stride in a more recent album, *Masters of Light* (2016), where they explicitly communicate inclusivity, specifically in the song, "Metal Is for Everyone." Freedom Call again evokes religious dimensions in a rhetorical fashion. In "Metal Is for Everyone," they proclaim that metal is "stronger than law." This is another nod to the transcendence of metal. Moreover, the line appears to be a gesture to The Gospel of Matthew where Jesus states: "For I tell you that unless your righteousness surpasses that of the Pharisees and the teachers of the law, you will certainly not enter the kingdom of heaven" (*New International Bible*, Matt 5:20). In a spirit similar to Christianity, metal surpasses the worldly law in an inclusive manner—and such transcendence will open up the heaven to all people. This harkens back to the "Metal Invasion" song from 2002. Freedom Call offers a transcendent universal appeal here. Much like Jesus's statement, Freedom Call alludes to the concept that anyone can enter the metal journey toward Truth, regardless of cultural standards and laws.

Powerwolf and Catholicism

German power metal band Powerwolf (2003–present) unapologetically amplifies Catholic motif as a means to assert metal as a religion. Unlike Freedom Call who does so subtly, Powerwolf visibly repurposes Catholic tradition, liturgy, aesthetics, and even traditional Catholic music. Similar to Manowar and Freedom Call, their goal is not to preach Catholicism or even Christianity. Instead, Powerwolf engages the rhetorical equipment of Catholic tradition to attract diverse audiences to their self-proclaimed "metal religion." Clearly, the religious rhetoric is effective: their 2013 album *Preachers of the Night* sailed to number one on the German music charts.

Powerwolf leads its audience through self-proclaimed "Metal Masses" or live shows. Each "Mass" begins with sacred organ and choir music. The vocalist, Attila Dorn, wears a priestly outfit on stage, albeit in a gothic fashion. The keyboardist, Falk Schlegel, plays an archaic organ while wearing a priestly stole. Images of stained glass windows act as a backdrop behind the band as they play. Their set includes songs from albums such as *Blessed and Possessed*, *Bible of the Beast*, *Blood of the Saints*, *Lupus Dei*, and *Preachers of the Night*, wherein they intersperse Latin phrases into their German and English lyrics. Musically, Powerwolf's melodies are fairly generic by power metal standards; yet the uniquely religious theatrics sets Powerwolf apart from other power metal experiences. The Catholic motif becomes their signature brand.

The integration of Catholicism provides Powerwolf with a unique rhetorical advantage within a large international market of power metal bands. Powerwolf's songs are catchy and the music is well orchestrated; but apart from this, how does the explicit Catholic motif work to successfully attract an audience to their artistic vision? And additionally, why use Catholicism? Why not use Lutheranism (After all they are a German band.)? Or, why not use pagan mythology like other metal bands? Firstly, Roman Catholicism highlights holy unification. In fact, "Catholic" in Greek (*katholikos*) means "on the whole" or "universal." According to the *Catechism of the Catholic Church*, the Church is "holy" and "one," "calling together" people from all over the Earth (*CCC* 750–751). The Roman Catholic Mass is a sacred event whereby Catholics reaffirm a pervading oneness with Jesus Christ and the entire Church, throughout the world, in heaven and on Earth, and with the living and the dead (*CCC* 1354). Powerwolf's image and attraction rely on such unification—and they are far from subtle in calling the audience toward this unity. For instance, during the 2015 Masters of Rock live show in Vizovice, Czech Republic, Attila demands that the packed crowd, "Celebrate the one and only metal mass with us!" (*Powerwolf: The Metal Mass*). This nod to the "one-and-only" uniqueness of Powerwolf's show fosters an appeal to "orthodoxy" that other metal bands do not express. This approach is similar to Manowar's insistence on "true metal"; however, Powerwolf offers a more inviting appeal: inclusive and evangelical about the "truth," rather than exclusive and cultish. Sycophants are welcome to join Powerwolf's metal masses and fall into communion with the metal ideal. About halfway through the "metal mass," Powerwolf blesses the audience using an incense burner and at the end of the "metal mass" he tells the audience to "Go forth!" The call to "go forth" is borrowed from the universal Catholic liturgy where the priest proclaims to the congregation at the conclusion of the Mass to "Go forth. The Mass has ended." The call reminds the Catholic congregation to act as a Christian outside of the walls of the church and spread the Good News. Similarly, Powerwolf wishes the audience to remain in communion with the ideals of metal when they leave the concert hall—and spread the message of heavy metal to the world.

Powerwolf additionally uses the Latin language in their albums and live show. Again, this rhetorically gestures to universalism. According to traditionalist Catholic scholar, Peter Kwasniewski: "Latin is universal and is not the daily language of any modern nation or people. There is no cultural imperialism in the use of Latin, but rather a visible sign [...] reaching out to all nations, leading them back to the unity in one faith, one communion" (159). As a champion of Catholic orthodoxy, Kwasniewski argues that denying Latin in the liturgical rites contradicts the universalism of the Church (160). He notes that Latin establishes a shared universal language of the Church wherein multilingual nations can unite (Kwasniewski 160). Ultimately, Kwasniewski implies that Latin is inclusively practical. In a similar rhetoric, Powerwolf's evocation of Latin suggests that the music—specifically, metal music and culture—is universal; therefore, "true metal" welcomes all people to their "congregation." Of course, Powerwolf is much more explicit about the rhetoric of Latin than Freedom Call: Latin language appears in nearly all of Powerwolf's songs.

In addition to the Latin, Powerwolf also uses pipe organ tones in their music. In favor of traditional organ music in the Catholic Church, Kwasniewski explains that the organ tone effectively communicates solemnity much like Gregorian chant. He notes that such solemnity allows congregations to see the world around them "differently," specifically with *sobria inebrietas* or sober inebriation (Kwasniewski 17). This sobriety adds *gravitas* to the music and the message. The solemnity of this musical choice is not lost on Powerwolf. Powerwolf's keyboardist Falk Schlegel, who is a trained church organist, defends their organ tones as more "ceremonial" than "sinister and scary." Therefore, a solemnity pervades Powerwolf's music through the ceremonial organ music. The ceremonial solemnity provides a layer of seriousness that reaches beyond the profane. Combined with references to Catholicism's sacred history and traditional liturgy, the organ transports Powerwolf's audiences beyond the profane toward something greater. Although, *Catechism of the Catholic Church* clarifies that song and music should seek "conformity with the Church's norms" (*CCC* 1158) and "should be drawn chiefly from Sacred Scripture and from liturgical works" (*CCC* 1158, quoting from Sacrosanctum concilium), Powerwolf uses Catholic traditions of solemnity to proclaim heavy metal as a religion: one that is more than a club but a meta-narrative that helps propel its listeners beyond the world of appearances.

Accommodating Difference Within Powerwolf

Apart from their very first album, Powerwolf's brand is based upon a particularly outlandish Eastern European werewolf legend: the "Lupus Dei," or "Wolf of God." This werewolf legend comes from the trial of Theis of Kaltenburg, a werewolf case from the 1690s. In this trial, Theis, the defendant, describes how he lived as a werewolf; additionally, he explained that he was not alone as a werewolf; rather he was part of a community of werewolves. However, Theis clarified that as a werewolf community, they were not "beasts of Hell," rather they were "hounds of God." According to Theis, who was presumably of "sound mind," he and other werewolves descended into Hell on holy feast days. On these feast days, their mission was to steal food and equipment from "wizards" who were appointed by the devil. After arriving back from Hell, Theis and the werewolf community distributed these goods to farmers on Earth to help flourish the harvest. Ultimately, their mission was pious. Unlike popular legend may suggest: Theis's werewolves were not evil creatures. Instead, they combated evil in the name of God (Blecourt 49–50).

Powerwolf's albums grow out of this pious werewolf tale as related in the historical trial of Theis. Consequently, Powerwolf similarly straddles discussions of Hell and Heaven, piety and evil, much like the legend that also blends both perspectives. Unlike metal bands such as King Diamond or Rhapsody of Fire, who narrate one full story throughout an entire album (or between several albums), Powerwolf's albums do not regularly convey closed linear narratives. Rather, Powerwolf's songs highlight isolated aspects of the fiction whereby werewolves are working with the Church, albeit militantly. Consequently, Powerwolf's approach fosters audience imagination. Via numerous cues, listeners can plug bits of information about the mythology into the wider thematic framework that has been established by Powerwolf. In other words, the legend's relative obscurity requires audience members to fill in the gaps with their own imagination and thus have fun participating in the narrative. The mystery and ambiguity of the mythology itself can kindle audience curiosity—and, consequently, increase audience connectivity to the music.

Powerwolf delicately crafts their songs with the audience in mind. Apart from situating their music on the mysterious "Lupus Dei" myth, they also implement irony to safeguard themselves from being identified as Christian zealots, or conversely, as Christian blasphemers. In Powerwolf's *Kruetweg: Of Wolves and Men* band documentary, Matthew Greywolf readily admits that Powerwolf deliberately uses irony to increase the playful elements of their albums (*Powerwolf: The Metal Mass Live*). This playfulness allows them not too be taken seriously and gives room for the audience to have fun with their music. Therefore, Powerwolf purposely incorporates ambivalence into their songs to signal to audiences that they are not religious zealots, nor are they anti–Catholic. For example, their *Bible of the Beast* album offers religious anthems like "Raise Your Fist, Evangelist" alongside ambivalent songs like "St. Satan's Day" and "Seven Deadly Saints." The contradictory song titles imply that Powerwolf is not seriously preaching a dogma. This intentional hedge allows them to appeal to diverse metal fans: ones that may enjoy horror, ones that may identify as Christian, ones that may identify as Pagan or Satanist, and ones that may merely enjoy creative artistic concepts. Therefore, Powerwolf's inclusivity is similar to Freedom Call's mission: albeit instead of using fantasy elements, Powerwolf develops a particular horror legend. Under the banner of "metal," Powerwolf synthesizes a patchwork of perspectives and mythologies. The patchwork—united within their storytelling, music, and culture—inclusively accepts difference while not compromising the spirit of those differences.

Despite sounding like an attack on traditional values by ironically blending two opposing perspectives (song titles such as "St. Satan's Day," "Catholic in the Morning, Satanist at Night," and "Amen and Attack"), Powerwolf primarily purposes the Roman Catholic tradition as means to reconcile diametrically opposed positions and demonstrate that contrasting positions can cooperate within the heavy metal arena. Powerwolf offers a version of the Roman Catholic meta-narrative in their music, lyrics, and references; however, the band does not take a definitive stance within that framework. Powerwolf offers a space for metalheads to pluralistically cooperate as long as they share in the communion of the metal mass. Therefore, Powerwolf accommodates difference of belief while uniting under a common heavy metal ideal.

The "Metal as Religion" Rhetoric

The roles of "metal as religion" rhetoric are twofold: it can (1) adhere listeners to heavy metal music and the culture, and (2) introduce participants to the value of religion, building an individual's appetite for sacredness. "Metal as religion" provides audiences exposure to sacred traditions, aesthetic iterations, and counter-cultural ideals that often remain hidden from mainstream visibility. This approach folds religious rhetoric into "metal as religion." In doing so, the stigma of religion in heavy metal culture can dissipate. Although the "metal as religion" approach may seem to want to supplant Christianity, it can actually introduce listeners to Christian history, culture, traditions, and truths. Merely by cooperating with Christian motif (rather than *against* Christian motif as seen in the Black Metal subgenre), the music can kindle an appetite for transcendence and plant a seed of spiritual curiosity, which can be potentially developed further through theological inquiry or participation in an institutional religion.

Several counterarguments commonly arise in this discussion. Skeptics may suggest that the repurposing of Christian/Catholic religion undercuts the solemnity of its Truths; therefore, they may deem the appropriation of religion as blasphemous or sacrilegious. Similarly, critics may see Powerwolf as play-acting, mocking, or poking fun at religion. However, in the "Kreutweg: Of Wolves and Men" Powerwolf documentary, Falk Schlegel (Powerwolf's keyboardist) explains that Powerwolf intentionally expresses religion with "a necessary distance to it." Schlegel further explains that he and his fellow band members are "not fanatics, not Satanists, not Christian"; instead, they are entertainers (*Powerwolf: The Metal Mass*). In other words, they are not mimicking Christian rituals to invert Christian ritual as seen in Black Metal songs, such as Cradle of Filth's "Dinner at Deviant's Palace," which includes a backwards version of the Lord's Prayer. Instead, Powerwolf pragmatically integrates Catholicism as a participatory rhetoric—and in doing so, they reveal a categorical appreciation for religious idealism.

Like Manowar and Freedom Call, Powerwolf's ideal does not have political aims or social commentaries in mind. They aim to entertain and comfort by fostering communal ideals. Christian rhetoric within heavy metal music offers a shared way whereby audiences can imaginatively perform the rhetoric alongside the artists themselves. This is a fundamentally positive activity. As James Folder and Stanley Hauerwas suggest in their essay, "Performing Faith: The Peaceable Rhetoric of God's Church," Christian rhetoric differs from other performative rhetorics in its "peaceable character" which gestures to the "peaceable drama" of the mystery of God and the trinity (386). As Fodor and Hauerwas explain, Christian rhetoric offers a blend or reconciliation of differences (389) similar to Freedom Call and Powerwolf's lyrical approach. Although Christianity "fights the world" much like all three metal bands discussed here, the Christian church is essentially "not called to exclude or reject but to affirm, welcome, and accept difference in the hope that everything will in the end be reconciled to God in Christ" (Fodor and Hauerwas 390). This type of hope is implicit in Manowar and Powerwolf, and even more explicit in Freedom Call's "heavenly kingdom on Earth."

In sum, power metal bands who claim "metal as religion" using Catholic motif and Christian references, rhetorically appropriate the Christian program. The "metal as religion" program strives to "out-narrate" the world by situating "givens" within a more peaceable and hence a more comprehensive narrative (Fodor and Hauerwas 391, quoting John Millbank). Rather than accept the world's program, "heavy metal as religion"—like Christianity—looks to challenge or change the presupposed requirements of the world (Fodor and Hauerwas 391).[1] Heavy metal becomes prioritized, not as a club or a hobby but as a vehicle of Truth itself: one that can be defined as religious. The approach provides heavy metal "congregations" purposeful equipment for pondering the trans-mundane and managing the world—and can be celebrated as such.

NOTE

1. Fodor and Hauerwas nod to the work of John Millbank (*Theology and Social Theory: Beyond Secular Reason* (Oxford: Basil Blackwell, 1990) and Samuel Wells's *Transforming Fate into Destiny: The Theological Ethics of Stanley Hauerwas* (Carlisle, U.K.: Paternoster, 1998).

WORKS CITED

Catechism of the Catholic Church. New York: Doubleday, 1995.
De Blecourt, Willem. "A Journey to Hell: Reconsidering the Livonian "Werewolf." *Magic, Ritual, and Witchcraft*, vol. 2, no. 1 (Summer 2007): 49–67.
Foder, James, and Stanley Hauerwas. "Performing Faith: The Peaceable Rhetoric of God's

Church." *Rhetorical Invention and Religious Inquiry.* Yale University Press, 2000, pp. 381–414.

Freedom Call. *Eternity.* SPV/Steamhammer, 2002. CD.

_____. *Masters of Light.* SPV/Steamhammer, 2016. CD.

Holy Bible: New International Version. Zondervan, 2015.

Kwasniewski, Peter. *Resurgent in the Midst of Crisis: Sacred Liturgy, the Traditional Latin Mass, and Renewal of the Church.* Angelico, 2014.

Manowar. *Into Glory Ride.* Magic Circle Entertainment, 1983. CD.

_____. *Fighting the World.* Atlantic Records. 1987. CD.

_____. *Louder Than Hell.* Geffen Records, 1996. CD.

_____. *Sign of the Hammer.* Virgin Records, 1984. CD.

Manser, Martin H. *The Westminster Collection of Christian Quotations.* Westminster John Knox Press, 2001.

Powerwolf. *Bible of the Beast.* Metal Blade Records, 2009. CD.

_____. *Lupus Dei.* Metal Bade Records, 2007. CD.

_____. *Preachers of the Night.* Metal Blade Records, 2013. CD.

Powerwolf: The Metal Mass Live. Napalm Records, 2016. DVD.

Sharpe-Younge, Garry. *Metal: The Definitive Guide.* Jawbone Press, 2007.

Christ from Chaos

*Redemption Through Rebellion
in Christian Hardcore*

KAREN FOURNIER

Punk and religion have had an uneasy relationship since the early days of the punk subculture in the mid–1970s. For their part, punks resisted any oppressive social institution that placed power in that hands of those at the top of the social hierarchy and viewed institutionalized religion as complicit in the marginalization of those at the bottom. Since Christian doctrine encourages its followers to tend to those who are disadvantaged, many Christians would have agreed with punks that the role of the Church should be to minister to those who are economically disadvantaged and otherwise vulnerable but nonetheless felt uncomfortable about the way that punk expresses this view. The wild behaviors, raw musical aesthetic, and anarchistic philosophy used by punk to challenge predominant taste cultures in Britain and the United States made the genre abhorrent to those who subscribed to the teachings of Christ. On the surface, one might expect any efforts to merge punk and religion into a new kind of protest to face enormous obstacles but, in the early 1980s, a Christian punk subculture emerged on the American West Coast that promoted a restorationist theology similar in its objectives to secular punk's call for the return of popular music to its musical roots in early rock'n'roll. In the same way that secular punk sought to subvert the authority of the music industry in the production of popular culture (so that anyone who could play three chords could form a band, as the famous directive from the 1977 punk fanzine *Sideburns* instructed its reader), Christian punk sought to facilitate redemption and salvation by rejecting any institutional intermediary between an individual and Christ. Both subcultures touted a DIY approach: anyone with a guitar could form a band in punk's secular do-it-yourself subculture, at least in theory, just as any person of faith would be invited to determine for themselves how to interpret and live by the teachings of Christ. The Christian punk journalist Alexis Neptune explains that "Christianity and punk were, at their roots, reactions to stale aesthetics: [Christian punks] rejected the hierarchies of organized religion, while punk shunned the pretensions of art and the music industry" (paraphrased in Luhr, 96).

Although the Christian punk subculture continues to thrive today across the United States and beyond, this study seeks to explain how and why the subculture came into existence in the early 1980s and therefore limits itself to a specific historical moment and to the seminal bands that coalesced into the emergent scene in Southern California at that time. The purpose of this study will be to explain how the existence of a "Christian" form of punk (hereafter called "Christian punk") might change our perception of the latent potential of secular punk (hereafter merely called "punk") to serve as a different kind of social critique. In the discussion to follow, I will seek to define Christian punk through illustrations of its multiple and coexisting alienations: from the Church and some of its established traditions, from punk and some of its rituals, and also from mainstream culture more broadly.

Redefining Punk Through Its Relationship to Christianity

In the weeks that followed their infamous expletive-laden television debut on the December 1, 1976, episode of Bill Grundy's *Today Show*, the Sex Pistols limped to the end of a promotional tour that was disintegrating around them. Protestors forced promoters of the band to cancel shows across the United Kingdom, but one hold-out was the elderly owner of the Castle Cinema in Caerphilly, Wales, who refused to be intimidated by local authorities. The Pistols' show went ahead as scheduled at the venue on December 14, but was met by a group of picketers from the local church who circulated a leaflet that proclaimed that "such trends [as those exhibited in punk] are clearly part of the fulfillment of Jesus' prophecy that before his return to earth, wickedness would multiply beyond all previous limits."[1] According to the Pistols' lead singer, Johnny Rotten, the damnation took a personal turn when a Protestant preacher from within the group shouted at the band that "God can forgive anyone … anyone except punk rockers, for they are the devil's children" (quoted in Strongman and Parker, 165).

Christian viewers of the Grundy interview had particular reason to vilify the Pistols because many of their songs engaged subjects that were deemed off-limits to public discussion by institutions like the Church. The tour would have included the song "Anarchy in the UK," for example, which had been premiered on July 20, 1976, and in which Rotten famously proclaims himself to be the "Antichrist" in a move that seems designed to rile those in Britain's Christian community (Heylin, 127). As 1976 drew to a close, the Pistols would also have added the infamous anti-anthem "God Save the Queen" to their set-list. In a recent reading of the song, Mark Johnson explains that "the tone of [Rotten's] voice is essentially one of sarcasm and his proclamation in the lyrics that God saves is clearly meant to be interpreted in the same vein. The plea for mercy appears to be no more than ironic ... for if there really is no future, and thus no future judgement, then how can there be sin for there is no penalty?" (Johnson, 62). Given that they hold no power, members of the class for whom Rotten's "Antichrist" speaks are therefore invited by the singer to resist the authority of a Church that promises redemption and salvation in the afterlife while simultaneously offering little hope for a meaningful life on Earth. Of course, dissatisfaction with seeming obliviousness of the Church to the plight of marginalized individuals was not a unique feature of the British punk subculture. A few years before the Sex Pistols broke onto the British scene, Patti Smith had already expressed her rejection of the concept of salvation through the embrace of Christ in the opening lyrics to "Gloria" (1975), which is likely one of the most overt critiques of religion to emerge from the early New York punk scene. Often said to be inspired by bands like the Sex Pistols, the hardcore scene that emerged in California in the early 1980s picked up the topic of sin and redemption where the Pistols left off in songs like Heart Attack's "God Is Dead" (1981), Bad Religion's "Voice of God Is Government" (1982), and the Feederz' "Jesus Entering from the Rear" (1983), the titles of which only hint at the harsh critique of the Church offered by the lyrics of each song.

For Christian protesters against punk who had limited exposure to the messages encoded in its lyrics, the visual landscape of the subculture offered a more accessible and immediate cause for concern. To a Christian viewer of the British subculture, one of the most offensive images would have been the iconic "DESTROY" T-shirt that was created by Vivienne Westwood and Malcolm McLaren and sold in their Kings Road store, SEX. The image features an upended crucifixion onto which a swastika is superimposed, with the hybrid image placed beneath a banner that gives the T-shirt its name. When paired with tokens of servitude and oppression (like jewelry made of chains or bondage trousers) and defaced symbols of the ruling class (like frayed images of the Union Jack or items of clothing made from torn pieces of the Monarch's Royal Stewart tartan), the DESTROY T-shirt signals not only "a sin [with] no penalty" but, perhaps more damning, "appears to be charging the church with complicity. While it viciously condemns the nation's authorities it also includes [among these] the established church" (Johnson, 28).

American punk imagery provided other examples of resistance to the Church, perhaps most notable among which is the famous "Crossbuster" logo that was designed and adopted by the LA punk band Bad Religion. Former band member Greg Hetson explains that the logo, which features a black cross within a red prohibition sign, was meant as a gesture of defiance against "any established set of rules," but concedes that "the church just seemed to be the easiest target ... [because] they say 'you either believe it or not, this is the way it is,' and that's not the way the world works" (quoted in Matthias Kollek and Thorsten Bach, 1990). Put differently, Hetson suggests that punks viewed the Church as just another institution that prescribed and censored human behaviors and interactions in the interests of preserving the hegemony of a ruling class to which the Church belongs.

Given the seeming antipathy towards organized religion that marked punk's earliest incarnations in Britain and the United States, and the view of punks as "wicked" and "beyond forgiveness" by some Christians, it might seem surprising that a subset of American youth in the early 1980s would fuse some of the rituals of punk with those of Christianity. However, punk's established reputation as a potential threat to mainstream values made it the perfect vehicle through which to target the Church in an era marked by the rising political activism of the Evangelical right in American politics and the concomitant Judeo-Christian moral traditionalism that they represented. If punk's role was to resist the secular authority of those in positions of political and economic power, one of early Christian punk's main of objectives would be to challenge the religious authority held by a small but powerful Evangelical cadre of self-appointed guardians of Christian morality.

Resisting the "For-Profit" Prophet in Christian Punk

In its alienation to certain aspects of the secular world, Christian punk builds upon some of the critiques of its secular counterpart: both subcultures exhibit a suspicion of government, a contempt for the marketplace as the site of consumer capitalism, and a rejection of suburbia as the idealized site of "mainstream" consumerist life. For early Christian punks, however, these three sites of resistance were seen to coalesce in the growing political aspirations of the Church, which were perceived as diametrically opposed to the humanitarian aims of the Judeo-Christian faith. In particular, Christian punks raised concerns about the political empowerment of certain American Evangelical leaders in the early 1980s who had adopted a marketing approach to religion through which they built their celebrity, and hence their power and influence over a growing number of Christians (and, importantly, their votes).

Christian punks maintained that a business approach that views salvation as a kind of transaction between a religious leader and a follower conflates religious capital with political and economic capital because it empowers a small number of individuals to identify themselves as prophets of God solely on the basis of their success at fund-raising, marketing, and gaining political authority. (I use the term "capital" here to refer to symbolic goods that are used to assert dominance in a particular field, following Bourdieu, 1984. In this theory, religious leadership would be asserted through the acquisition of "religious capital," for example, which might manifest as an expertise in a particular theological area, a claim to a unique connection to God, a seeming ability to perform miracles, possession of coveted religious artefacts, and so on. As Bourdieu demonstrates, both the political and economic arenas have their own forms of symbolic "capital.") Christian punk sought, among other things, to disrupt the messages of Evangelical "for-profit" prophets who had risen to positions of political power and influence by the early 1980s because, in their view, these religious leaders were too closely aligned with secular politics and the business world to be taken seriously as "true" followers of Christ. To demonstrate how this disruption took place in the early days of the Christian punk movement, we must look at the historical and cultural circumstances out of which the subculture emerged and against which it offered itself to disenfranchised Christian youth as an alternative.

Though Christian punk did not emerge until the early 1980s, the political and economic ambitions of the Church leaders to whom punk responded traces its multiple origins back through the 20th-century. In their earliest incarnations, these ambitions were facilitated by technological innovations that were used by a few individuals to spread the teachings of Christ. One of the first was Father Charles E. Coughlin, a Detroit priest, who decided to reach out to a broad audience with a weekly radio broadcast on CBS in which he frequently weighed in on politics and international affairs. By 1932, a year before Franklin Delano Roosevelt's inaugural "Fireside Chat" on March 12, 1933, Coughlin had built an audience of almost 45 million listeners, and though his radio show would be cancelled by 1939 because of his anti–Semitic rhetoric and his vehement opposition to Roosevelt's New Deal, it served as a model for religious leaders who aimed to reach beyond their immediate congregations (Hadden, 115). The advent of television helped to broaden this reach and spawned a new generation of "celebrity" religious leaders when, starting in 1977, Pat Robertson's Christian Broadcasting Network became the first to transmit all-day religious programming by satellite to viewers across the United States. Pastors Paul Crouch and Jim Bakker would follow suit, with the Trinity Broadcasting Network and the PTL ("Praise the Lord") Network, respectively. By the early 1980s, these three networks were broadcasting to an audience of about 25 million as they supported such offshoot projects as religious theme parks (like Heritage USA), colleges and universities (notably, Regent University), and bricks-and-mortar churches. The televangelist movement also helped to draw attention to, and boost attendance at, churches that were headed by noted televangelists. Religious leaders like Ernest Angley (Grace Cathedral), Joel Osteen (Lakewood Church), and Robert Schuller (Crystal Cathedral), to name just three, became television celebrities in their own right by hosting religious-themed television programs tied to, and sometimes broadcast from within, their churches. In microcosm, the phenomenon of the megachurch, whose numbers began to grow through the 1980s, reflected at the local level what televangelism sought to achieve at the national level, which was to build congregations for the purposes of empowering certain religious institutions and their leaders. The "megachurch," which describes any church with at least 2,000 weekly attendees, operates on a belief system in which "an individual consumes both secular and religious goods. The secular good is considered a private good in which the individual receives all the benefits of its consumption (i.e., none of the benefit goes to a third party). The individual's consumption of the religious goods has a public goods nature to it in that its consumption affords the participant beliefs as well as other participants benefits" (von der Ruhr and Daniels, 472–3). Von der Ruhr and Daniels explain that the megachurch attracts potential recruits with secular "group" activities (sports, games, crafts, and so on) that serve as the foundation upon which faith communities are built. Secular goods draw recruits to the Church, where they gain the "religious goods" that will allow them to function, define value, and interact with others in the faith community. Like televangelism, the megachurch offers a kind of "trickle-down Christianity" premised on an inherently top-down political structure that is dominated and driven by a religious leader who defines the value of religious capital to those within the community.

Christian punk's complaint about the state of religion, like that of its secular counterpart, has been that religious institutions reproduce exclusionary hierarchies present in the political sphere, where those at the bottom have little power to determine how they will live/worship. In his study of the globalization of punk, Kevin Dunn explains that "in large part, the emergence and success of [secular] punk was a response to … capitalist relationship to culture. At its core, punk was a dual rejection. On one level, punks were rejecting the banal cultural products that were being sold to them, from music to fashion…. On a more important level, punk involves a rejection of the passive role of consumer. By tearing down the artificial boundaries between performer and audience, punk proclaims that anyone can be a cultural producer. But more significantly, it states that everyone *should* be a cultural producer" (Dunn, 12). Similarly, Christian punk resisted any notion of a symbolic "marketplace" in which "the product is Jesus Christ and his gift of eternal salvation for all who will accept" (Hadden, 117) and spurned the idea of salvation as a transaction between a religious authority who is licensed to speak to, and sometimes through, God or the Holy Spirit/Ghost and a passive audience that is there to listen but not to partake as a cultural producer in its own right. The subculture advocated, instead, for a "DIY" approach to worship that finds its parallels in secular punk's "DIY" rejection of mainstream consumer culture. Accordingly, Christian punk's adoption of a restorationist theology invited participants to interpret and live by the teachings of Christ for themselves, unencumbered by the interpretations of Church leaders. Further, Christian punks resisted the same kind of banality that was rejected by their secular counterparts and argued that teachings of Christ were lost in places of worship that seemed designed, in the words of Steinberg and Kincheloe, to provide gimmicky "Christotainment" in lieu of social advocacy (2009). Matt Theissen, the lead singer of the American Christian punk band Reliant K, expresses a common punk complaint when he observes that, in America, suburban Christians increasingly "meet in big expensive buildings that resemble arenas more than temples. Starbucks is served before the sermon. Papa John's dominates the Friday night lock-ins…. This causes the Christian church to mirror consumer America as a whole" (quoted in Heisel, 100). In the United States in particular, secular punk's contempt for the ruling class and its consumerist ethos translated into an aversion of the suburban lifestyle that was touted in advertising as an aspirational goal for American youth. For secular punks, the image of "suburbia" that was marketed to mainstream consumers was condemned because of its narrow conception of gender roles and its exclusion of participants on the basis of economic class, sexual orientation, and race. Moreover, punk's dim view of suburbia represented a shift in generational values, so that a teenaged rebellion against parents necessarily included a rejection of their suburban way of life. For Christian punks, the denunciation of suburbia also extended to a rejection of the "suburban church" as a site of worship that was typically embraced by parents and that reflected a conservative lifestyle that curbed the "DIY" aspect of punk. For Christian punks, then, it was both the spiritual emptiness of consumer culture *and* the Church's apparent mirroring of secular capitalism that came under scrutiny within the subculture.

Perhaps most troublesome to Christian punks was that that the consumerist Church seemed to exist as a training ground for religious leaders who aspired to public office. One of the driving forces behind Christian punk, as for its secular counterpart, was its suspicion of the Church's entanglement in the affairs of state and its belief that, in their quest for political influence, some religious leaders turned a blind eye to some of the contradictions inherent in public life, where politicians who claim to embrace Christ as their Savior during political campaigns often show little consideration for His teachings as they write and enact legislation. The Christian punk subculture emerged during the first term of the Reagan presidency, likely in response to the candidate's courtship of the Religious Right, whose members were invited, during Reagan's acceptance speech to the 1980 Republican National Convention, to follow him as "we begin *our crusade* joined together in a moment of silent prayer" (quoted in Miller, 61, italics original). To those on the outside, the speech would have been taken as a thinly veiled pitch for the Christian vote, but for Evangelicals who sought to reinstate prayer in public schools, Reagan's public support for one of their keystone causes would have been seen as long overdue. Within a year of his historic 1980 land-slide victory, Reagan rewarded some of his most ardent Evangelical supporters with key appointments to the newly formed conservative think-tank, the Council for National Policy (CNP), where such founding members as Jerry Falwell, Tim LeHaye, and Paul Weyrich (from the Moral Majority movement) and Pat Robertson (who was the founder of the Christian Broadcasting Network and who would make his own bid for president in 1988) would pursue a conservative social agenda designed to place their interpretation of "Christian morality" at the center of American politics and life. In an advisory role to the President, the CNP pushed for legislation that would protect against any perceived threats to the "traditional" view of the family, including the Equal Rights Amendment, access to birth control and abortion, and gay rights. Further, Christian punks pushed back against the inherent contradiction in Evangelical politics, in which "the core evangelical belief is that love and forgiveness are freely available to all who trust in Jesus Christ … many evangelicals have claimed the role of moral gatekeeper, judge, and jury" (Dickerson, online). Christian punk would also question the political awakening of the Evangelical Right in the wake of the failure of the Vietnam War (which had been supported both philosophically and economically by Reagan's predecessors) and during the escalation of Cold War tensions, as the "détente" of the 1970s was replaced during Reagan's administration by a more defensive (and therefore more expensive) approach to the perceived threat of communism. Reagan's controversial "Strategic Arms Initiative" of 1983, colloquially known as the "Star Wars" program, would divert needed funding away from social programs with the excuse that national security was at risk. Coupled with a supply side economic policy (known by the portmanteau "Reaganomics") that afforded tax cuts to the wealthy while it froze minimum wages at $3.85, slashed public housing and Section 8 vouchers by half, and cut social programs like Medicaid and food stamps, Reagan's geopolitical ambitions seemed to come at an enormous social cost. For those who coalesced into the Christian punk subculture, some of the more exclusionary and repressive political objectives of the Reagan Presidency would seem to stand in diametric opposition to the teachings of Christ, which made the growing political aspirations of the newly empowered New Christian Right anathema to Christian punks. The seeming subordination of social justice to political ambition by Evangelical leaders who allied themselves with the Republican Party became a common subtext in Christian punk, where it was observed that politicians aligned themselves with religious leaders, in the words of one punk, "*only* for personal and political power and gain [and] not to spread the true teachings of Christianity, which they are very far from" (Heisel, 94). At the same time, Christian punks would argue that, in their quest for political influence, some religious leaders lost sight of Jesus as "a person who loved everyone, including the outcasts" and who "rebuked the 'religious leaders' and did not get caught up in politics. This [i.e., Christ] is who Christians should be following" (Heisel, 94). For Christian punks, the political hierarchy that empowered certain Evangelical leaders reflected a policy of exclusion that was at odds with the inclusionary spirit of Christianity.

Rebels Without a Cuss

Members of first-wave Christian hardcore bands like The Altar Boys (formed in Southern California in 1982), Scaterd Few (Burbank, 1983), The Crucified (Fresno, 1984), One Bad Pig (Austin, 1985), and Nobody Special (Orange County, 1985) may not have fully embraced their secular counterpart's rejection of religion, but that did not prevent them from identifying more broadly with secular punk's "outsider" status in relation to mainstream culture. In the same way that punk was driven by the desire to up-end a system that privileged the goals and values of the hegemonic class, Christian punk sought to challenge the authority held by those who were viewed as God's official or self-appointed intermediaries on Earth. Despite its adoption of many punk rituals, its rejection of others from its secular counterpart marked Christian punk as a unique form of the genre, and one that was alienated from its secular counterpart. On the later Christian punk album *Dead to the World* (Screaming Giant, 1998), the West Coast Christian punk band Officer Negative likely provides the most succinct account of their alienation from punk in the song "JCHC." The title, which is an acronym for "Jesus Christ Hardcore," is a double entendre. On its surface, the term "hardcore" connects the band to its secular punk counterpart whose music is typically more aggressive and abrasive than other forms of punk. At the same time, a more colloquial interpretation of the term "hardcore" in the title of the song can also suggest an intense enthusiasm for the Christian faith (as in a "hard core commitment to Christ"). The lyrics of the song tease out these two readings with sonic features that recall such secular hardcore bands as Black Flag or Bad Brains and lyrics that describe the ideal Christian life, in which anyone who seeks to convene with Christ in a "hard core" manner will eschew vices like drugs and alcohol. By pairing punk's hallmark sonic landscape (suggestive of its secular roots) with faith-inspired text, the song becomes a broader condemnation of the mainstream popular music industry, which markets an image of "sex and drugs and rock'n'roll" as normative behaviors for those who have achieved success in the industry. Further, the song also models Christian behavior in its eschewal of obscene language and its reiteration of "Jesus Christ" in the chorus in a literal sense, to emphasize the objectives laid out in the song (which is to foster and nurture a relationship with Christ).

Just as the near-absence of obscenities in Christian punk serves to highlight a difference with punk, the visual element of the former both recalls and resists its secular antecedent. Punk fashion, for example, remains somewhat consistent across the two subcultures, although Christian punks adorn themselves with various symbols of their faith (like the cross, the ichthys or "Jesus fish," and the crown of thorns). One important schism between the two subcultures lies in Christian punk's resistance to anarchy as a political philosophy that opposed any form of hierarchy and authority, including Christ or God. Although favored by some secular punks (like Crass, Poison Girls, and Subhumans in Britain or Reagan Youth or MDC in the United States), anarchy was seen as antithetical to the objectives of Christian punk to reestablish the primacy of Christ in the Judeo-Christian religion. Using the process of *détournement* that was common in punk art and borrowed from the Situationist movement, some Christian punk bands adapted the "circle-A" anarchy symbol into an amalgam of the first and final letters of the Greek alphabet (Alpha encircled by Omega). The "Christian anarchy symbol" that ensued was meant to signify both the omnipresence of God (that is, from "beginning to end") and Christian punk's resistance to all forms of authority except that of Christ.

While Christian punk might have expressed its alienation from some of the rituals associated with its punk counterpart in subtle ways, its various and varied responses to the political aspirations of some religious leaders the 1980s were direct. With a sneer that was typical of hardcore punk vocals and the genre's characteristically abrasive performance aesthetic on full display, one of the subculture's earliest bands, Undercover, unleashed an aural assault on all who aspire to political power in the title track to their debut album *God Rules* (A&S Records, 1982). The song advocates for a clear separation between Church and state when it urges its listener to abide only by the teachings of Christ because "God [and presumably *only* God] is in control." Given that God is all-powerful, as the title of the song suggests, any leader who claims to hold power either misunderstands or misrepresents God as the ultimate, and the only, authority over human-kind. Like Undercover, the seminal Christian punk band The Crucified also tackled the issue of politics in many of its earliest songs, perhaps one of the most telling of which is the song entitled "Problem-Solution," which circulated within the subculture as a demo in 1985 and was released nine years later on the album *Nailed/Take Up Your Cross* (Tooth and Nail Records, 1994). In its opening verse, the song lists a variety of social ills facing American youth (like drug abuse, gun violence, urban decay, and the lack of opportunities) that have gone unnoticed by politicians and religious leaders. To solve these problems, according to the song, American youth should shun leaders on Earth and seek their counsel in God. A similar message is conveyed in the song "Kingdom Come," released by the early Christian punk band One Bad Pig on their second album, *Smash* (Pure Metal, 1989). Like the other songs cited here, "Kingdom Come" suggests that salvation will never happen until a time when "no man rules a nation." Taking direct aim at televangelists who offer salvation at a price, Crucified's "A Guy in a Suit and the Pope," released on their self-titled debut (*Crucified*, Narrowpath, 1989), warns of a reckoning for anyone who partakes in the greed that lies behind many consumerist religious enterprises. On the same album, "Your Image" exposes the vanity that lies behind the religious leaders who place greater emphasis on their own public images than they do on the teachings of Christ.

Like its secular counterpart, the Christian punk subculture arose as a response to a particular configuration of historical events as these were read through the lens of religion. At the same time, the subculture also resisted some of the more secular practices of punk. While the notion of a Christian variant of punk might seem like a contradiction in terms, this study has illustrated how these two terms, and the rituals associated with each, coalesced into an active form of resistance on many fronts.

NOTE

1. Quoted in "The Sex Pistols in Caerphilly" (December 14, 2011), online. http://www.bbc.co.uk/wales/music/sites/history/pages/sex-pistols-caerphilly.shtml.

WORKS CITED

Abraham, Ibrahim. "Christian Punk and Populist Traditionalism." *United Academics Journal of Social Science* (May/June 2012): 23–37.
Abraham, Ibrahim. "Innovation and Standardization in Christian Metalcore: The Cultural Influences of Church and Market." In Toni-Matti Karjalainen and Kim Kärki (eds.), *Modern Heavy Metal: Markets, Practices and Cultures*. Helsinki: Aalto University, 465–473.
Abraham, Ibrahim. "Postsecular Punk: Evangelical Christianity and the Overlapping Consensus of the Underground." *Punk and Post-Punk* 4/1 (2015): 91–105.
Abraham, Ibrahim. "Punk Pulpit; Religion, Punk Rock, and Counter (Sub)Cultures," *The CSSR Bulletin* 37/1 (February 2008): 3–7.
Anonymous author. "The Sex Pistols in Caerphilly (December 14, 2011), online. http://www.bbc.co.uk/wales/music/sites/history/pages/sex-pistols-caerphilly.shtml.
Anonymous author. Thumper Punk blogsite. http://www.webring.org/l/rd?ring=cheeyupunk;id=537;url=http%3A%2F%2Fthumperpunk%2Eblogspot%2Ecom%2F.

Bourdieu, Pierre. *Distinction*. Cambridge: Harvard University Press, 1984.

Dickerson, John. "The Decline of Evangelical America." *The New York Times Sunday Review* (December 15, 2012), online. http://www.nytimes.com/2012/12/16/opinion/sunday/the-decline-of-evangelical-america.html.

Gololobov, Ivan. "There Are No Atheists in Trenches Under Fire: Orthodox Christianity in Russian Punk." *Punk and Post-Punk* 1/3 (2012): 305–321.

Graffin, Greg, and Steve Olson. *Anarchy Evolution: Faith, Science, and Bad Religion*. New York: Harper Perennial, 2010.

Hadden, Jeffrey K., and Anson Shupe. *Televangelism: Power and Politics on God's Frontier*. New York: Henry Holt, 1988.

Hebdige, Dick. *Subculture: The Meaning of Style*. London: Routledge, 1979.

Heylin, Clinton. *Never Mind the Bollocks: The Sex Pistols*. New York: Schirmer, 1988.

Hiesel, Scott, ed. "Building the Church on the Punk Rock." *Alternative Press* 208 (2005): 87–102.

Johnson, Mark. *Seditious Theology: Punk and the Ministry of Jesus*. Farnham, UK: Ashgate, 2014.

Knight, Michael Muhammad. *The Taqwacores*. Berkeley, California: Soft Skull, 2009.

Kollek, Matthias, and Thorsten Bach. *Along the Way* (Bad Religion concert video). Epitaph Records, August 25, 1990.

Laing, Dave. *One Chord Wonders: Power and Meaning in Punk Rock*. Milton Keynes: Open University Press, 1985.

Luhr, Eileen. *Witnessing Suburbia: Conservatives and Christian Youth Culture*. Berkeley: University of California Press, 2009.

Malott, Currie, "Christotainment in Punk Rock: Complexities and Contradictions." In Shirley Steinberg and Joel Kinchlove (eds.), *Christotainment: Selling Jesus through Popular Culture*. Boulder: Westview, 247–268.

Miller, Steven Patrick. *The Age of Evangelicalism: America's Born-Again Years*. London: Oxford University Press, 2014.

O'Hara, Craig. *The Philosophy of Punk: More Than Just Noise*. Oakland, California: AK, 2001.

Schaeffer, Dan. "McChurch: Fast Food Christianity." *The Plain Truth: A Magazine of Understanding* (2002).

Thornton, Sarah. *Club Cultures: Music, Media, and Subcultural Capital*. Hanover, NJ: Wesleyan University Press, 1995.

Von der Ruhr, Mark, and Joseph P. Daniels. "Subsidizing Religious Participation through Groups: A Model of the 'Megachurch' Strategy for Growth." *Review of Religious Research* 53/4 (January 2013): 471–491.

Wellman, James K., Jr. "Turning Word into Flesh: Congregational History as American Religious History." *The Journal of Presbyterian History* 91/2 (2013): 68–77.

Religious Aesthetics
of Nine Inch Nails

Negative Theology as Mediation
of Transcendence

JAMES E. WILLIS III

Nine Inch Nails and the Study of Religion

Trent Reznor's influence through the industrial metal band Nine Inch Nails is unflinchingly adaptive to the fluid musical dissemination of twenty-first century technology (Belskey et al. 8–10). Ever the critic of systems of oligarchy, monetized and corporatized control, and institutionalized religion, Reznor's lyrics and music have been sustained across three decades of significant change. Emerging prior to the Internet and continuing through new models of technological influence, Nine Inch Nails continues to be redefined with each album. There has been notably little written about Nine Inch Nails from an academic perspective; while it would be unhelpful to speculate why, it suffices to say that Nine Inch Nails is a topic usually consigned to music magazines and internet forums. This is an unfair or, perhaps unaware, standpoint of academe: Reznor's lyrics convey a rich and trenchant engagement with systems warranting further consideration, particularly religious criticism.

Through the agency of music, Reznor becomes a seraph of faith cleansed of religious filth, hypocrisy, and logical inconsistency. His songs become a prayer of agony, of loss, of absence, but in so doing, his prayer reaches a truth far beyond some hymns. It is this deprivation which perverts the usual categories of religion, and thus makes Nine Inch Nails no mere metal band, but rather a mouthpiece to something greater underfoot in comprehending how

74

transcendence is possible in post-industrial, scientifically fixated, technologically nihilistic society.

Reznor's theme of absence is akin to medieval Christian apophaticism, specifically negative theology associated generally with mystics and other contemporaneously marginalized thinkers. Though scholars today consider negative theology an important artifact in Christian theology, the role of it as a current method for religious reflection is perhaps minimal. In recent decades, the philosopher Jacques Derrida leveled the most damning criticism of negative theology as "hyperessentiality," or that pursuing God through negation is still, nevertheless, pursuing God (Derrida 79). Yet, the logic of negation offers compelling opportunity for reflection, especially on transcendence, which may be the most confounding religious abstraction. By con sidering the intersection of Reznor's thought, as expressed in his music with Nine Inch Nails, with the insights of Meister Eckhart, John of the Cross, and Julian of Norwich, negative theology is recast as mediation of transcendence. This mediation includes examining themes of going beyond the profane and sacred as dialectics of belief, finding freedom from the psyche as reli-gious violence, and asserting the nothingness of death in the meaning of hope. Reznor's version of negative theology demonstrates a new epoch in religious thought: one that actively embraces loss, abandonment, and absence.

Inquiry: The Case for Nine Inch Nails and Christian Apophaticism

The dearth of scholarly literature treating Nine Inch Nails is surprising given the socio-cultural impact of the music.[1] Themes spanning political, economic, philosophical, apocalyptic, and religious agendas are embedded in Reznor's lyrics. Save that of a 2005 article, "Transgressing Boundaries in the Nine Inch Nails: The Grotesque as Means to Sacred" (Tatsuko), a 2009 doctoral thesis, "Subjectivity in American Popular Metal: Contemporary Gothic, The Body, The Grotesque, and The Child" (Thomas), and a 2011 undergraduate thesis, "Narrative Music and the Concept Album: A Case Study of the Nine Inch Nails, the Downward Spiral," (House)[2] neither Trent Reznor nor Nine Inch Nails are discussed in terms of philosophical or religious ideas. The aforementioned commentators utilize the category of the "grotesque" as a descriptive foil to understand Reznor's sometimes shocking lyrics, music, and videos. Andrew Tatsuko's study of Reznor focuses on the divisions of the sacred and the profane, through particularity in the grotesque, offering the following helpful analysis: "Reznor transports the viewer through a blurred boundary or a simulacrum of boundedness in order to face the possibility of annihilation; and rather than run away or turn back from it, look at it with ... perverted gaze" (5).

While there has been scant scholarly attention to Reznor in particular, there are rich Christian theological traditions examining the role of music and spirituality.[3] Recent studies, for example, approach varying topics like the intersection of modern music, Deleuze, and religion (Pickstock 173–199), or Christian theology, music, and creation (Begbie), or music, theology, and ideology (Engelhardt 32–57). While there may be some methodological similarities (namely, of selecting a specific musical or lyrical theme and pairing it with religion, no matter how congruent or misaligned), the attempt to review a selection of Reznor's music within the specific optics of medieval negative theology does not fit well within a genre or scholarly category of inquiry. Instead, an experimental approach of positioning the lyrics of a contemporary metal band alongside Christian thinkers of some five hundred or six hundred years ago is done so with the goal of uncovering a new transcendence.

While some summary remarks may be made about the types of themes encountered in Reznor's music, and indeed for the complexity of Eckhart, John, and Julian, direct engagement with the primary sources helps connect the ideas. The purpose is not to treat the entire work or discography, but rather to cross-section in a way that exposes ways of further study of the alignment of what might appear initially as incompatible subjects.

Detachment and the Self Crucified

Though now widely regarded as a pivotal medieval mystic, Meister Eckhart's renaissance is improbable due to official Church condemnation of his writings not long after his death (Davies 28–45). His writing style can be surprising for its candor, but Eckhart's fidelity to Biblical interpretation, with the logical conclusion that a person must forsake God for God's own sake, suggests a corollary with Reznor: to relinquish the idol of the divine is to gain the sacredly profane. That is, beyond the artificial dialectic of the sanctified and the godless, where the self no longer detracts purity from thought and experience, both Eckhart and Reznor detect a beautiful gulf.

When Eckhart refers to the *Gottheit* (Godhead) as beyond God, he is likewise appealing to the ground of being; that is, the ground unites human experience with existence. Readily Neoplatonic in influence, Eckhart contributes profound insight to Christian theology through connecting *Gottheit* with detachment: "We must train ourselves in self-abandonment until we retain nothing of our own. All turbulence and unrest comes from self-will, whether we realize it or not. We should establish ourselves with all that we might wish or desire in all things, in the best and most precious will of God through a pure ceasing-to-be of our will and desire" (Eckhart, "Talks of Instruction," 42). The *danger* of Eckhart's thought to orthodoxy, and his Church investigators sensed this, though failed to adequately articulate it in their condemnation, is the tenuous relationship between the self (in modern usage, the ego) and God-as-other. At once, Eckhart argues that the self and God become one in their mystical union, yet this is only possible in detachment and subsequent shedding of the ego. The ground of being, then, is the negated space of unification and annihilation. The mutual loss and gain of the soul with identification of God becomes the crucible for God's self-preservation in the *Gottheit* and God's self-annihilation. The co-/mutual dependency of the soul and God creates a third space that is both neither/nor the self and God.

Reznor likewise operates at the periphery of this third space, where the soul is lost in its journey. In the song "Underneath It All," Reznor sings against up-tempo electronic percussion with direct reference to self-crucifixion and death. Besides the direct reference to crucifixion, Reznor is also creating alienation with his lyrics: the dualistic tension between *you* and *I* envisage how the latter is entrapped. Such entanglement is also found in "Every Day Is Exactly the Same," expressed as numbing stasis. The journey of this third space operates where Reznor's lyrics struggle against the music and where meaning becomes an appreciable narrative. The intra-musical struggle creates a skillful dialectic to consider a mystic's path to God: alienation generates a locus where the sacred and the profane no longer define experience; rather, the in-between is where loss and absence have fullness in their meaning*less*ness. In "All Time Low," Reznor paints a dystopic chronology of the forever couched within the fullness of loss and absence, without resolution.

Eckhart and Reznor share a belief that goes beyond the merely sacred and profane. Eckhart's detachment from God and Reznor's loss haunted by chronology of absence suggests a third space of mystical insight: the beyond (whether God or meaning) is not a place, nor an experience, nor a logical negation. The beyond remains an eschatology of beautiful finality ("Various Methods of Escape") or "infinity shall fill my emptiness, and … immeasurable, incomprehensible Godhead shall fill my base and wretched humanity" (Eckhart, "Talks of Instruction," 35). Neither demonstrate an entirely orthodox or heterodox consummation of absence, but rather the beauty of loss. The dialectic proposed in Eckhart and Reznor's thought is courageous because it entails profound loss, so much so "that God should reduce himself to nothing in the soul so that the soul may lose herself" (Eckhart, *Selected German Sermons*, Sermon 30, J 82, 244).

Violence and Disorientation

History is replete with examples of violence motivated by religious ideology, hatred, and difference. Outward acts are demonstrations of volition against competing groups or ideas. Yet, few consider the interior, or emotional, reasons for religious violence. Are acts of barbarity or brutality in the name of God or the gods motivated by surety in one's beliefs? Or, could the banality of violence be perpetuated by doubt and insecurity? In other words, does outward violence reinforce emotional confidence in the rightness of one's religious position? The role of anxiety, in this case the misplaced relation of the self to the world, should be more readily coupled with religious violence. The psyche, then, becomes mediator between outward and inward violence.

The violence enacted on others may stem from the anxiety of religious doubt. Well known to many Christian mystics, doubt served the dual purpose of sharpening one's specific beliefs while also preventing definitive presumption that one's personal perspective indeed apprehends *truth*. Sustained doubt, which often embodied the angst of feeling the absence of God, is sustained in several Christian traditions as the "dark night" from the thought of the Spanish mystic, St. John of the Cross. In his "Dark Night of the Soul," John describes "spiritual darkness," (73) the "dark, painful, and gloomy water of God" (117), and "hidden[ness] in the face of God" (117). John's dark night shows a maturity gained in the unsure, doubt-filled path to God, or "to enter the ineffable emptiness and darkness of the Abyss, beyond the reach of all natural faculties" (Green 29). Today, the alienation felt by John might be called a form of anxiety because it entailed loss, indecision, and disorientation. Without the philosophical baggage of psychoanalysis, Denys Turner calls this alienation an "emotional crisis" because "ego-dependent agency is destroyed as such only to reveal the presence within us of other sources of agency which, without the disablement of our active natural powers, we could not have detected" (Turner 236). The disorientation of the dark night causes not only angst and pain, but the potential for growth and freedom. The psyche can be re-oriented as the catalyst for shifting common views of religious violence through the disorientation of religious certainty.

Reznor's disorientation and anxiety are recurring throughout his discography. Reznor's meaninglessness ("Various Methods of Escape,") prefigures remorse as described in the desire to repeat aspects of his life ("In This Twilight"). Endless depression in the recurrence of daily sameness ("Every Day Is Exactly the Same") demonstrates how emotional turmoil is subsumed to the psyche's induction of violence as being external to the self ("In Two") and self-loathing ("Getting Smaller"). While religious violence often takes on external meaning, for Reznor that violence is directed inward; this type of violence seemingly takes on an irritable spirituality in solitude ("Only"). The inversion of psychological pain and spiritual dislocation culminate in a violent breakdown between the isolation of the self and the banality of religious imagery and vapid promises ("Right Where It Belongs").

The dark night for Reznor and St. John of the Cross is bipartite psychological violence and spiritual disorientation. The notable difference between the two thinkers is the ends: for John, hope in finding God beyond the absence is sufficient to struggle, but for Reznor, the dark night is compounded in further withdrawal. The inward struggle, then, is the juxtaposition of where spirituality can be both hopeful and aimless: "God, being now … the Teacher of this poor blind soul, well may she, when at last she comes forth into light, and perceives the steps whereby she has been led, rejoice with exceeding joy and cry: 'In darkness and yet safe'" (St. John of the Cross 114). Yet for Reznor, the psychological toll of aimless spiritual wandering culminates in one of his most poignant critiques of religion: the potential meaninglessness of religious belief and action and the ills of humanity fighting itself in the shadow of God who may or may not be existent ("The Hand That Feeds"). For both Reznor and John, religion is not synonymous with spirituality, yet psychological violence is wrought with disorientation and anxiety.

Nothingness and Despair

Death and decay are familiar themes in Reznor's lyrics; they are seen as omnipresent and grotesque reminders of the nothingness that awaits all life—eventually. Rather than standing in dialectical opposition to life affirmation, death takes on a special place, an otherness that becomes *more than* integrated with life. Reznor's thoughts on decay as a process mirror of reality because no matter the spiritual belief, everyone still experiences death ("Hurt"). Death befalls all while carrying an apocalyptic meaning wrought only in fear and pain ("The Day the World Went Away"). Such apocalypticism, or in this sense the culmination of all meaning within its own finitude, is inextricably warped with nothingness and annihilation ("Suck"). Further, Reznor's early song "Terrible Lie" aptly connects a type of religious nothingness in his versioning of an apocalyptic, if not entirely cosmic, farce. Yet within this outwardly dismal view, there is something like *hope* in Reznor's lyrics; stupendously defiant, Reznor's hope emerges only after absolute collapse ("The Big Come Down"). This breakdown is indicative of what is beyond the collapse because in at least two references Reznor indicates, given another chance, he would live a different life ("Hurt" and "In This Twilight"). These references create death within the narrative, where annihilation becomes intertwined with hope, and where collapse and meaninglessness become meshed with the power of memory ("Hurt").

The strained affinity between death, annihilation, and something like hope finds its parallels in Julian of Norwich, an English mystic. Her *Revelations of Divine Love* subtly questions the post–Augustinian entrenchment of salvation through the blood of Christ, and rather recast Jesus as Mother. Notably, Julian also reasserts the role of grace and mercy, even to the extent that some scholars suggest a type of universalism (Windeatt 3). Julian's writing contains a strong, if not emphatic, pastoral character. The comfort she displays to her readers extends beyond the expected reaches of the institutional church. For example, when speaking of salvation, Julian speaks of God as though "we are his bliss: for in us he liketh without end; and so shall we in him, with his grace" (43). In direct contrast to a very robust orthodox theology of hell, Julian seems to embrace a grace that pits sin as the separation from God, not hell (34). As Bernard McGinn comments, "Sin separates us from God, but, from the viewpoint of divine love, the pain that sin causes in us is a necessary part of the purgative process of falling and rising that we must undergo throughout this life" (204). Julian talks about despair as in the same strong terms as sin and hell, but yet despair has an almost critical inverse: not hopelessness, but lack of love (69). Love and suffering are bound for Julian, "an high knowing of love that he hath in our salvation" (44), by which death is a mechanism of hope, "for [Julian] desired to be soon with [her] God" (4). Pastorally, by appealing to what later thinkers labelled universalistic tendencies, Julian creates an interesting space with mystical understanding of death, annihilation, and hope: faith means the soul comes into direct challenge with despair, that the precipice of angst and pastoral relinquishment are wrought in "mercy and grace working" (111).

Julian's connection with Reznor is found in the role of despair as a capitulation of death and hope as incomplete manifestations of the much more salient nothingness and mercy. Though death is a recurring theme in Reznor's discography, "In This Twilight" is perhaps his most direct reference in the biblical reference to dust. The most curious lyrics in this song reflect a heavenly vision of sky and light which shares affinity with Julian's vision of heaven: "And this shall [God] do as long as any soul is in earth that shall come to heaven—and so far forth that if there were no such soul but one, he should be withal alone till he had brought him up to his bliss" (162). For both Reznor and Julian, nothingness and mercy are linked through the despair of suffering, whether at the end of life, seeking the beyond, or in the final twilight ("In This Twilight"). The despair in both thinkers, however, ultimately fades into a hope beyond. The mystical beyond, then, is the locus of how nothingness is *the* religious aesthetic.

A New Epoch and Lack of Faith

Reznor's close affiliation with religion extends well beyond the casual, passing reference. As intensely personal and acerbic societal critique, Reznor's lyrics also venture into the difficult territory of the mystic. Far from atheistic, yet not entirely theistic, Reznor's thought appears to rest on the periphery of social religion and personal struggle ("Closer"). The same might be said of Eckhart, John, and Julian: while the mystical path appears to be ardently singular and lonesome, the self either becomes no-thing or is subsumed into God. This annihilation of the self, the disappearance of the ego, creates nothingness as the path to God and as the protective agent against idolatry. By examining Reznor's music with three medieval mystical thinkers, the revealed nothingness stemming from loss, abandonment, and anxiety pivot into a new way of conceiving of transcendence in a post-industrial, scientifically fixated, technologically nihilistic society.

Through Nine Inch Nails, Reznor signals a sustained meditation of the grotesque, criticism of artificial power, and demonstrable beauty of religious fracturing at the cusp of the person and the institution. In this signaling, Reznor transgresses how religious language can delimit categorical knowledge: in his envisaging of the absence of belief, a "new" negative theology emerges. A *pièce de résistance* against institutionalized religion, Reznor's negative theology is an aesthetic wrought with nothingness and new transgressions. Those transgressions begin with language and their paradoxical relationship with expressing transcendence. For if modern language is dependent upon the maddening confines of a scientific and empiricism-obsessed vocabulary, Reznor's negative theology breaks open paralyzing doubt and spirituality in the absence of God.

Today's religious experience is not unlike the medieval mystic. Fraught with doubt and absence, the path to God is one of self-annihilation and nothingness, where "[t]he emptying of the self is only one half of a process, of which the complementary half is far from being annihilistic or negative, for it consists in receiving God in the depths of the soul" (Green 34). Reznor's lyrics carry on the revealed knowledge of transcendence because, somewhere buried in the lines of death, remorse, and doubt, beauty is found once again ("My Violent Heart").

NOTES

1. This is a commentary, too, on the state of the academy and its privilege over some subjects and outright ignoring of others. While in a previous day the lofty ideals of scholarly inquiry may have been more homogenous, the advent of the Internet, along with attendant deep connectivity and communication, renders such provincialism obsolete. Reznor has an interesting history of using technology to make, distort, remake, and synthesize music, perhaps even calling into question the very definition of "music." So, too, are the scholarly intentions with such technological communication, for the dissemination of music and lyrics is

unshackled from boundaries of record production. This is evidenced best, perhaps, by the fact that Reznor released his 2008 album, *Ghosts*, on the internet for free, as well as the files for his 2007 *Year Zero* for the explicit purpose of remixing. Reznor also has a documented, contentious relationship with record production companies. See Wikstrom or Bruno.

2. House makes passing reference to religion in two instances, but neither are essential to the argument, nor are they explored in depth.

3. For example, members of the Institute for Theology, Imagination and the Arts at the University of St. Andrews study the role of art and music as a theological discipline.

WORKS CITED

Begbie, Jeremy S. *Theology, Music and Time*. Cambridge: Cambridge University Press, 2000.

Belsky, Leah, Byron Kahr, Max Berkelhammer, and Yochai Benkler. "Everything in Its Right Place: Social Cooperation and Artist Compensation." *17 Mich. Telecomm. & Tech. L. Rev.*, vol. 1 (2010): 8–10.

Bruno, Anthony. "Reznor Sounds Off on Pricing, UMG." Billboardbiz. Retrieved from: http://www.billboard.com/biz/articles/news/1323614/reznor-sounds-off-on-pricing-umg.

Davies, Oliver. *Meister Eckhart: Mystical Theologian*. London: SPCK, 1991.

Derrida, Jacques. "How to Avoid Speaking: Denials." *Derrida and Negative Theology*, edited by Harold Coward and Toby Foshay, Albany: State University of New York Press, 1992, 73–142.

Engelhardt, Jeffers. "Right Singing in Estonian Orthodox Christianity: A Study of Music, Theology, and Religious Ideology." *Ethnomusicology*, vol. 53, no. 1 (Winter 2009): 32–57.

Green, Deirdre. "St. John of the Cross and Mystical 'Unknowing.'" *Religious Studies*, vol. 22, no. 1 (March 1986): 29–40.

House, Allison. "Narrative Music and the Concept Album: A Case Study of the Nine Inch Nails, The Downward Spiral." *Wesleyan University*, Honors Thesis, 2001.

Julian of Norwich. *Revelations of Divine Love*, New York: Cosimo, 2007.

McGinn, Bernard. "The English Mystics." *Christian Spirituality: High Middle Ages and Reformation*, edited by Jill Raitt, Bernard McGinn, and John Meyendorff. New York: Crossroad, 1987, 194–207.

Meister Eckhart. Selected German sermons. In *Selected Writings*, edited and translated by Oliver Davies. London: Penguin, 1994.

_____. *The Talks of Instruction: On Spiritual Endeavor*. In *Selected Writings*, edited and translated by Oliver Davies. London: Penguin, 1994.

Nine Inch Nails. "All Time Low." *Hesitation Marks*, Columbia, 2013.

_____. "The Big Come Down." *The Fragile*, Nothing/Interscope, 1999.

_____. "The Day the World Went Away." The Fragile, Nothing/Interscope, 1999.

_____. "Every Day Is Exactly the Same." *With Teeth*, Nothing/Interscope, 2005.

_____. "Getting Smaller." *With Teeth*, Nothing/Interscope, 2005.

_____. "The Hand That Feeds." *With Teeth*, Nothing/Interscope, 2005.

_____. "Hurt." *The Downward Spiral*, Nothing/TVT/Interscope, 1994.

_____. "In This Twilight." *Year Zero*, Interscope, 2007.

_____. "In Two." *Hesitation Marks*, Columbia, 2013.

_____. "My Violent Heart." *Year Zero*, Interscope, 2007.

_____. "Only." *With Teeth*, Nothing/Interscope, 2005.

_____. "Right Where It Belongs." *With Teeth*, Nothing/Interscope, 2005.

_____. "Suck." *All That Could Have Been*, Nothing 2002.

_____. "Terrible Lie." *Pretty Hate Machine*, TVT, 1989.

_____. "Underneath It All." *The Fragile*, Nothing/Interscope, 1999.

_____. "Various Methods of Escape." *Hesitation Marks*, Columbia, 2013.

Pickstock, Catherine. "Messiaen and Deleuze: The Musico-Theological Critique of Modernism and Postmodernism." *Theory, Culture & Society*, vol. 25, no. 7–8 (2008): 173–199.

St. John of the Cross. *The Dark Night of the Soul*, introduction by Margaret Kim Peterson. Barnes & Noble, 2005.

Tatusko, Andrew. "Transgressing Boundaries in the Nine Inch Nails." *Journal of Religion and Popular Culture*, vol. 11, no. 1 (Fall 2005).

Thomas, Sara Ann. "Subjectivity in American Popular Metal: Contemporary Gothic, the Body, the Grotesque, and the Child." *Faculty of Arts, University of Glasgow*, retrieved from http://theses.gla.ac.uk/644/1/2009thomasphd.pdf.

Turner, Denys. *The Darkness of God: Negativity in Christian Mysticism*. Cambridge: Cambridge University Press, 1995.

Wikström, Patrik. *The Music Industry: Music in the Cloud*. Cambridge: Polity, 2013.

Windeatt, B.A. "Julian of Norwich and Her Audience." *The Review of English Studies*, vol. 28, no. 109 (1977): 1–17.

Duncan Sheik's Human Revolution in Sound/Buddhist Search for the Perfect Sound

Erika M. Nelson Mukherjee

"Nam-myoho-renge-kyo, nam-myoho-renge-kyo, nam-myoho-renge-kyo," these are the words Duncan Sheik chants daily as part of his Nichiren Buddhist practice, which has informed, guided, and shaped the evolution of his life, career, and music, underscoring how deeply interwoven his practice of Buddhism is not only with his personal beliefs but with his artistic expression and professional development. Given that "life itself is based on constant change" (Sheik "Preface" v), one constant in Sheik's eventful life has been his Buddhist practice with the Soka Gakkai ("Value Creation Society") International, also known as the SGI, lay organization since the age of 19. Ginia Bellafante acknowledges both the continuity and connection between Sheik's Buddhist practice and his evolution from early pop stardom with his breakout hit "Barely Breathing" in 1996 to Tony Award–winning success with the musical *Spring Awakening* in 2006 and beyond, stating: "how Mr. Sheik came then to compose a hit Broadway musical requires a digression into the matter of his spiritual life." Indeed, the singer-songwriter considers Buddhism a key influence in his life and readily shares details about his practice with others in interviews, articles, and posts on his social media sites.[1] Especially since the form of Nichiren Buddhism Sheik practices is not typically as familiar as the traditions of Tibetan or Zen Buddhism to many people in the West, these explanations of his practice and the SGI accompany most reviews of Sheik's work. Numerous interviews also include recordings of Sheik chanting, either alone or with other collaborators.[2] "Those who chant together, work together.

Or so it seems," Robert Simonson noted about Sheik's work with other Buddhists, most notably the playwright Steven Sater, with whom Sheik wrote *Spring Awakening* but Sheik has also collaborated with such Buddhist singer-songwriters as Howard Jones and Suzanne Vega.

What they chant as Nichiren Buddhists is the "mantra-like title" (Strand) of the Lotus Sutra (Myōhō Renge Kyō), considered to be the highest teaching of Shakymuni or Gautama Buddha, coupled with *nam* from Sanskrit, meaning "to devote or dedicate oneself." This chant was introduced as a Buddhist practice for the modern world by the 13th century Japanese reformist priest Nichiren[3] (1222–1282) before being exiled to Sado Island, possibly the "cold and barren place" Sheik references in his song "Nichiren." According to Nichiren Buddhists, Nam-myoho-renge-kyo is "the Mystic Law of life and the universe" (Ikeda, xiii), and by chanting it, one reveals the law within one's own life, putting oneself "in harmony or rhythm with the universe" (Ikeda xiii). As such, the mantra is revered as "a great teaching of supreme hope" (SGI "Esablishment") and said to be "the sound that awakens the Buddha nature of all humankind" (SGI "Establishment). It roughly translates as "devotion to the Wondrous or Mystic Law of the Lotus of the Supreme Teaching," or more practically as "I dedicate myself to the Mystic Law of the simultaneity of cause and effect through the teaching or sound of Buddha."[4]

Along with other members of the SGI, Sheik and his Buddhist collaborators recite this mantra and two chapters from the Lotus Sutra every morning and evening "as a way of harnessing the universal life force" (Strand 5) inherent within. The words acknowledge the Buddhist idea of the interrelatedness of all phenomena, known as "dependent origination," as well as the simultaneity of cause and consequence. Chanting Nam-myoho-renge-kyo encompasses the heart of the SGI's Buddhist practice, encapsulating an "expression of determination" to embrace and manifest one's inner Buddha nature, a "pledge to oneself to never yield to difficulties and to win over one's suffering," and also a "vow to help others reveal this law in their own lives" (SGI "Meaning") through care and heart-to-heart dialogue, so they may similarly express their own vast potential and establish lives of unshakable or "absolute" happiness.[5]

Stephen Holden suggests that a sense of chanting is audible in Sheik's music, especially on his third album *Phantom Moon* (2001), where "the droning consistency of Mr. Sheik's incantatory, vibrato-less crooning, which at different moments echoes Jackson Browne, Leonard Cohen and Elvis Costello, lends the music a chantlike pulse." Keith Powell similarly observes that Sheik's music, particularly in his more recent work *Whisper House* (2010) conveys a deeper, spiritual message, saying: "when you listen to Duncan's older or newer records, it's kind of like he's talking or whispering in your ear" (qtd. in Wren). This intimate form of address, Powell suggests, is heartfelt "without being cloying or saccharine" (qtd. in Wren). Sheik, however, denies trying to give his music an overt religious message and shuns prose-lytizing in his music. When asked how his practice of Buddhism finds its way into his music, Sheik suggests that it doesn't, at least not in any overt or "straight ahead manifest way" (qtd. in Martin), stating: "God forbid that it did 'cause I—there's nothing I like less than music that kind of, like, tries to insert some sort of spiritual message inside it. That, to me, is nails on the chalkboard" (qtd. in Martin). Nevertheless, Sheik acknowledges that given that he does practice Buddhism, "I do have a worldview and a way of looking at humanity's place in the universe. And that does kind of seep into some kind of moral outlook that's in the songs" (qtd. in Martin). Sheik also acknowl-edges that "Buddhism is kind of the underpinning to all I do; it's understand-ing that you are not your little problems, that everything is flux" (qtd. in Finn).

The idea of flux aptly applies to all aspects of Sheik's creative life. Sheik's career, as Angie Romero notes, "has taken so many twists and turns," and as Jenna Scherer notes, "few musical careers are as varied as Duncan Sheik's." Sheik remains best known for his 1996 hit song "Barely Breathing," a song whose message appears to have little to less to do with Buddhism and more to do with heartbreak. The song remains Sheik's most successful hit to date, and, as Sheik noted in a recent interview, "it kind of took on a life of its own" (qtd. in Romero), having been featured on shows like *Glee* and *Girls* in recent years. As Romero suggests of Sheik, "he looks back only for a split-second and strictly for nostalgia's sake." The singer has evolved significantly from his '90s stardom to become an experimental artist, musical theater composer, and more recently to electronic musician, known for his ability to find "bal-ance in an off-kilter world" (Scherer).

This theme of finding footing and calling forth one's best amid chal-lenging circumstances belongs to key teachings of the Buddhism Sheik prac-tices, namely undergoing one's own heart-centered "human revolution," by bringing out the highest potential of one's Buddha nature in every action, thereby creating value for one's self and society, and thus "turning poison into medicine," or any suffering into a so-called "benefit." The essence of Nichiren Buddhism is the conviction that each person has within them the ability to overcome any problem or difficulty they may encounter in life and find ultimate happiness. Each person's life possesses this power "because they are inseparable from the fundamental law that underlies the workings of all life and the universe" (SGI "Meaning"). Changing oneself from the inside out is called "human revolution" (SGI "Human Revolution"),[6] which describes a fundamental process of inner transformation whereby people are able—through the recitation of the mantra Nam-myoho-renge-kyo and the practice of Nichiren Buddhism—to break through the shackles of their "lesser selves," which are "bound by self-concern and the ego" and develop greater sense of empathy and "altruism toward a 'greater self' capable of caring and taking action for the sake of others—ultimately all humanity" (SGI "Human Revolution"). The lotus flower, symbol of the SGI organization, not only represents the beautiful thousand-petaled flower often considered to represent spiritual consciousness, but also the simultaneity of cause and consequence with its ability to seed and blossom beautifully amid the dirtiest mud of the swamps of daily life. Like the lotus, a person who undergoes human revolution, as Nichiren Buddhists believe, can fully bring out the characteristics of their unique personality and reveal their true brilliant potential, i.e., their inherent Buddha nature.

Given the often somber tone of Sheik's music, one might assume that the Grammy-nominated, Tony Award–winning indie pop-rock singer-songwriter's unique characteristics reveal a bit of a brooding Buddhist. Over the past twenty years, he has honed his own particular sound of haunting melancholic, meditative introspection and soulful, spiritual stream-of-consciousness musings, favoring the exploration of the darker tones of emotional human experiences in his music, a characteristic Misha Berson describes as "dark-themed, sonic Gothic brooding." Robin Finn has called Sheik a "supersensitive, superspiritual pop troubadour," while Dan Harris offers a slight variation, suggesting Sheik's an "emo-troubadour." Holden considers Sheik one of the "poets of melancholy," alongside such others as Bob Dylan, Donovan, Jackson Browne, Leonard Cohen, Tim Buckley, and Cat Stevens, who has "reinvented the 'Sgt. Pepper' idea of rock or folk as 'art'" in the soft-rock genre and emerged as a "contemporary descendant of a 19th-century literary type, the dreamy moonstruck man-child on an obsessive quest for erotic and spiritual transcendence. The stereotype of this figure is a gauntly handsome, porcelain-skinned, raven-haired poet brooding behind a black cape, his gaze turned toward a sky churning with storm signals."

Sheik's music would indeed suggest he is an introspective, religious aesthete. When asked what role his interest in Buddhism plays in his music, Sheik admits that "it's the darker parts of our psyche and our behavior that are much more interesting" (qtd. in Martin) to him than the "shiny, happy, hippy-dippy version of Buddhism that some people might like to think about" (qtd. in Martin). This is perhaps what drew him to Nichiren Buddhism's active meditative practice. Unlike other sects of Buddhism, which focus on silent, contemplative forms of meditation as a means of overcoming desire, Nichiren Buddhism, as practiced by the SGI, is a dynamic practice for modern day life. It espouses the idea that "earthly desires equal enlightenment." Hence practitioners chant about their daily needs and struggles, which may well include specific problems, including gaining money, success, and fame.[7] Sheik said this difference is what drew him to the practice. "This particular form of Buddhism attracted me because it is so proactive," Sheik explained in an interview with Gina Bellafante in 2006, saying, "It is very much not about detachment. It's about getting out into the world. It is a source of creative energy" (Bellafante).

Critics are quick to note that in spite of his moving melancholic music and his penchant for often dark and "morbidly wry" (Berson) tones and themes, Sheik "is no downer" (Berson) and "lacks the wan look of an alternative rocker" (Bellafante). Rather he's "engaging and genial" and "musically adventuresome" (Berson) with a "happy, welcoming face and comports himself with no signs of angst" (Bellafante) as he "assembles complex and often-lovely arrangements around his thoughtful songs and pleasing tenor vocals" (Berson). Sheik has also "remained consistently immune from the grip of creative block" (Bellafante) throughout the past two decades of his ever-evolving career. Sheik manages, as Holden suggests, a fine balance, noting about Sheik's songs that "for all their gloom, the songs don't feel depressed."

Sheik's emotional range of expression suggests that there are indeed many sides and surprises to discover about Duncan Sheik. Often considered an oddity in the music world, Sheik is not your average pop star. He is "simultaneously an old-fashioned folk-singer of the Bob Dylan school and a modern electronic musician of the Brian Eno school" (Scaruffi), schooled in semiotics, the study of signs and symbols, and not music. Although immersed in music for most of his childhood and adolescence, Sheik didn't seriously consider music until college, when he was in Lisa Loeb's band Liz and Lisa as her lead guitarist. Bellafante notes that Sheik is often considered to be "blessed" in his career, although the adjectives resilient and versatile are perhaps more apt in describing the singer-songwriter's ability to resurrect, reorient, and redefine his career on numerous occasions over the course of the past two decades. Nevertheless, Sheik is no stranger to heartbreak and struggle. His early beginnings in music were anything but easy and often full of dashed hopes and disappointments. Yet Sheik's easy disposition, grounded sense of humor, and charm, as well as the wisdom and vision he has gained through his Buddhist practice, seem to have also served him well as he's navigated through the ups and downs of the music business.

In many ways, his Buddhist practice appears inextricable from Sheik's life. One might believe that Sheik's connection to Buddhism might well have been fated by birth. Born on November 18, 1969, in Montclair, New Jersey, to a single mother, Sheik shares his birthday with the founding of the very Buddhist organization Sheik considers his spiritual home. Thirty-nine years earlier, on November 18, 1930, in Tokyo, Japan, the reform educator Tsunesaburo Makiguchi and his disciple Josei Toda founded the precursor of the modern SGI, the *Soka Kyoiku Gakkai* ("Society for Value-Creating Education"), when they published their first volume in a series of four writings entitled *Soka kyoikugaku taikei* (The System of Value-Creating Pedagogy). These writings outlined the methodological, theoretical, and practical system of *"soka,"* a word Toda coined by combining Chinese characters for "create" and "value" to stress that their educational pedagogy's purpose was the creation of value ("Theory of Value Creation") in support of their desire to foster the unique creative ability of each child and the life-long happiness of all learners, which they saw as the true goal of education, which Makiguchi believed could be further strengthened by the philosophy and practice of Nichiren Buddhism which similarly stresses developing the vast untapped potential of every individual. Thus, this fateful date, November 18, marks the founding of the SGI's headquarters in Japan, but also the death of Makiguchi, who after being arrested, along with Toda, in July 1943 as "thought criminals" for openly criticizing and opposing the militarist Japanese government, which opposed any form of independent or dissident thought or instruction, died in 1944 in prison, refusing to recant his beliefs. The SGI's connection to both educational philosophy and Nichiren Buddhism makes the practice of modern-day SGI unique from many other forms of Buddhism. Central to the SGI is the tenet of raising youth to be "protagonists of peace within their local communities" (SGI "Nov 18th"), i.e., capable, contributive global citizens in society and happy, courageous individuals, able to stand up against oppressive tyrannies of abuse and power. Sheik seems to have inherited some of Makiguchi and Toda's "soka" spirit, especially in his undertaking with Steven Sater to write *Spring Awakening* to encourage today's young people, who might, as he did, be struggling to find their way through life.

The SGI practice often appeals to people in distress. It gained greater popularity in the West with Japanese war brides who came to the United States, often disillusioned and unhappy in their marriages. They turned, as did many U.S. youth and spiritual seekers in the 1960s, to Buddhism, looking for answers to the deeper essence of life and its infinite mysteries amid the complexities, conflicts, and rapid changes of modern life. Sheik reflected on the beginnings of his own practice in a foreword he wrote in 2000 for a book called *The Way of Youth: Buddhist Common Sense for Handling Life's Questions*[8] by Daisaku Ikeda, a Buddhist philosopher, poet, and third president of the SGI. In it, Sheik describes his own search for meaning, stating:

> At the age of nineteen, profoundly dissatisfied with my inability to steer the course of my life and less than impressed with the direction the modern world seemed to be taking, I began practicing Buddhism. It seemed to be the only philosophy that, while never contradicting my rational, scientific view of the universe, acknowledged its mystery and wonder. Buddhism imbued the universe and our human place in it with great dignity and freedom ["Preface" v].

Sheik also acknowledged that since he began practicing, his "appreciation for Buddhism has only deepened" and more importantly, his personal practice has "galvanized" his life in ways he "never could have imagined." Sheik credits much of this to Daisaku Ikeda,[9] who as leader of the SGI "has worked tirelessly to encourage and enlighten millions of people around the world" ("Preface" v). Ikeda's writings have been a source of inspiration and wisdom for Sheik, reminding him "that life is based on constant change" ("Preface" v) and "on a practical level, Buddhism is reason, it is no different from common sense" ("Preface" v). Sheik explains, "Buddhist philosophy, particularly as it is expounded by Daisaku Ikeda, comprises a world of ideas that can be enormously beneficial to Buddhists and non–Buddhists alike" ("Preface" vi). Noting that especially in a world of change, when "from all reports, the coming decades will be filled with changes we can't even imagine—changes that will completely alter the landscape of our society socially, culturally and politically," Sheik recognizes the importance of good guidance:

> This is why it is imperative to find a philosophy that can carry us through these times, to embrace the positive changes and show us how to deal with the negative ones. The truly important point Mr. Ikeda constantly underlines is that it is up to us, the generation of youth, to guide these changes and to create this new world. Not only do we have the inherent ability to affect these changes, but we have the responsibility to do so in a wise, compassionate manner ["Preface" vi–vii].

In his book about the SGI entitled *Waking the Buddha*, Clark Strand notes that "one of the most striking things about the Soka Gakkai from a Buddhist point of view is its emphasis on attaining victory in ordinary life—sometimes under *extra*ordinary circumstances" (4). Strand also notes, "by chanting Nam-myoho-renge-kyo and working for the happiness of others, Nichiren Buddhists seek to improve their current life condition and demonstrate "actual proof" of the Buddhist principle that all things are interconnected—that an inner change in the life of one individual can trigger changes in their community, their environment, and ultimately the world at large (5).

Sheik experienced something akin to "actual proof" of his Buddhist practice early on. In a *New Yorker* article entitled "Enlightened," Michael Shuman similarly traces the beginnings of Sheik's Buddhist practice almost verbatim from an interview with the singer-songwriter, writing:

> When the composer Duncan Sheik was nineteen, he visited Los Angeles, hoping to land a meeting with a music publisher. He stayed with an older relative, a longtime member of the Soka Gakkai International, a Buddhist lay organization headquartered in Japan. She and Sheik debated spiritual matters, until she told him, as he recalled the other day, "Unless you actually sit down and practice, it's not really going to have an effect on your life." So Sheik kneeled before her Gohonzon—a Buddhist scroll—and chanted. Then the music publisher called. "I thought, Oh, wow, Buddhism works!"

Sheik continued to chant since that moment, even though the music deal never materialized as he had expected. What the experience did offer him was a new focus and a felt sense that he could affect the outcome of his career through own efforts. He has continued to practice ever since. "I use the practice to focus on how can I create value in the world, in society, how can I create value for myself, for the people in my environment," Sheik explained to Schulman in the same interview, saying "As somebody who makes art for a living, how can I do that in the best way possible—That's what chanting gives me."

In practical ways, his continued Buddhist practice also helped him overcome challenges he faced creatively, including stage fright. As Sheik explains, he used the guidance he received from his study of Buddhism to change aspects of his life:

> Fortunately, the advice I did take strengthened my resolve to change the things about myself that were holding me back from accomplishing my creative goals. Before I started practicing Buddhism and reading Daisaku Ikeda's guidance, I couldn't bear to sing in public—I didn't like the sound of my own voice and was painfully self-conscious on stage. It is no coincidence that seven years later, my first album went gold, I was nominated for a Grammy for Best Male Vocal performance, and I toured all over the world, performing in front of millions of people ["Preface" vi].

Sheik chronicles many of his personal dilemmas in his music or readily shares stories of setbacks in interviews and online with fans, including for instance what Sheik calls his "Lost California years" (Schulman) before success when he was signed a record deal with Immortal Records, which went nowhere, leaving Sheik in limbo for at least two years. He challenged his frustration and misery into writing songs, and eventually in 1994, Atlantic Records bought him off his contract with Immortal.

The rest is history, as one might say. While signed with Atlantic and still in his twenties, Sheik released his eponymous debut album, *Duncan Sheik*, on June 4, 1996, to glowing reviews, receiving a rating of four out of five stars from *Rolling Stone* magazine. The single from the album, "Barely Breathing," a ballad borne out of heartache, which was originally considered a "throwaway" track, conceived and composed simply to complete his album ("Atlantic Hopes") became a breakout hit and the fourth longest running top 100 single in *Billboard* history after being listed for 55 weeks ("Duncan Sheik" On Tour). It also won the Broadcast Music Inc. (BMI) Award for 'Most Played Song of the Year' in 1997. Sheik's album later went gold. Although Sheik remains grateful for his overnight success, "he has not always been happy with its trajectory" (Bellafante), especially as he felt the song misrepresented his repertoire. But as Miller explains, Sheik's first album went gold "just in time for the mass adoration of the sensitive singer/songwriter to be redirected toward an oversexed adolescent army led by the likes of Britney Spears,

Christina Aguilera, 'N Sync and other 'pop music with a capital P,' as Mr. Sheik calls it" (Miller). As Ann Powers also adds, the success of "Barely Breathing" "did what uncharacteristic chart-toppers often do for pop musicians: made him seem both more commercial and less interesting than he is."

Few music insiders anticipated Sheik's long, illustrious, and varied career in the business. As Powers describes, "Sheik is a pop songcrafter turned Broadway composer who knows what it's like to be dismissed as a lightweight." For many people, "his name conjures acid-washed memories" (Scherer) of "Barely Breathing," which Berkowitz aptly describes as a "breezy" hit song and "an inescapable staple of mid–90s rock and pop radio." Branded early on as a one-hit wonder by skeptics following his meteoric rise to Top 40 fame, Sheik struggled with the marketing of his image and sought to distance himself from some of his early Top 40 fame, refusing at times to even play his famous hit. Sheik's music post–Top 40 sucess more readily reflects his style and his interest in developing new styles and sounds. Sheik's second album, *Humming* (Atlantic, 1998), for instance, featured more of Sheik's characteristic introspective searching and social critique and was described by critics as "a lovely mesh of sense and sonics" (Johnson) and "a spiritual exercise and philosophical essay" (Scaruffi) with "more atmospheric lushness" (Johnson) thanks to "a more profound and resonant base, complemented by accentuated drums and various string elements" (Blanford), in addition to orchestral pianos and flutes throughout. The first single from the album, "Bite Your Tongue," allowed him to express some self-deprecating admonishment for buying into his own fame and quickly became the most requested track in the country. It also earned Sheik staying power. The album *Humming* also received glowing reviews, earning Sheik the status of the most important new singer-songwriter of the decade ("Duncan Sheik" On Tour).

The album also pays subtly tribute to his Buddhism with its final track, "Nichiren." Tucked away in the middle of the track "Nichiren" is a hidden song titled "Foreshadowing" that appears to describe a gathering at an SGI discussion meeting where people study and discuss Buddhist concepts through "heart-to-heart dialogue."[10]

It was in 1999, at such a meeting in New York City, that Sheik met Stephen Sater, a fellow Buddhist, playwright, and at the time the SGI Arts Division leader. Sater, who had had a near-death experience in college that made him want to "create works of literature that could become part of the world,"[11] describes this first encounter as "the most remarkable meeting of my lifetime" (qtd. in Finkle). The two of them "fell to extended post-chanting chatting about their careers" (Finkle), during which Sater at some point mentioned that he needed a song for a "radical rewrite" (qtd. in Finkle) he was doing of Shakespeare's *The Tempest*. Sater then "emailed Sheik a lyric and was informed—practically in return email—that a tune was ready" (Finkle).

Sheik, who had a recording studio in his downtown Manhattan loft, could record songs as master quality demos there, and "that's what he did then and does whenever Sater fires off a newly minted lyric" (Finkle). Sater hadn't really considered himself a lyricist before this venture and admitted that he "didn't know the difference between a verse and a chorus" (qtd. in Finkle). Sheik had always approached his "songwriting as a kind of solitary pursuit" (qtd. in Finkle) and jokingly calls this unique working arrangement with Sater "a completely noncollaborative collaboration" (qtd. in Finkle). Nevertheless, the efforts of their first collaboration was included in Sater's play *Umbrage*, which premiered at Manhattan's Here Arts Center.

The next set of Stephen's lyrics that were turned into songs within the space of six months became Sheik's third album *Phantom Moon*, released in 2001 (Nonesuch Records). For Sheik, this album marked a new venture, one was far more introspective and daring artistically and, as Holden suggests, "not poised to hurtle up the charts anytime soon" (Holden). In his review of this primarily acoustic album, Holden recognized the chemistry in the Sater-Sheik collaboration, recognizing that Sater was Sheik's "artistic soulmate whose lyrics recast the sometimes bluntly didactic sentiments of his own lyrics in a more elevated and arty diction." The result is what Holden describes as "orchestrated meditations" that link together to tell the story about a struggling hero's "romantic loss and deepening spirituality as a heroic quest." Holden views the album as an "interior pilgrimage" from "a landscape desolate of life and hope" to a return "at the end to the same motif fleshed out with a string arrangement that adds color and feeling to that scene along with a sense of restoration and release." Seeing this voyage as an "album of moods to set you drifting and dreaming," Holden suggests that if one surrenders to the album's spell, one "might find it has healing powers."

The song-stories on the album *Phantom Moon* rely heavily on evocative imagery taken from mythology, chess, literature, Tarot cards, and the Bible and on "rich" language and foreshadows many songs from their later collaborative project *Spring Awakening*. "Sad Steven's Song," for instance, speaks of mermaids with portrait faces that are pale, tempting the singer into a treacherous dream realm of coral cavern halls while the blend of Sheik's voice and his own overlaid guitars are, as Holden suggests, "too beautiful." Similarly, in the lullaby "Far Away," the guitars played by Sheik and Bill Frisell are otherworldly, transporting "listeners to the musical equivalent of an enchanted island." Holden remarked the songs pulsed with the rhythm of chanting and also recognized in Sheik's melodies a "circular pattern also implies ritualized prayer." However, Sheik and Sater's Buddhist beliefs is only expressed more directly in the song, "A Mirror in the Heart." The song appears to reference the Gohonzon, or scroll, which is enshrined in a case on the altar that SGI members have in their homes. Considered an object of devotion, the Gohonzon is like a spiritual mirror for self-examination. The song's lyrics acknowledge the true intent of the scroll, upon which Nichiren is said to have inscribed his life and enlightenment in sumi ink. The song also enacts the ritual of chanting in front of the Gohonzon.

The success and fruitful collaboration on *Phantom Moon* inspired a further and far bolder new undertaking for Sheik and Sater—a new version of famed German playwright Frank Wedekind's 1891 classic *Spring Awakening: A Children's Tragedy* as a rock musical. Sater had long loved the provocative piece that follows the lives of three German schoolchildren—Melchior Gabor, Wendla Bergman, Moritz Stiefel—and their schoolmates as they deal with challenges of innocence, adolescence, and their own blossoming of sexuality and had wanted to adapt the play for modern audiences. As Sater recalls, he felt the piece's frank presentation of problems plaguing the youth, including sex, homosexuality, abortion, masturbation, and suicide still held valuable lessons for today's youth:

> It was indeed the turn of a new century when I first gave Duncan a copy of the play. Some months later, in the wake of the shootings at Columbine, its subject felt all the more urgent[....] These days, a short eight years later, in the shadow of the shootings at Virginia Tech, I am often asked why I ever thought Spring Awakening could work as a musical. And my only real answer is that I knew and loved the play, that I had long felt it was a sort of opera-in-waiting, and that somehow I could already "hear" Duncan's music in it [vii].

This choice surprised many. When Sheik first start composing music for the theater in 2006, several critics had "to clarify, 'yes, *that* Duncan Sheik'" (Berkowitz). Duncan Sheik devotees, however, were "less surprised when the creatively restless multi-instrumentalist emerged as the architect behind the Tony Award–winning soundscapes of 2006's *Spring Awakening*" (Berkowitz). It seemed "a natural progression" (Berkowitz) for a musician who throughout his career consistently broke with convention and changed the script in favor of embracing new experimentations. Nevertheless, even for Sheik, this new project pushed beyond the boundaries of his own comfort zone and expectations for his career.

The last thing he had anticipated was becoming involved in musical theater. When Sater first suggested appropriating Wedekind, Sheik recalls that he was at first very wary and "a little reticent" (Wren) about the project. Like many of his generation, Sheik had little interest in musical theater. He didn't like musicals. To him, musicals were "inherently problematic as a genre" (qtd. in Bellafante) and "showbiz scores and popular music sounded like different species" (Wren). Sheik felt that there is "a pandering aspect to a lot of musicals, the sense that they ought to be fun with a capital F" (Bellafante). Sheik also wasn't sure what kind of music he'd write "for a late-19th-century play about adolescent sexual awakening, parental oppression, suicide, and forced abortion. Would it be music meant to evoke the Bavaria of 100 years ago? Should it be updated to the 1960s with appropriate music? Those kinds of questions nagged at him" (Finkle). However, as Sheik read that play, he found it to be "really eccentric and racy" (Scherer), as well as "really bizarre but cool and interesting." *Spring Awakening* portrays a complicated story of several young people's struggles from adolescence to adulthood. Sheik describes as it as "obviously not an evening's light entertainment. There's comedy and there's tragedy, there's love, there's lust, there's betrayal, there's heartbreak and all kinds of other scandalous things that go on. It's definitely representative of the fullness and richness of life." The fact that it had repeatedly been banned also intrigued him. Sheik noted that "the controversy that surrounded the play was a plus for me in many ways. The fact that … people were so scandalized by it, that's only a good thing in my book" (qtd. in Besenyodi). Sheik also came to realize that "If I can write music that's the style of music I'm interested in and get away with it, and you don't expect me to do some weird ersatz version of Sondheim, then yeah, let's do it" (Scherer). His one stipulation was that "the music would have to make sense" to people, especially young people, of his generation (qtd. in Bellafante).

So, they started writing songs for the piece. Yet Sheik couldn't help wondering if he'd be "biting off more than I could chew" (qtd. in Finkle). Sater, on the other hand, had already recognized that Wedekind's "gorgeous threnody" already had the "soul of song within it" (viii). Yet even Sater was surprised by the effect adding music had on Wedekind's text, remarking that "I never dreamt that, by letting his characters actually sing, we would end up so profoundly transforming his work" (viii). What Sater and Sheik recognized as they began to work was that they had "access, through song, to the inner workings" of the characters' heard and minds" and thus "engaged with them differently." As Sater describes, "we embarked on journeys with them. Before long, we found ourselves altering the structure, even the substance, of our source material, to account for the places those songs had taken us" (viii).

Sheik and Sater soon also realized they "could fill a niche: craft a musical with an authentic contemporary sound, whose songs could slip onto portable media players and the radio" (Wren). Unlike typical musical theater numbers whose songs when heard out of context don't make sense, Sheik and Sater "wanted to do things that were universal enough, in a certain way, that the song could exist on its own" (qtd. in Wren). Thus, the two broke with a long-standing musical theater convention "in place at least since 1943's *Oklahoma!*—that a song further a musical's story and characterization" (Wren). Instead, their songs would "function as interior monologues. Characters would not serenade one another in the middle of scenes. Rather, each student would give voice to his or her inner landscape" (viii). This worked well for Sheik, who believes that a "song is one emotional moment. It's not necessarily part of this larger story. It's deepening the moment" (qtd. in Wren). For Sater, these moments reminded him of a quote by Ludwig Wittgenstein: "What we cannot speak about, we must pass over in silence." Sater also found that "song seems to let us pause within that silence, to find ourselves articulate within it" (viii). Thus within the show, the "songs soon came to function as subtext" (viii), giving the characters—and today's youth—vocal expression of their inner most anxieties and transforming them into beautifully sung shared experiences of struggle, an appropriate rendering of the Buddhist heart-to-heart dialogue they practice for wide audiences.

Wedekind's piece, as Sater notes, was already "full of exquisite monologues" but Sater describes that their new "monologues were meant to be truly interior—a technique more familiar in twentieth-century fiction." Thus, as Sater describes in his preface to the play,

> Instinctively, I felt I did not want to write lyrics which would forward the plot, and so chose not to follow that golden rule of musicals. I wanted a sharp and clear distinction between the world of the spoken and the world of the sun. And yet, I also wanted to create a seamless and ongoing musical counterpoint between the languages of those distinct worlds [viii].

Sheik and Sater had other ideas that veered from the original text. As Sater explains, in their show: "the scenes set out the world of nineteenth-century repression, while the songs afford our young characters momentary release into contemporary pop idiom. (Caught in the relentless dramas of our adolescent lives, we are all still rock stars in the privacy of our bedrooms.) The time-jumping structure of our show is meant, thus, to underscore the sadly enduring relevance of our theme" (ix). Thus, Sheik and Sater wrote modern pop songs one can rock out to, and indeed that is what their character often do on stage, namely pull a microphone from inside his vest and rock out as if no one was watching them. The characters sing songs of desire, songs of confession, songs of denial, songs of defiance, songs of loss, and *cris de coeur* songs. There is even a song ("Bitch of Living"), which deals with masturbation and shame. In many ways these songs give voice to what Ikeda in his chapter on how the "Arts Transform the Heart" in his book *Way of Youth* calls the "voiceless cry resting in the depths of our souls, waiting for expression" (83). As Sater explains, "Then, perhaps there is something in the nature of song itself that opens the door to story—that admits us to the heart of the singer—as if every story tells a sort of unacknowledged "I want." For, what we sing is unspoken, what is hidden. The "real story" (viii). Sater found in Sheik an extremely capable and equally expressive individual, able to capture the wide range of human experiences and emotions in such moments in extraordinary ways. Sater sums up the experience of working with Sheik with the following anecdote from the preface to the play when Sheik crafted one of the more memorable pieces: "who can explain the mystic thing that happens when I hand him a lyric and he somehow hears a song in it. When (in a moment indelibly etched in my memory) he first looks through those words, picks up his guitar and strums." Sater emphasizes that they "didn't set out to revolutionize the musical theater" (xiv-xv). Rather, as Sater emphasizes: "we had a story we wanted to tell, and a way we all felt we wanted to tell it" (xiv-xv).

In their adaptation, Sater and Sheik did far more than simply adding new scenes or rewriting extant ones. They re-envisioned the piece, and as Sater explains, "we created journeys for our three lead characters which did not exist in the original dark fractious fable" (x). Their version, for instance, chose to depict Melchior's rape of Wendla as consensual and pleasurable. Similarly, their addition of music also enabled them to dispense with Wedekind's haunting but highly problematic Masked Man, who "appears— literally out of nowhere—in the last scene of Wedekind's text" (x) as a *deus ex machina* figure. Sater and Sheik understood that their "music already performs the role of the Masked Man, for it gives our adolescent characters a voice to celebrate, to decry, to embrace the darker longings within them *as part of them*, rather than as something to run from or repress" (xi). Yet, in their reworking of the original text, they feel they "remained true to the inchoate yearning of Wedekind's youths."

They also—whether intentionally or not—shared in numerous ways their own Buddhist beliefs with the world, allowing millions of people to experience the relief of making conscious inner experiences that are often unacknowledged and unspoken. As Sheik explains, "Buddhism is about life in all its complexity and intensity. I think for us, as Buddhists, it's acknowledging what the human condition is" (qtd. in Ulaby). Schulman suggests, Sater and Sheik's *Spring Awakening* "may be the only Broadway musical with deliberately Buddhist underpinnings." Sheik agrees wholeheartedly, stating, "In Buddhist epistemology, there's this idea, the ten life states that every human being shuttles between," among them hell, hunger, animality, realization, bodhisattva, and Buddhahood" (Schulman). *Spring Awakening*, Sheik notes, hits all of them and emphasizes the potential within each life state for transformation, i.e., the potential of human revolution by harnessing hope and bringing out the Buddha potential in even the worse of circumstances and "turning poison into medicine."

In Sater and Sheik's sake, they turned this piece into gold—albeit only after seven long years of work. Theater producers were "leery of rock musicals" (Scherer), and many simply didn't understand Sater and Sheik's style. It didn't sound much like musical theater (Scherer). "But we showed them," Sheik noted, saying that in a certain way, he felt "vindicated" that he was perhaps "leading the charge of showing people that it's OK if the music that happens onstage reflects the taste of what the people are listening to in the wider culture" (Bellafante). In many ways, Sheik has a right to feel vindicated, as *Spring Awakening* helped "usher in an era of rock musicals, from *Bloody Bloody Andrew Jackson* to Green Day's own *American Idiot*, and these days Broadway is even embracing other popular forms—just look at the runaway success of Lin-Manuel Miranda's hip-hop-indebted *Hamilton*" (Scherer).

When the piece premiered at New York's Atlantic Theater Company in June 2006 and then opened at the Eugene O'Neill Theatre on December 10, 2006, Sheik and Sater's musical adaptation of the piece, which was directed by Michael Mayer, it quickly became "Broadway's favorite ingénue" (Hiser), hailed for "its inventive use of music and lyrics, and its ability to tackle difficult subject matter in an accessible manner" (Hiser). Writing about the show in *The New York Times*, Charles Isherwood raved about its brilliant and "honest" depiction of "the confusion and desperation that ensue when the onrushing tide of hormones meets the ignorance of children raised by parents too embarrassed or prudish to discuss what those new urges signify" (June 2006). Isherwood even proclaimed that Broadway "may never be the same" (Dec. 2006), referencing in particular Sheik's score.

The musical was a great success in part because of Sater and Sheik's ability to give expression to teenage angst. As Jose Solis suggests, Sheik "dives deep into his characters to find a beating heart that finds a commonality between money-driven America in the 1980's and angsty teenagers in late 19th century Germany, all of whom were lost and tried their best to reclaim their souls in their corresponding eras" (Solis). The musical won eight Tony awards: including Best Musical, Best Book (for Sater), and Best Score (a shared honor for Sheik as composer and Sater as lyricist). The musical has also toured the globe, earning rave reviews, and many members of its original cast, including Jonathan Groff, Lea Michele, Skylar Astin, and John Gallagher Jr, have gone on to highly successful careers in show business.

For Sheik, the long and often arduous process resulted in one of his works of which he's most proud. It also opened up new understandings and abilities. The experience of working on *Spring Awakening* taught Sheik to collaborate, not only with Sater, but with the whole cast, including the director, choreographer, and producers. "If you're making a solo album, you call the shots," Sheik says. He recalls early on that he wanted to direct the way the cast sang his songs, saying, "I was probably really pretty bratty about it. Because I was: 'It's my song, and they're going to sing it how I tell them to sing it!' But in truth, I had to learn that musical theater is a major collaboration between many people, with many diverse points of view" (Wren). Sheik learned "the incredible power of storytelling" and "what narrative can do to make the songs more powerful," noting that his "big realization over the course of that seven years" was how much he really enjoys "telling stories with songs."

Sheik has continued to write for the theater and tell more stories with his music for such projects as *Whisper House*, a tale of a boy in a haunted lighthouse during World War II, *The Cake Eaters*, Mary Stuart Masterson's directorial debut film, CSC's productions of Brecht's *Mother Courage and Her Children* and *The Caucasian Chalk Circle*, and the musical *Because of Winn Dixie*, to name just a few. Included in this new trajectory are new struggles and challenges, including Sheik's struggle with finances and also with alcohol that sent him to seek professional help. In 2010, Sheik checked into rehab the very same day his album *Covers 80's* was released, telling the staff there, "My record is coming out and I'm checking in." Sheik takes these struggles in stride, seeing them within the context of Buddhism as a part of his practice and process. In a letter to his fans on his website, Sheik shared his insights gained through the process, which he considered "all of it a good thing, a new challenge, an interesting riddle, a gift" ("Message"). He also shared with fans what he learned about the reward centers in the brain and how he feels it relates to his Buddhist practice—that when his practice is stronger and more consistent, the more capable he is with dealing with life's unexpected ups and downs. Sheik also promised more new concerts and music, perhaps even "God forbid, music people will want to dance to" ("Message") and the reassurance that "both he and his music will be the better for having gone through these experiences" ("Message").

New projects emerged again after his return, including an unexpected re-adaptation of *Spring Awakening*. Six years after it left Broadway, it returned to enjoy "a second life on Broadway" (Scherer) in a groundbreaking and reconceived new production by Deaf West Theatre, a Los Angeles–based company that creates theatrical productions for another new audience group, namely the hearing-impaired by including both deaf and hearing performers. As Scherer describes, the Deaf West production was "a whole different animal, double-casting some roles with deaf actors who sign and hearing doppel-gängers who sing for them." This version also incorporated "a seamless critique of how deafness is treated in the educational system into a show" (Scherer), highlighting, as Sheik points out, that "the theme of the show is really about the inability of parents and children to communicate" (qtd. in Scherer). Sheik altered and adapted his original arrangements to suit Deaf West Theatre director Michael Arden's production, which emphasized this problem of communication. As Sheik notes, "When you introduce deaf actors into the scenario, it just doubles down on the difficulty of that communication. It packs a huge emotional punch" (qtd. in Scherer).

Most recently, Sheik also wrote the music and the lyrics for Roberto Aguirre-Sacasa's musical adaptation of the Bret Easton Ellis novel *American Psycho*, turning to electronic music (as he did on his album *Legerdemain*, released 2015) to tell the story of the Wall Street status-obsessed serial killer Patrick Bateman. With *American Psycho: The Musical*, Sheik has not only embraced a new sound—"one indebted to '80s Chicago house music and New Order" (Scherer)—but he has also ventured into new territory and taken on the role of a Broadway lyricist for the first time. Sheik admits he thought it was an odd idea for a musical, until he reread the book and was inspired by its satire and its 1980s setting (Lunden). Sheik's choice to give *American Psycho* an all-synth score with "no guitars whatsoever. Just analog synthesizers and drum machines" (qtd. in Scherer) harks back to the genre of low budget sci-fi and horror's reliance on synthesizers for otherworldly sounds. But it also came in reaction to what he saw as "the overflow of rock musicals flooding Broadway" (Scherer) in more recent years following *Spring Awakening*. As Sheik explains "It's jumped the shark so badly," Sheik says, thus he wanted a sound that would fit for the piece: "It's set in 1989 in New York, and all those guys were going to clubs where they were playing early versions of house music and techno. It made sense, stylistically." In a different interview, Sheik suggested: "I also saw the possibility of doing a piece of musical theater where the score was completely electronic, where the band in the pit, so to speak, could be like Kraftwerk of Depeche Mode" (qtd. in Lunden).

It shouldn't be surprising that critics have again found, there are still many Buddhist themes interwoven into his music. In the song "Common Man," for instance, from *American Psycho*, the main character Patrick sings "I'm needing something more, every pleasure is a bore," and when asked whether he'd "wish enlightenment for Patrick," Sheik responded with a knowing laugh:

> I definitely think that is a very Buddhist song in a certain way, and I have had those sort of moments in my life when everything was going perfectly, I maybe had a lot of money in the bank, and I should have been the happiest person in the world, but when you get in that zone you're just always looking for something more intense, and more pleasurable. It's a crazy hamster wheel where you're never going to be satisfied. So I feel in my very small way I had an understanding of Patrick Bateman, just from the handful of moments in my own life when I've gotten too big for my britches [qtd. in Solis].

Sheik also believes this new version of *American Psycho* will bring a new audience to Broadway, noting that the 1991 novel and the 2000 film starring Christian Bale have "rabid fans who are not your usual Broadway crowd" (qtd. in Scherer). *American Psycho* had successful runs in London and L.A., and Sheik continued to work on getting the score right for New York audiences, saying "I've just continued to refine the sound of it, to make it hit harder and be more muscular and be a little cooler." He acknowledges that he could have done a version "that's totally campy and silly and ridiculous." Instead, he says, "I definitely did not want to do that. There's a lot of stuff in there that has teeth and is quite serious and hopefully will really mess with people's heads" (qtd. in Scherer).

It's clear that Sheik continues to defy odds, evolve, experiment, and change, while still finding ways to remain relevant. Sheik clearly "enjoys the kind of recognition and fulfillment that comes only when you're brave enough to take risks" (Romero). Thus, in addition to being a "pop troubadour and musical-theater composer" (Bellafante) Sheik has also "added a new notch to his belt: electronic musician" (Scherer). In addition to his work on *American Psycho*, in late 2015, Sheik released *Legerdemain*, his first non-musical solo album since 2006's *White Limousine*. *Legerdemain* is "half layered electronic music, half analog acoustic tunes—and, as such, a departure from what the artist describes as 'ye olde Duncan Sheik'" (qtd. in Scherer). But Sheik doesn't mind "that he's working all over the sonic and genre map" (Scherer). As he explains, "I just try to keep my head down and do the best work I can do, and to do it for the right reasons." For him, it's the search for the right sound: "For me, it's always been: How can I make music that's going to make the listener feel some undefinable, wonderful, excellent feeling? And the only arbiter you have of that is: Does it do it to me?" (qtd. in Scherer). Clearly, Sheik lives the maxim that "the only constant is change," ("Preface" vi), and for Sheik this change includes seeking the perfect sounds and creating meaning songs in many different forms of manifestation, and when challenges arise, Sheik knows he can always retreat to his Buddhist altar to chant, noting that "If I'm at sea, I know I can chant for an hour or so, and things will get better" (qtd. in Bellafante).

NOTES

1. Duncan Sheik regularly posts updates to his official website, www.duncansheik.com; his Twitter account, https://twitter.com/TheDuncanSheik; and Facebook page, https://www.facebook.com/DuncanSheik/.

2. Both Sheik and Sater chant together in Ulaby's interview, and Sheik chants in Harris's interview.

3. As the official SGI "The Meaning of Nam Myoho Renge Kyo" website explains: "Several hundred years after Shakyamuni, amidst the turbulence of 13th-century Japan, Nichiren similarly began a quest to recover the essence of Buddhism for the sake of the suffering masses. Awakening to the law of life himself, Nichiren was able to discern that this fundamental law is contained within Shakyamuni's Lotus Sutra and that it is encapsulated and concisely expressed in the sutra's title—Myoho-renge-kyo. Nichiren designated the title of the sutra as the name of the law and established the practice of reciting Nam-myoho-renge-kyo as a practical way for all people to focus their hearts and minds upon this law and manifest its transformative power in reality."

4. "To briefly explain its component parts: Nam (devotion)—To fuse one's life with the universal Mystic Law, drawing from it infinite energy for compassionate action. Myoho (Mystic Law)—The fundamental principle of the universe and its phenomenal manifestations. Renge (lotus flower)—The lotus blooms and seeds at the same time, symbolizing the simultaneity of cause and effect. The lotus, which grows in a muddy swamp, also symbolizes the emergence of Buddhahood in the life of the ordinary person. Kyo (sutra, teaching of a Buddha)—More broadly, it indicates all phenomena or the activities of all living beings." Ikeda, xii

5. Buddhists differentiate between "relative" and "absolute" happiness. Relative happiness is often temporary, mutable, and dependent on external circumstances, whereas

absolute happiness is forged from within and unshakeable, regardless of external circumstances.

6. Second Soka Gakkai President Josei Toda first used the term "human revolution" to describe "a fundamental process of inner transformation, and the third Soka Gakkai President Daisaku Ikeda further clarifies this process, explaining: "There are all sorts of revolutions: political revolutions, economic revolutions, industrial revolutions, scientific revolutions, artistic revolutions...but no matter what one changes, the world will never get any better as long as people themselves...remain selfish and lacking in compassion. In that respect, human revolution is the most fundamental of all revolutions, and at the same time, the most necessary revolution for humankind" (SGI "Human Revolution").

7. Strand notes the hypocrisy the SGI faces from other sects of Buddhism, explaining that the SGI is often criticized in the United States "for its focus on such middle class values as economic success and security" (12) and judged for encouraging its members to chant for "stuff like cars and money" by upper middle-class Buddhists of American and European descent (12–15).

8. In his book, Ikeda responds to the complicated issues facing American young people in a straightforward question-and-answer format. He addresses topics that include building individual character, the purpose of hard work and perseverance, family and relationships, tolerance, and preservation of the environment. The book offers young people straightforward answers and advice to specific questions and concerns they face in life, such as "How can I tell who my real friends are?" as well as straightforward advice to concerns young people face—including such issues dealing with family, friendship, love, learning, work, as "I recently broke up with someone, and I am really depressed." Or "the more "The more I study history, the more I find out what I've been taught isn't true." "How can I tell who my real friends are?" "Sometimes I get confused between what other people want for me and what I want for myself."—These are some of the concerns Ikeda addresses, providing an optimistic yet grounded view of life.

9. "Daisaku Ikeda is a peacebuilder, Buddhist philosopher, educator, author and poet. He was president of the Soka Gakkai lay Buddhist organization in Japan from 1960 to 1979 and is the founding president of the Soka Gakkai International (SGI), one of the world's largest and most diverse community-based Buddhist associations, promoting a philosophy of empowerment and social engagement for peace. He is also the founder of the Soka Schools system and several international institutions promoting peace, culture and education. [...] In 1975, he became the founding president of the SGI, now a global network linking over 12 million members in some 190 countries and territories" ("Overview").

10. Buddhist meetings are held in SGI members' homes or in cultural centers, and during the meetings, people often share their experiences of transformation. Schulman describes attending such a meeting with Duncan Sheik in his article "Enlightened."

11. In her interview with Sater, Wadler tells the story of Sater's fall from his third-story apartment during a fire and the lasting "effect of leaping out of a burning building on one's creative life," which Sater described as his realization: "I felt I wanted to create things that could last. Really what I felt was I wanted to create works of literature that could become part of the world."

WORKS CITED

"Atlantic Hopes Radio Makes Mad Dash for Duncan Sheik's 'She Runs Away.'" *Billboard*, 5 July 1977, p. 88. Web. 14 July 17.

Bellafante, Ginia. "Broadway Is Rocker's Latest Alternative." *The New York Times*. The New York Times, 25 Dec. 2006. Web. 14 July 2017. http://www.nytimes.com/2006/12/26/theater/26shei.html.

Berkowitz, Joe. "How Duncan Sheik Reinvented Himself from Radio Hits to *Fast Company*." Fast Company, 13 May 2016. Web. 14 July 2017. https://www.fastcompany.com/3059509/how-duncan-sheik-reinvented-himself-from-radio-hits-to-american-psycho.

Berson, Misha. "Nightclub Review: Duncan Sheik Brings a Just a Taste of 'Spring' to Triple Door." *The Seattle Times*. The Seattle Times Company, 28 Feb. 2009. Web. 14 July 2017.

http://www.seattletimes.com/entertainment/nightclub-review-duncan-sheik-brings-a-just-a-taste-of-spring-to-triple-door/.

Besenyodi, Adam. "Très Sheik: An Interview with Duncan Sheik." *PopMatters*. 7 June 2007. Web. 15 July 2017. http://www.popmatters.com/feature/tres-sheik-an-interview-with-duncan-sheik/.

Blanford, Roxanne. "Humming—Duncan Sheik: Songs, Reviews, Credits." *AllMusic*. N.p., n.d. Web. 14 July 2017. http://www.allmusic.com/album/humming-mw0000600975.

"Duncan Sheik." *Duncan Sheik: On Tour: WHYY*. N.p., n.d. Web. 14 July 2017. http://whyy.org/cms/ontour/duncan-sheik/.

Finkle, David. "Duncan Sheik and Steven Sater: Awakening Broadway." Backstagewww. N.p., 01 Nov. 2006. Web. 14 July 2017. https://www.backstage.com/news/duncan-sheik-and-steven-sater-awakening-broadway/.

Finn, Robin. "Decisions, Decisions. Name Recognition or Nirvana?" *The New York Times*. The New York Times, 01 July 2002. Web. 14 July 2017. http://www.nytimes.com/2002/07/02/nyregion/public-lives-decisions-decisions-name-recognition-or-nirvana.html.

Harris, Dan. "10% Happier with Dan Harris—Featuring Duncan Sheik." *ABC News*. ABC News Network, 29 Oct. 2016. Web. 15 July 2017. http://abcnews.go.com/Entertainment/video/10-happier-singer-songwriter-duncan-sheik-43163109.

Holden, Stephen. "A Throwback to the Poets of Melancholy." *The New York Times*. The New York Times, 10 Mar. 2001. Web. 14 July 2017. http://www.nytimes.com/2001/03/11/arts/music-a-throwback-to-the-poets-of-melancholy.html.

Ikeda, Daisaku. *The Way of Youth: Buddhist Common Sense for Handling Life's Questions*. Santa Monica, CA: Middleway, 2000. Print.

Isherwood, Charles. "In 'Spring Awakening,' a Rock 'n' Roll Heartbeat for 19th-Century German Schoolboys." *The New York Times*, 16 June 2006. 14 July 2017. http://theater2.nytimes.com/2006/06/16/theater/reviews/16awak.html?scp=3&sq=spring%20awakening&st=cse&gt.

Isherwood, Charles. "Sex and Rock? What Would the Kaiser Think?" *The New York Times*, 11 Dec. 2006, Theater sec. 11 Dec. 2006. 14 July 2017. http://theater2.nytimes.com/2006/12/11/theater/reviews/11spri.html?scp=1&sq=spring%20awakening&st=cse&gt.

Johnson, Beth. "Humming." EW.com. 09 Oct. 1998. Web. 14 July 2017. http://ew.com/article/1998/10/09/humming-2/.

Lunden, Jeff. "Can Pop Musicals Bring New Audiences to Broadway?" *NPR*. NPR, 20 Apr. 2016. Web. 15 July 2017.

Martin, Rachel. "The Eclectic World of Duncan Sheik, from Billboard to Broadway." *NPR*. NPR, 04 Oct. 2015. Web. 15 July 2017. http://www.npr.org/templates/transcript/transcript.php?storyId=444779540.

Miller, M.H. "Duncan Sheik, Better than Barely Breathing, Reinvents Himself." *Observer*. Observer Media, 13 Aug. 2013. Web. 14 July 2017. http://observer.com/2011/06/duncan-sheik-better-than-barely-breathing-reinvents-himself/.

"Overview: Daisaku Ikeda Website." *Home*. N.p., n.d. Web. 15 July 2017. http://www.daisakuikeda.org/main/profile/bio/bio-01.html.

Powers, Ann. "Duncan Sheik Uncovers Hope for the '80s." *NPR*. NPR, 07 June 2011. Web. 14 July 2017. http://www.npr.org/sections/therecord/2011/06/07/137029238/duncan-sheik-uncovers-hope-for-the-80s.

Romero, Angie. "10 Questions with Duncan Sheik." BMI.com. 15 Dec. 2015. Web. 15 July 2017. https://www.bmi.com/news/entry/10_questions_with_duncan_sheik.

Sater, Steven, Duncan Sheik, and Frank Wedekind. *Spring Awakening: A New Musical*. New York: Theatre Communications Group, 2011. Print.

Scaruffi, Pierro. *The History of Rock Music. Duncan Sheik: Biography, Discography, Reviews, Links*. N.p., n.d. Web. 14 July 2017. http://www.scaruffi.com/vol5/sheik.html.

Schulman, Michael. "Buddhism on Broadway." *The New Yorker*. The New Yorker, 19 June 2017. Web. 15 July 2017. http://www.newyorker.com/magazine/2015/10/19/enlightened.

SGI (Soka Gakkai International). "Human Revolution." *Soka Gakkai International (SGI)*. N.p., 17 July 2008. Web. 14 July 2017. http://www.sgi.org/about-us/buddhism-in-daily-life/human-revolution.html.

SGI (Soka Gakkai International). "November 18: Celebrating the Founding of the Soka Gakkai." *Soka Gakkai International (SGI)*. N.p., 14 Nov. 2011. Web. 15 July 2017. http://www.sgi.org/resources/study-materials/celebrating-the-founding-of-the-soka-gakkai.html.

SGI (Soka Gakkai International). "The Establishment of Nichiren Buddhism." *Soka Gakkai International (SGI)*. N.p., n.d. Web. 15 July 2017. http://www.sgi.org/resources/study-materials/the-establishment-of-nichiren-buddhism.html.

SGI (Soka Gakkai International). "The Meaning of Nam-myoho-renge-kyo." *Soka Gakkai International (SGI)*. N.p., 17 July 2008. Web. 14 July 2017. http://www.sgi.org/about-us/buddhism-in-daily-life/the-meaning-of-nam-myoho-renge-kyo.html.

Sheik, Duncan. "Message Song from Duncan." *Duncan Sheik*. N.p., 24 Aug. 2010. Web. 15 July 2017. http://duncansheik.com/message-song-from-duncan/.

Simonson, Robert. "Pop Idol Duncan Sheik Lends Music to HERE's Umbrage, Feb. 11–28." *Playbill*. N.p., 01 Feb. 1999. Web. 14 July 2017. http://www.playbill.com/article/pop-idol-duncan-sheik-lends-music-to-heres-umbrage-feb-11-28-com-79809.

Solis, Jose. "Not a Common Man: Duncan Sheik and the Crafting of an American (and London) Pyscho." *PopMatters*. N.p., 7 Apr. 2016. Web. 15 July 2017. http://www.popmatters.com/feature/not-a-common-man-duncan-sheik-and-the-crafting-of-an-american-and-london-py/.

Strand, Clark. *Waking the Buddha: How the Most Dynamic and Empowering Buddhist Movement in History Is Changing Our Concept of Religion*. Santa Monica, CA: Middleway, 2014. Print.

"Theory of Value Creation." *Theory of Value Creation: Tsunesaburo Makiguchi Website*. N.p., n.d. Web. 15 July 2017. http://www.tmakiguchi.org/timeline/Theoryofvaluecreation.html.

Ulaby, Neda. "'Spring Awakening' Brings Teen Angst to Broadway." *NPR*. NPR, 27 Jan. 2007. Web. 15 July 2017. http://www.npr.org/templates/transcript/transcript.php?storyId=7032516.

Wadler, Joyce. "Storming Broadway from Atop a Fortress." *The New York Times*. The New York Times, 13 Dec. 2006. Web. 15 July 2017. http://www.nytimes.com/2006/12/14/garden/14dakota.html.

Wren, Cecilia. "How Duncan Sheik Went from 'Barely Breathing' to 'Spring Awakening.'" *The Washington Post*. WP Company, 05 July 2009. Web. 14 July 2017. http://www.washingtonpost.com/wp-dyn/content/article/2009/07/03/AR2009070300061.html.

Criticism and Confusion in the Spiritual Transformation of Matisyahu

ERIN E. BAUER

Matthew Paul Miller, best known by his Hebrew name and stage name, Matisyahu, achieved fame in the first decade of the twenty-first century as a Hasidic, reggae rapper and alternative rock musician. The most notable part of that equation, at least within the Jewish community and momentarily disregarding the equally inimitable combination of reggae, rap, and rock (not to mention the incorporation of beat-boxing, scat singing, and the Jewish *hazzan* style of songful prayer), was the distinctively religious aspect to Matisyahu's public identity as well as his music, particularly given the musician's positionality within the more mainstream world of American popular culture. Yet, in December of 2011, Matisyahu posted a picture of himself on Twitter without a beard, explaining, "No more Chassidic reggae superstar. Sorry folks, all you get is me … no alias," and creating confusion and controversy among his Jewish (and other) fans. In June of 2012, the musician appeared without a yarmulke, adding fuel to the already blazing media frenzy. This essay traces the spiritual journey, musical evolution, and complicated public reactions to the Hasidic reggae superstar, considering the meaning of religious identity within the modern rock community and the dichotomous commitment of fans to music and meaning alike.

Matthew Miller to Matisyahu: Initial Transformations and "Pre-Shave" Music

Born in West Chester, Pennsylvania, in 1979, Matthew Miller grew up in White Plains, New York. He was raised as a Reconstructionist Jew, attending Hebrew school at a synagogue in White Plains.[1] As a teenager, Miller struggled with issues of personal identity and a number of addictions. In 1995, he attended a two-month program at the Alexander Muss High School in Israel. As the musician explains, while his interest in attending the program centered primarily on getting out of high school for a few months, his time in Israel became an important catalyst for his developing sense of identity and musicality. According to Matisyahu, "I started listening to Bob Marley, and that informed some of my identity in terms of music and spirituality, and seeing a lot of Jewish references within reggae music was kind of a pull for me towards piquing my interest in Judaism" (qtd. in Horn). Upon returning to New York, Miller dropped out of high school, attended a drug rehabilitation program in upstate New York, followed the band Phish on a nationwide tour, and ultimately finished school at a wilderness expedition program in Oregon. After moving back to New York, Miller began to develop his version of reggae music, while also taking classes on Jewish spirituality at The New School. By 2001, Miller had officially joined the Chabad-Lubavitch movement and had taken Matisyahu as the Hebrew form of his name. As the artist explains, "I was wearing a jacket and hat before I knew it. And before I knew it, I was in Crown Heights [in Brooklyn] and completely indoctrinated into the Chabad way of life" (qtd. in Horn).[2]

In 2004, Matisyahu signed with JDub Records (a nonprofit label that promotes Jewish musicians) and released his first album. Noting the innovation in *Shake Off the Dust ... Arise*, the artist explains, "It was like, taking the roots-reggae thing and connecting it with all the elements of this Chabad Hasidish knowledge" (qtd. in Grossman). In 2006, Matisyahu released a live album from a concert in Austin, Texas, called *Live at Stubb's*, followed closely by *Youth*. The live version of "King Without a Crown," originally on *Shake Off the Dust ... Arise*, became widely popular, reaching No. 28 on the Billboard Hot 100 and No. 7 on Billboard Hot Modern Rock Tracks. A shorter studio version of the song was included on *Youth*, which reached No. 4 on the Billboard 200 album chart. Right before the release of *Youth*, Matisyahu broke his contract with JDub Records, moving his representation to Gary Gersh (a prominent Hollywood agent, formerly president of Capitol Records).

While the musician's religious identity certainly seems to be a genuine component of his popular appeal (as will be discussed in more detail below), Matisyahu also seems acutely aware of the connection between appearance and commercialism. As the artist explains, "I don't feel great about labels, but I've used them to my advantage. I wasn't stupid, I knew there was a moment of surprise that was going to attract people to who I was" (qtd. in Weingarten). In this context, the musician's decision to move to a manager more attuned to popular commercialism seems to relate to some of the criticism he has received within the Jewish community of selling out. In an interview, the artist admits, "Who doesn't want success? There's some artists that say they don't, and they're not looking for it, but I'm not one of those artists" (qtd. in Mobius). Despite his position within the religious community, Matisyahu seems to remain closely linked to the secular practicalities of making money. Yet the response to this pursuit of commercialism (even before the shaving incident) is often harsh:

> [T]he men who broke their backs to make [Matisyahu] a star, Aaron Bisman and Jacob Harris [JDub Records], have been hung out to dry by a man I now recognize to be a false prophet of our own making, who traded in his most devout "true believers" merely to maximize his cashflow potential…. So much for "I owe it all to G-d" [Mobius].

While *Live at Stubb's* and *Youth* both went gold, leading to mainstream popularity and a widespread touring program, a fourth studio album, *Light* (2009), did not achieve this same level of success. Writing for *Tablet Magazine*, David Meir Grossman even attributes Matisyahu's later re-identification outside of the Hasidic community at least in part to the need for a clean slate following the flop of *Light*. As Grossman asserts, in the three years between the release of *Light* and the infamous beard shaving, Matisyahu released only small live EPs and a sequel to *Live at Stubb's*, called *Live at Stubb's, Vol. 2*. Accordingly, and beyond an outcry of loss from the Jewish community, the eventual alteration of the musician's spiritual identity was sometimes treated as a joke or a publicity stunt. As a 2011 headline in the New York City blog *Gawker* flippantly announced, "Matisyahu Shaves Beard, Reminding World of His Existence" (Read). While the musician seems to be sincere in his personal spiritual journey, the sense of rejection following the release of *Light* is a plausible factor in the artist's ultimate dismissal of his earlier religious identity.

Matisyahu as Symbolic Representation: Musical Meaning for a Diverse Audience

Upon initial consideration, the character of Matisyahu can seem like a novelty act with limited popular appeal, particularly among a secular audience. However, during the 2000s, the artist was surprisingly successful with not only the Jewish community, but also among a diverse, popular crowd. As *Slate* writer Jody Rosen affirms, "Whatever you think of the music, there's no denying the powerful novelty of the singer's shtick." Yet, perhaps part of the artist's appeal is that his Jewish image is not just a shtick designed to sell records. The musician seems genuinely committed to his complex, but deeply personal, religious journey. Tracing his background through addiction, religious transformation in the form of community-based commitment, and continued spiritual transformation through the ultimate revoking of this community, Matisyahu seems to be, at his core, merely a human being searching for answers to the difficulties of life. The musician explains part of this continuing, complicated journey in a recent *Reddit* post responding to questioning fans (in recent years, Matisyahu has become a master of social media, using Twitter, Facebook, and Instagram to connect with audiences, promote his music, and counteract the controversy surrounding some of his decisions of identity):

> I have always been a very expressive individual. For example, when I was a kid I loved to play war. We watched movies like *Rambo* and *Commando* and my dad built me a club house in the backyard which became our weapons den…. By putting on the clothing and strapping all the weapons I felt I became a soldier. This continued for me throughout my life, i.e. when I got into Bob Marley I grew dreadlocks and painted the cover of his record *Uprising* on my wall.

Yet, Matisyahu's childhood experiences taking on and expressing himself through alternative roles is not limited to simple costumes, decorations, and role-playing. As the artist continues, he used these roles- particularly the reggae influences of Bob Marley- to reach into himself and find an individual mode of expression: "Looking the part was not enough. The music made something inside me come alive and as I was listening I realized that it was touching my soul deeply and leaving a mark. I felt deep down even though I was a white kid from the suburbs that I could express myself in this mode."

Within this context, it seems fitting that the artist would eventually express himself through the lens of Hasidism. Taking on that particular role took him deeply into his religious beliefs and gave him the opportunity to express himself in a highly visual context- related to the idea of costumes and role-playing, but pushing beyond this simplistic explanation to create a deeply individual form of expression. As Matisyahu continues in the same *Reddit* post, "When I got interested in Judaism it wasn't enough to read about it in books, I felt I needed to become it and part of that meant expressing it via my looks." However, the artist also explains that his ultimate dismissal of Hasidism related to a newfound ability to drop the role-playing, the lifelong need for expression through alternative characters, and instead rely on himself for expression. As Matisyahu concludes, "About three years ago I found something I had been looking for, for my whole life and all of a sudden I felt I didn't need to look the part anymore. The part had become a Part of me and that was enough." In this regard, while Matisyahu's distinctive look has probably attracted a diverse audience, at least in terms of an initial, perhaps largely curious, form of recognition, this Orthodox image seems to have served a deeper, genuine role in the artist's spiritual transformation. This religious authenticity helps to contextualize the innate meaning of the music for early Jewish fans, as well as to explain much of the vehement backlash upon its removal, particularly among the Hasidic community. For religious fans who took Matisyahu as a personal example of a sense of balance between Jewish values and a secular world, the ultimate rejection of this religious image became a rejection of the religion itself. Many Jewish fans viewed the artist's spiritual reorientation as a dismissal and trivialization of their own personal beliefs, ultimately questioning the authenticity of the original Orthodox image.

In addition, the seemingly unusual juxtaposition of reggae and Judaism in the music of Matisyahu becomes less of a novelty when viewed through an earlier lens of American popular music. Compared to generations of minstrelsy performances by Jewish musicians, tracing a path through Irving Berlin, Al Jolson, Mezz Mezzrow, Bob Dylan, and the Beastie Boys, Matisyahu becomes just another Jewish artist fascinated by—and a successful practitioner of—black musical culture. As Rosen notes, "[S]uccessive generations of Jewish musicians have used the blackface mask to negotiate Jewish identity and have made some great art in the process." Yet Matisyahu adds an additional layer of exoticism (and corresponding commercialism) with the (for many) striking image of Hasidism. Regardless of intent, the beard and sidelocks presented within a secular setting make the artist stand out, drawing audiences to the music in a way that necessarily disappears with the later change in imagery. Furthermore, the pentatonic scales and minor-key melodies of Jewish liturgical music and Hasidic folksongs are common to the sounds of reggae, as are Rastafarian themes of Exodus and a longing for Zion. In many ways, Matisyahu's appropriation of the Jamaican style is simply a reappropriation of symbolic themes originally drawn from the Torah and a common musical language.[3] As journalist Hampton Stevens notes, "There is something bizarre yet poignant and undeniably American about a Jewish kid from the suburbs who found a path to his own ancient faith by hearing Jamaicans sing about it."

For Jewish audiences, Matisyahu's (Hasidic) image, as well as the use of traditionally Jewish imagery and religious values, typically held much greater significance than the music itself. This deeper sense of meaning for the community closely contributed to the backlash the artist experienced from religious audiences following his withdrawal from Hasidism. As Elad Nehorai, a blogger within the Chabad-Lubavitch community of Crown Heights, explains, Matisyahu's simultaneous position within Orthodox Judaism and mainstream popular culture provided an inspiration for the Jewish community—particularly the younger generation—to take pride in their unique religious customs. He enabled people to see a possibility to combine aspects of devotion with the modern world. The musician's role within mainstream society also served as a valuable representation of the Hasidic culture to the outside world. In addition, the music itself remained deeply connected to Judaism through the lyrics and thematic materials, combining an enjoyable, secular sound with religious values and beliefs. As Nehorai explains,

> It might be hard to understand if you aren't a religious Jew, but there was an amazing joy that we got out of finally being able to dance, to sing, to music that was connected to us and our beliefs. That we no longer had to compromise and listen to music we felt didn't represent us or our values just because we liked the beat. Now we could like the beat, and connect to the music. We could even let our children listen to it. You have no idea what a blessing that is.

For many fans in the Jewish community, Matisyahu was a validation of their religion, customs, and beliefs. For the younger generation, he brought a new sense of relevance to Jewish culture—particularly within the Orthodox realm—and provided an example for fans to remain strictly religious while simultaneously assimilating into popular society and pursuing secular activities like concerts.

In the sphere of popular music, fans often gather in genre-specific groups based on some sort of common cultural understanding. A certain similarity of background drawn from commonalities of upbringing, socioeconomic circumstance, education, or belief system creates what George Lipsitz has called a "family of resemblance," in which seemingly disparate cultural groups draw from parallel life experiences to cultivate a cohesive understanding from individual elements; in Marshall Berman's words, a "unity of disunity" (136). In this regard, religious fans of Matisyahu formed a community based on a (presumably genuine) perception of shared beliefs. The music itself became less important than the cultural cohesion that the artist represented. The removal of Matisyahu's religious foundation thus eliminated the collective understanding binding many of the fans to the music, leaving them longing "desperately for something solid to cling to" (Berman 18).

According to a number of religious studies scholars, the cultural practice of religion is, at its core, a product of materialities (c.f. Engelke, Asad). In essence, and through a diverse array of global customs, religion constitutes material objects, including images, idols, and manner of dress, as well as actions, words, music, and, in recent years, various manifestations of media (c.f. De Vries and Weber). In this regard, the Hasidic image and initial musical product of Matisyahu created a material component of religious practice among the artist's Jewish fanbase. The music became more than music itself, serving instead as a material representation of religious beliefs. This aspect of Jewish materiality is what was lost for Orthodox fans when Matisyahu shaved his beard. The religious audience gave the musician's music a type of semiotic ideology (a semantic approach developed by anthropologist Webb

Keane), using the creative product to represent an important balance between religious Judaism and the modern secular world. In many ways, the loss of this musical product brought the mainstream/religious balancing act into question as well. In fact, Matisyahu's public shift in spiritual orientation challenged the entire system of beliefs for certain religious fans. With the loss of their religious role model, these fans were confused about their own continuation of religious practices and spiritual positionality in a secular world. In this regard, the music itself was largely irrelevant.

Revoking Hasidism, or the Shaving Incident

In December of 2011, Matisyahu shaved his beard, ostensibly stepping away from his role as cultural icon for the religious Jewish community. In the years leading up to this most visible decision, the musician explains, his religious identity had been slowly changing: "Chabad has been a bit of a roller coaster for me. It was very pure in the sense that I totally divested myself from all of the confusion that I was living in…. [But] I definitely lost myself, as well, in the process, in the sense that I somehow stopped thinking for myself. I became completely dependent on other people for my sense of what was right and wrong. I felt incapable of making my own decisions. I was borderline completely losing my mind" (qtd. in Horn). At that point (2008), the artist pulled himself out of the Chabad-Lubavitch movement and stopped identifying with any specific Jewish group, but still considered himself an Orthodox Jew. After struggling for the next few years with continuing questions of spirituality and identity (a process similarly reflected in the sonic and thematic eclecticism of *Shattered*, an innovative EP released in 2008), Matisyahu finally decided to let go of the beard. He explains, "I remember the moment when it hit me, I was walking down Amsterdam Avenue on the Upper West Side and it felt like I was literally walking out of a jail cell that I had been in. At that moment I realized I could shave if I wanted. It was up to me and no one else" (qtd. in "Matisyahu"). A year later, the artist continues, "In a certain way, my growing of and shaving of the beard had a similar meaning" (qtd. in Grossman). Matisyahu's act of shaving represents a continuation of the lifelong journey to find meaning in his own spiritual identity. Unfortunately, many of his fans in the religious community did not interpret his spiritual journey as their own, instead experiencing only loss and pain in the act.

Matisyahu's public announcement of his change in religious identity came through a clean-shaven picture posted on Twitter, accompanied by a message: "At the break of day I look for you at sunrise/When the tide comes in I lose my disguise"—lines from the song "Thunder" on the album *Light*. The musician quickly offered a further explanation on his official website:

> This morning I posted a photo of myself on Twitter. No more Chassidic reggae superstar. Sorry folks, all you get is me … no alias. When I started becoming religious ten years ago it was a very natural and organic process. It was my choice. My journey to discover my roots and explore Jewish spirituality- not through books but through real life. At a certain point I felt the need to submit to a higher level of religiosity … to move away from my intuition and to accept an ultimate truth. I felt that in order to become a good person I needed rules- lots of them- or else I would somehow fall apart. I am reclaiming myself.

Addressing subsequent confusion, Matisyahu clarified on Twitter that he had not rejected his Jewish faith, but had just decided to leave behind the more stringent rules of Hasidism. However, despite this and later attempts at clarification by the artist, reactions among fans—particularly in the religious community—typically included confusion, pain, anger, and a sense of loss. As noted above, Matisyahu had become more than just the music, often serving as a material manifestation of the Jewish religion itself. Matisyahu symbolized a successful navigation of both religious and secular practices in modern society. The artist's public shift in spiritual orientation—coupled with an altered visual image—thus trivialized Hasidism, destroyed the idea of a secular balance, and brought personal religious practices into question for many fans who had looked to Matisyahu as a semiotic model.

A Sense of Loss: Public Reactions to Personal Identity

For the religious Jewish community, Matisyahu's decision to move away from Hasidism (and the clear outward appearance it provided to the outside world) was not merely a personal decision. For fans who had used Matisyahu as a religious inspiration and secular representation of Jewish culture, the musician's decision took away a significant source of pride within the modern world. For these fans, Matisyahu's role was never truly about the music, but rather his representation as a Hasidic musician within a secular market. While the removal of their role model saddened and angered religious audiences, the stark realization of the value of his symbolism for fans, rather than his actual music, deeply affected the musician himself. Following the artist's public shift in religious orientation, religious Jews lashed out emotionally—and publically—on social media and blogs. As Nehorai explains, "We were all mourning…. He had taken off the mantle of leadership. He had 'left' in a public way, in an insensitive and humiliating way. And we were broken hearted." In dismissing Hasidism, the religious Jewish fanbase felt that

Matisyahu had dismissed them. After holding the artist up as a spokesman, ambassador, and mentor, his withdrawal from Orthodoxy left him without a role among many of these fans. Meanwhile, the musician's other fanbase— the wider audience of non–Jews, secular Jews, and such—wondered what all the fuss was about. This second group had always been attracted to the music, and Matisyahu's change of religious identity, while confusing to some, did not change this purpose.

In addition, many religious Jews—in retrospect—saw both Matisyahu's adoption and ultimate dismissal of Hasidism as a trivialization of their own religious practices. They asserted that his role as a public figure made the decision far more significant than mere personal identity, as the fallout reflected upon and influenced the entire community. These fans also argued that it was impossible to separate the music from the religious message. Since, to them, the artist's shift in religious orientation negated the significance of his message, the music itself was no longer important. Furthermore, for many of these fans, Matisyahu's position as a religious figure within a secular world-and the corresponding implications for audience members themselves in modern society- was destroyed by his suddenly secular appearance. In this interpretation, Matisyahu compromised his own beliefs (and the personal projection of these beliefs among an Orthodox audience) in pursuit of popular success. The symbolism was removed, and many religious fans were left with no real connection to the musician, since his role had never really been about the music. As the musician explains, "It was really hard for me because it turns out these people were not really fans of my music. Those people that made the comments, they were just I guess followers or fans of me representing them or making Judaism cool or whatever it was" (qtd. in Ghermezian).

Popular music scholar David Hesmondhalgh discusses the importance of music as a combination of two complementary dimensions of musical experience in modern society (1). Music is simultaneously an emotional manifestation of the private self and the foundation for many collective, public experiences (such as live performance, dancing at a party, and basic common consciousness). For fans of Matisyahu, the initial product served as a dichotomous representation of personal beliefs and a collective religious community. For religious Jews, the separation of the artist from his collective identity brought into question the continuing value of the music. Beyond mere aesthetic experience, Matisyahu's music had become a form of cultural communication; a common materiality linking fans to contemporary religious practices. Without this collective basis, many fans were left only with an individual sense of aesthetic satisfaction. While music in modern culture often functions as simple sonic entertainment, it also derives meaning as an avenue of emotional expression, a process of relaxation or invigoration, the communication of power and politics, and—as in the case of Matisyahu—the representation of a system of beliefs. Thus, in removing the music from its perceived purpose, the musician loses meaning for fans disinterested in the aesthetic capabilities of the creative product. In other words, the music cannot be separated from its symbolic representation. For many fans, the value of the music lies in the semiotic interpretation, and the removal of this meaning fundamentally destroys the musical experience.

Matisyahu to Matthew Miller?: Later Transformations and "Post-Shave" Music

Despite pain and a sense of rejection following the realization of his role—and not really the role of his music—among many religious audience members, Matisyahu has slowly started to recover from the rather dramatic fallout that came from shaving his beard. For better or worse, as Rabbi Ben Greenberg writes, "[T]he circle has been completed from Matthew Miller, Westchester-raised secular Jewish kid, to Matisyahu, icon and inspiration for thousands of his fellow Jews, back to Matthew Miller." The musician has come out with three new albums (*Spark Seeker* in 2012, *Akeda* in 2014 and *Undercurrent* in 2018) and now focuses on fans who respect his continuing journey and enjoy his music (rather than the symbolism alone). In a recent interview, he explains,

> I think my fans, get me, they understand me. The general population, *if* they've heard of me, don't know who I really am. They think—He was Hassidic. Or maybe they just think I was a gimmick.... There are some people who think that now that I've shaved, I've succumbed somehow and couldn't hack the hard parts and proved their point. But my fans are the only ones who really know what I do. They know exactly who I am [qtd. in Weingarten].

Akeda (2014) is perhaps Matisyahu's most self-reflective and emotionally raw album. It largely lacks the popular hooks of the artist's most commercially successful earlier works but in many ways serves instead as a sonic representation of the musician's continuing spiritual journey. Throughout the album, an underlying idea of sacrifice adds a further dimension to the musical significance. Perhaps unavoidably, since popular music often signifies more than the music itself, the music remains a symbolic representation of spiritual understanding, but the semiotic interpretation has changed. The term *akeda* signifies the biblical "binding" of Isaac to the rock by his father Abraham (at God's command). Accordingly, Matisyahu's album explores the worldly price of faith and the aftermath of his own decision to follow his own interpretation of religious devotion. The artist explains:

> The theme of the *Akeda*, of Abraham and Isaac and the idea of sacrifice, means listening to the word of God whatever that might mean. Going against the grain and

what people might expect of you. Abraham was at a stage in his life when he had everything he wanted. And then he heard a voice telling him to do the most outrageous thing. Basically, that's the theme in my life. Sacrifice. Following that inner voice even when everyone is telling you that you can't do that and it doesn't make sense. The theme of binding is literally what *Akeda* means. In my life I was bound to a lot of things and I found myself unraveling [qtd. in Weingarten].

Through this new musical offering, Matisyahu seems to be dealing with his own spirituality and evolving role in a secular world, while now providing a creative representation not only for religious Jews, but for a diverse audience attracted to his music and working through their own struggles of humanity. The essential sense of collectivity previously achieved through a religious context has shifted to a wider public, with a new fanbase collectively experiencing the deeper meaning of Matisyahu's music through a personal sense of reflection. For these fans, the music has not yet been separated from its semiotic value, creating a certain aesthetic satisfaction apart from strict religious identification.

As Hesmondhalgh explains, "Music is always embedded within complex networks of meaning and affect" (23). With the artist's public shift in orientation, many religious fans lost the personal meaning in Matisyahu's music. However, other audiences have subsequently gained a new sense of meaning through entertainment value and an alternative spiritual representation. Through this case, it is evident that music in modern society holds value beyond mere aesthetic enjoyment. Instead, popular music generates a symbolic system of meaning for its listeners that, when removed, leaves the material product only partially intact. Cultural communities are drawn from perceived commonalities of backgrounds, interests, and beliefs. The shifting devotion to an artist like Matisyahu shows clearly that the music itself is only one small component of a fan's attraction to a particular act. Instead, fan groups constantly separate and categorize and realign themselves with different musical styles based partly on aesthetic attraction, but more notably on the sense of community generated through the sociocultural traits- perceived or otherwise- of any given artist in any given moment.

NOTES

    1. Reconstructionist Judaism promotes modernity within Jewish customs, regarding Judaism as part of a continuously evolving culture in which traditions are questioned, challenged, and ultimately viewed through the lens of modern education. As such, there is substantial theological diversity within the movement. Jewish Law (Halakha) is not considered obligatory, but it is treated as a valuable component of the traditional culture and disregarded only after careful examination and for good reason. Within this context, Matisyahu's decision to shift from his upbringing as a Reconstructionist Jew to embrace Hasidism—a movement at odds with Reconstructionism in its conservative beliefs related to the infallibility of Jewish Law, gender roles, social seclusion, intellectualism, and others—is a particularly prominent move."
    2. Chabad-Lubavitch, also known as Chabad, Lubavitch, or Habad, is an Orthodox

Jewish, Hasidic (referring to the promotion of spirituality through Jewish mysticism) movement. Chabad is a Hebrew acronym for Chochmah, Binah, Da'at (Wisdom, Understanding, and Knowledge), while the term Lubavitch refers to the Belorussian village of the movement's leaders. Chabad-Lubovitch is one of the world's best-known Hasidic movements and the largest Jewish organization in the world today. Corresponding to the customs of Hasidic Judaism, male members of the movement typically wear dark jackets and trousers, white shirts, black shoes, and black hats. Following a biblical command not to shave the sides of the face, male members of Chabad-Lubovitch wear a beard and long sidelocks called payot.

3. For a further exploration of the connections between Judaism and Rastafarianism, see the 2009 documentary *Awake Zion*, directed by Monica Haim.

WORKS CITED

Asad, Talal. "Reading a Modern Classic: W.C. Smith's *The Meaning and End of Religion*." *History of Religion* 40.3 (2001): 205–222. Web. 8 Feb. 2015.

Berman, Marshall. *All That Is Solid Melts into Air*. New York: Simon & Schuster, 1982. Print.

De Vries, Hent, and Samuel Weber, eds. *Religion and Media*. Stanford, CA: Stanford University Press, 2001. Print.

Engelke, Matthew. "Material Religion." *The Cambridge Companion to Religious Studies*. Ed. Robert A. Orsi. New York: Cambridge University Press, 2012. 209–29. Print.

Ghermezian, Shiryn. "Exclusive: Matisyahu Provides Most Extensive Analysis Yet of His Religious, Musical Evolution (Interview)." *The Algemeiner Journal*. Algemeiner.com, 17 Dec. 2014. Web. 6 Feb. 2015.

Greenberg, Rabbi Ben. "Matisyahu and the Pitfalls of the Charismatic Leader." *The Huffington Post*. TheHuffingtonPost.com, 5 June 2012. Web. 6 Feb. 2015.

Grossman, David Meir. "King Without a Beard: The Rise and Fall and Rise of a Former Reggae Star." *Tablet: A New Read on Jewish Life*. Nextbook, 29 Aug. 2013, Web. 6 Feb. 2015.

Hesmondhalgh, David. *Why Music Matters*. Chichester, West Sussex: Wiley-Blackwell, 2013. Print.

Horn, Jordana. "Evolution of an Icon: Matisyahu's Musical and Spiritual Journey." *The Jewish Daily Forward*. The Forward Association, 18 Dec. 2008. Web. 6 Feb. 2015.

Keane, Webb. *Christian Moderns: Freedom and Fetish in the Mission Encounter*. Berkeley: University of California Press, 2007. Print.

Lipsitz, George. *Time Passages: Collective Memory and American Popular Culture*. Minneapolis: University of Minnesota Press, 1990. Print.

Matisyahu (Matisyahu). "I am Matisyahu, a reggae/rapper/alternative rock musician chatting with you from Los Angeles, CA." *Reddit*. Reddit, 28 Jan. 2015. Web. 6 Feb. 2015.

"Matisyahu: Exclusive Interview." Aish.com. Aish.com, 30 June 2012. Web. 6 Feb. 2015.

Mobius. "Honor Not a False Messiah." *Jewschool: Progressive Jews and Views*. Jewschool, 14 Mar. 2006. Web. 6 Feb. 2015.

Nehorai, Elad. "Matisyahu's Public Transformation: What the World Doesn't Understand About Religious Jews' Reaction." *The Huffington Post*. TheHuffingtonPost.com, 5 June 2012. Web. 6 Feb. 2015.

Read, Max. "Matisyahu Shaves Beard, Reminding World of His Existence." *Gawker*. Gawker Media, 13 Dec. 2011. Web. 7 Feb. 2015.

Rosen, Jody. "G-d's Reggae Star: How Matisyahu Became a Pop Phenomenon." *Slate Magazine*. The Slate Group, 14 Mar. 2006. Web. 6 Feb. 2015.

Stevens, Hampton. "How Matisyahu's Hasidic Reggae Music Made Me Cry." *The Atlantic*. The Atlantic Monthly Group, 22 Jul. 2010. Web. 6 Feb. 2015.

Weingarten, Rachel. "Matisyahu on Sacrifice, Unraveling, and Prayer." *Parade Magazine*. Parade Publications, 22 Sept. 2014. Web. 6 Feb. 2015.

Tracing a Dis/Harmony of the Spheres

SABATINO DIBERNARDO

> What indeed has Athens to do with Jerusalem? What con-
> cord is there between the Academy and the Church? What
> between heretics and Christians?
>
> —Tertullian

By reformulating Tertullian's oft-cited question, a contemporary, but no less intriguing, musico-religious variation on this theme presents itself for our consideration: What has rock to do with religion? What concord is there between rock and religion? Indeed, what happens when a rebellious, "distorted," and "noisy" form of music is coupled or copulates with religion? One need only recall the sexual significance of rock's founding euphemism—rock 'n' roll—to get a sense of the diametrically opposed moral and existential sensibilities represented by rock and religion in their Western Christian manifestations (other religions might look less askance at this "immoral" coupling). What happens to rock music when it brings into its orbit the themes, beliefs, and ecstatic fervor mediated by the language of religion? Conversely, what happens to religion when it exerts a gravitational pull on an alien "rock" hurling through the heavens on a collision course with itself? Why do rock musicians and fans reach for religious language in describing a musico-aesthetic experience? And why does religion reach for musical inspiration and expression for a religio-spiritual experience? These questions may be distilled into a more basic interrogation around which this essay finds its own orbit: Why does each sphere appeal to something outside of itself?

By way of a preliminary response to the first set of questions, one historically vociferous, and on occasion histrionic, Christian response from the sphere of religion has been to repel or deflect the threatening trajectory of rock from the path of religion by means of a denunciation, denigration, and demonization of rock, which achieves its ironic culmination in heavy metal's appropriation and celebration of the demonic. Evangelical Christians were among the first to recognize this threatening form of (satanic) religiosity and the force of attraction it posed. However, another more congenial trajectory of rock has been charted by Evangelical Christians for its utilitarian or missionary ends. From the sphere of rock, similar reactionary and appropriative gestures appear throughout its history by incorporating religious themes in the form of denigration, mockery, or rebellion, while, ironically, miming the very religious themes, beliefs, rituals, and experiences that it sought to subvert. In the following sections, this essay will explore the trajectories sketched here between rock and religion, ancient metaphysical speculations regarding the relationship between music and metaphysics, and the ironic structure (i.e., the conflated coexistence of contrary or opposite others) that makes possible the relational and experiential coupling of these signifiers—*rock 'n' religion*.

Theoretical Trajectories of Rock and Religion

Given the scholarly work that has been done in this area, it will be useful to begin with some representative theoretical trajectories.

In *Hungry for Heaven: Rock 'n' Roll and the Search for Redemption*, Steve Turner notes the commonplace assumption "that rock 'n' roll is irreligious, if not completely antireligious, and that it meets religion only in combat— or because a particular religious group has decided to 'use' rock 'n' roll as a 'tool' to 'reach young people'" (11). Contrary to this uncritical perspective, Turner argues "that religion has had a profound effect on almost all of rock 'n' roll's innovators and has helped to shape the music at key stages in its development. Even avowedly secular rock 'n' roll often has at its heart a quest for transcendence that uses the language of religion" (11).

In Turner's view, the sphere of rock is neither simply irreligious nor merely a utilitarian tool for evangelism. Rather, rock has shaped the trajectory of the development of the genre precisely because it has at its "heart" or *essence* a religious quest. Two crucial elements are evident here: rock's religious *essence* and rock's religious appropriation of *religious language*. In Turner's account, the use of religious language is not predominantly a semiotic or structural matter. It is simply the appropriation of the "language game" of one sphere, to use Wittgenstein's phrase, by another. Rock's religious orientation toward transcendence and redemption is metaphysically *manifested* through its "use" of religious language rather than this "essence" being an aftereffect (or the product) of language:

I came to believe that there is something in the essence of rock 'n' roll that mirrors the religious search, and my ... task is to try to distill that essence.... I became convinced that one of the reasons so many rock 'n' rollers eventually embrace a religious worldview is that the best rock 'n' roll is itself a crying out for an experience of transcendence that the modern secular world doesn't offer [14].

Since the metaphysical essence of rock mirrors the metaphysical essence of religion, rock and religion share a *sui generis* essence that provides the foundation for their point of contact. It should be noted (but not dismissed) that Turner's view represents a confessional Christian account of the relationship, which helps to contextualize the view that rock is a conduit for religious transcendence rather than a religion in its own right.

David Chidester's essay "The Church of Baseball, the Fetish of Coca-Cola, and the Potlatch of Rock 'n' Roll" provides a similar historical narrative regarding the ambivalent relationship between these spheres. He notes both that rock "has sometimes embraced explicitly religious themes, serving as a vehicle for a range of religious interests, from heavy metal Satanism to contemporary Christian evangelism" and that it "has often been the target of Christian crusades against the evils that allegedly threaten religion in American society" ("Potlach of Rock" 222). Indeed, from the point of view of the latter, "rock music appears as the antithesis of religion: not merely an offensive art form but a blasphemous, sacrilegious, and antireligious force in society" (222.). The difference between Turner's view and Chidester's view regarding the relationship between rock and religion turns on a crucial theoretical point. In Chidester's analysis, rock music's "inherently religious character," even if it is not readily apparent, has provided opportunities for scholars "to theorize rock 'n' roll as religion" (223).

In Chidester's account, attempts at theorizing rock *as* religion are based on rock's "inherently religious character." Much turns on the "as" (and the "inherent") in terms of the differences between essentialist, functionalist, or family resemblance approaches to defining religion. Nevertheless, the broader context of Chidester's argument allows for "the strangely religious forms of popular culture ... to become refamiliarized as if they were religion" (229). Furthermore, he asks: "Why not? Why should these cultural forms not be regarded as religion?" (229). Thus, questions of classification and authority are crucial: what gets to count *as* religion, and who gets to authorize it? Contrary to J.Z. Smith's contention that "'[r]eligion' is not a native term; it is a term created by scholars for their intellectual purposes and therefore is theirs to define" (281), Chidester provides a forceful response: "The determination of what counts as religion is not the sole preserve of academics. The very term 'religion' is contested and at stake in the discourses and practices of popular culture" (229). In the process of a call to refocus definitions, Chidester also recognizes an appeal to religious language by way of evoking "familiar metaphors" (229) to explain aesthetic experiences in secular phenomena *as* somehow religious.

In *Authentic Fakes*, Chidester makes use of a philosophy of "as if" as he explores "authentic fakes" that "look like religion" or are treated "as if they were religions" (viii). The ironic mode operative in the title and its strategic deployment are evident when he notes, "None of these things are religions, of course. Except: people say they are; they fit 'classic' academic definitions; and they do authentic religious work by negotiating what it means to be a human person in relation to transcendence, the sacred, or ultimate concerns" (viii). Commenting on his earlier essay, Chidester explains that he was willing to treat popular culture phenomena as religion precisely "because participants, real people, characterized their own involvement in these enterprises as religious" (17). Any notion of an "inherently" religious phenomenon gives way to a functionalist (and family resemblance) view of the linguistic and emotive habits of participants.

Robin Sylvan's *Traces of the Spirit: The Religious Dimensions of Popular Music* provides an account of the historical emergence of popular music from West African possession religion through contemporary popular music and a phenomenology of musico-religious experiences of the numinous through fan testimonies and a "functionalist" matrix of levels (viz., physiological, psychological, sociocultural, semiological, virtual, ritual, and spiritual) "that can be directly accessed and powerfully experienced" (21). Furthermore, he asserts that:

> religion and God are not dead, but very much alive and well and dancing to the beat of popular music; the religious impulse has simply migrated to another sector of the culture.... Yet, because conventional wisdom has taught us to regard popular musics as trivial forms of secular entertainment, these religious dimensions remain hidden from view, marginalized and misunderstood [3].

Sylvan notes that "music functions in the same way as a religion, and the musical subculture functions in the same way as a religious community, albeit in an unconscious and postmodern way" and that these musical subcultures provide "an encounter with the numinous" (4). He adds, "this is not religion in the traditional form grounded in a stable cultural context, expressing some essential defining quality ... but it is, I contend, religion nevertheless" (4). Although there is an explicit denial of some essence or defining characteristic in the traditional religious sense, Sylvan's functionalist approach is ultimately grounded in an essentialist experience of a *sui generis*, numinous experience, following Rudolf Otto, or a religiosity that is the essence of all culture, following Gerardus Van der Leeuw. The most important of the levels, the spiritual, is predicated upon an illumination of "the central mystery of the spiritual realm" (39). Indeed, Sylvan argues that rather than trying to explain it away or suspending judgment on "the sacred, the holy, the numinous, the absolute, the place of the archetypes, the world of the spirits, the realm of the gods, or God … one needs to take seriously the notion that there is such a thing as the spiritual realm" (39). Thus, according to Sylvan, there really is a religio-spiritual realm (a *sui generis* essence) that, although hidden, is able to manifest itself or migrate across cultures, traces of which may be found in all cultures, including popular music and its subcultures such that: "The real power of popular music is spiritual and religious" (12).

In Rupert Till's *Pop Cult: Religion and Popular Music* the signifier of choice is not *religion* but, rather, *cult*. As a musician and former Christian, Till recognized "the same human functions, experiences, and feelings" in both traditionally religious church settings and secular music settings (xi). Till's primary question is not whether popular music *is* religion but "whether functions formerly served within society by religions are now being addressed by cults of popular music" (ix). Till argues, "Within contemporary post-modernity, in liquid times, religion is being deregulated, and belief, meaning, faith and religion are to be found in popular culture as well as in traditional organized religions" (xi). A provocative, rehabilitative, and celebratory deployment of the term "cult" is proffered in a somewhat Nietzschean fashion to describe "popular music scenes and movements as cults … as a joyous affirmation of their glorious transgression of all those things that those who would use the word cult negatively hold dear" (1). Till's project is:

> to show how popular music mixes, confuses and plays with imagery and traditions that are traditionally regarded as either sacred or profane, transgressing borders and creating a "Sacred Popular" set of popular cults that lie between the two, in the realm of a popular culture often thought of as secular, but in fact drenched in meaning, belief, faith, worship and ritual, and thus presented here as religious [5].

Through his deployment of the term cult across both popular music and religion, Till provides another relational trajectory of these spheres and, concomitantly, calls traditional religion to task for its contradictory (or ironic) attempts to exclude or expel the cultic and/or idolatrous elements that inevitably arise within its own sphere—religious metaphors that will be appropriated for secular purposes.

These and other theorists have broadened the taxonomic canopy of religion by charting the interweaving trajectories of rock and religion through redefining rock music, its performers, and fan culture as religious across a wide spectrum of essentialist, functionalist, and family resemblance approaches to religion. Although these perspectives present different theoretical options in rethinking classic definitions of religion, and rock's inclusion into that family, they do not exhaust the theoretical possibilities of the proximal orbits of these two spheres.

Metaphysical Trajectories of "Music/Noise"

Long before scholars of religion and popular culture began thinking about the relationship between rock and religion, in the ancient testimonies of philosophers we read of those who "heard" metaphysical "music/noises" at the source or origin of a spiritual relationship between music and socio-political order. Basil Cole, referencing Aristotle on Pythagoras' views of music, notes that "music must be an imitation of the unheard harmony of the spheres" and that "Pythagoras was the first among the Greeks of whom we know to develop the idea of music as ethical and therapeutic, capable of strengthening or restoring harmony to the soul" (26). In the Greek philosophical tradition, most notably Plato and Aristotle, it was maintained that musical modes created different moods and dispositions in the individual, culture, and the state (27–42): "Therefore, great music associated with the virtues should be taught to future leaders of the State. Bad music associated with vice eventually will change the laws of the State for the worse and aid in bringing it down. Music, then, has no role as pure entertainment" (34). Similarly, with respect to Confucius in the East, Cole explains, "The whole purpose of life for the ancient Chinese was to align earth with heaven, man and his culture with the celestial principle of harmony. It was firmly held that music intrinsically and objectively produced energy and force for good or bad" (22). This "harmony of the spheres" and other analogous treatments of the relationship between music and the individual soul (e.g., being "in tune" with oneself) are predicated upon a number of metaphysically inflected binary oppositions. Contemporary reverberations of this inflection may be heard as an ancient musico-metaphysical anxiety resonating across the centuries in the declamations of rock music in certain Christian sectors in order to keep order.

Given my own ironic appropriation of this ancient metaphysical analogy, it is important to emphasize that for ancient philosophers as geographically, culturally, and philosophically diverse as Pythagoras, Confucius, and Plato, this was no "mere" analogy. Indeed, there was an underlying, even if unheard, metaphysical force that instantiated the "proper," "true," or "right" (i.e., sanctioned or authorized) tones in relation to the proper metaphysical functioning of existence (viz., cosmological, socio-political, moral, etc.). The musico-metaphysical sphere and the socio-cultural sphere intersected in a causal relationship that constituted and governed existence in a binary manner such that a harmony/disharmony in one created order/disorder in the other. Any *musical composition* or performance of unsanctioned or unauthorized music (i.e., immoral "noise") would transgress the metaphysical laws or the socio-political order of things and, consequently, would introduce a disharmonious or "noisy" distortion into socio-political networks and moral order resulting in a *spiritual decomposition*—not unlike traditional religious criticisms of rock/metal music. In Jacques Attali's *Noise: The Political Economy of Music*, he notes, "The idea that noise, or even music, can destroy a social order and replace it with another is not new. It is present in Plato" (33). Attali adds:

> In China as in Greece, harmony implies a system of measurement, in other words, a system for the scientific, quantified representation of nature. The scale is the incarnation of the harmony between heaven and earth, the isomorphism of all representations: the bridge between the order of the Gods (ritual) and earthly order (the simulacrum).... An ideology of scientific harmony thus imposes itself, the mask of a hierarchical organization from which dissonances (conflicts and struggles) are forbidden, unless they are merely marginal and highlight the quality of the channelizing order [60, 61].

Although a metaphysical ontology is replaced by political motivations and a structural relationship between music/noise and socio-political order/disorder, it is no less efficacious in its desired implementation of "noise control" (122–124). Indeed, if music is defined as "the organization of noise" (4), then, as Attali states, "Listening to music is listening to all noise, realizing that its appropriation and control is a reflection of power, that it is essentially political" (6). Consequently, "Subversion in musical production opposes a new syntax to the existing syntax, from the point of view of which it is noise" (34). Furthermore, Attali notes that "noise carries order within itself.... There is no order that does not contain disorder within itself" (33, 34). But it is precisely the status quo that cannot be kept, maintained, or strictly policed for the purposes of order, since order carries within itself its own potential undoing—its own disorder—which is the necessary condition for any order to have coalesced in the first instance (i.e., order out of disorder). A parallel distortion of the linguistic code (i.e., order) occurs in the structure of irony. Linda Hutcheon explains that:

> in ironic discourse, the whole communicative process is not only "altered and distorted" but also *made possible by* those different worlds to which each of us differently belongs and which form the basis of the expectations, assumptions, and preconceptions that we bring to the complex processing of discourse, of language *in use* [89].

Rewinding to the 1960s, we find an iconic example of the insights provided by Attali and Hutcheon regarding a distortion of codes through an ironic noise. Approximately six years after a juridical ruling in favor of an "objective" teaching of religion in public schools and, concomitantly, the non-establishment of "secular religion" (*Abington School District v. Schempp*, 374 U.S. 203 1963), a "noisy" progenitor of "distorted" guitar playing, Jimi Hendrix, became the prophet of a new noisy and distorted evangel announcing an "Electric Church." Although the blues had a long history of dealing with religious themes, in Hendrix's testimony we find an explicitly confessional statement about an aesthetico-spiritual desire filtered through a religious significance by means of a chain of associated (religious) experiences. In an interview in 1969, Dick Cavett asks Jimi Hendrix about "an Electric Church" and whether Hendrix was "speaking metaphorically or poetically" (*The Dick Cavett Show*). Hendrix responds "that's just a belief that I have ... [and through the use of loud electric guitars] the belief comes through the electricity to the people ... inside the soul of the person" (*The Dick Cavett Show*). This self-reflexive articulation by the guitar god and rock idol Hendrix makes evident an appeal to religio-spiritual language in order to put into words the visceral power of music, especially, as he suggests, when "words are empty" (*The Dick Cavett Show*). Hendrix appropriated religio-spiritual language in the service of a musical/noisy aesthetic that signified in ironic fashion its contrary other; that is, secular rock music as the basis for an Electric Church. This appeal to something beyond an aesthetic experience marks a desire to name as religio-spiritual the *aesthetic* power of his music mediated through his Fender Stratocaster and Marshall amps by means of distorted noises and sonic disturbances. In the process, Hendrix opened up a new musical discourse on musico-spiritual experience—one in which the album title and song "Are You Experienced" may be read as something other than just a "simple" reference to a drug-induced hyper-reality (of course, drugs and religion have a long history). In the context of Hendrix's belief in an "Electric Church," this becomes a religio-spiritual question that parallels a structurally similar religio-spiritual question: are you saved?

During the late '60s and early '70s, other "noisy" and "distorted" bands such as Black Sabbath and Led Zeppelin were experimenting with their own religio-mystical spin on rock, which would thereby engender other taxonomical categories; namely, hard rock and heavy metal. One thematic thread from Sabbath onward in much of heavy metal would be its focus on the darker themes of Christian religion. Although conventionally viewed as an irreligious form of music, metal, and its association with the "dark side" of religion—from band names and lyrical content to the ritualized "demonic" stagecraft—is arguably among the earliest genres to explicitly conjoin rock and religion or rock/metal *as* religion (e.g., Satanism and mystical or pagan religions).

Meanwhile, with the advent of Christian rock and the Jesus movement during roughly the same period, the antagonistic relationship between rock 'n' roll and (Christian) religion largely gave way to an appropriation of the former's "noisy" and "distorted" tones by some evangelical segments of the latter in a parallel religio-musical trajectory that would culminate in the contemporary Christian music industry machine. When a couple of decades later Christian Death Metal becomes yet another subgenre of metal, an unmooring and ironic comingling of supposedly contrary spheres would suffice to suggest a very different orbital relationship; one where a previously "demonic" *noise* is transubstantiated miraculously into salvific Christian *music*. Notwithstanding the previously dominant ideology, axiological disparity, and metaphysical incongruity between the mundane or worldly "playfulness" of rock and the "ultimate concern" or metaphysical orientation of religion, a gravitational attraction between the spheres developed and continues unabated. Moreover, the religious denunciations of rock, past and present, bear witness less to the "frivolous" or "merely entertaining" nature of rock and more to the (sometimes threateningly) *serious* nature of this genre—to its *gravitas*.

If anything is revealed in tracing a history of these metaphysical trajectories by virtue of the music/noise dichotomy, it is that the instability or lack of some fixed orbital trajectories (or essences of the spheres) provides the condition of possibility for dramatic shifts, even complete reversals and transvaluations, in orbital trajectories: either prophetic declamations of an impending apocalyptic collision and subsequent collapse of Western culture or the not-so-apocalyptic, surreptitious, and subtle fusion of the spheres that pass without much notice or attention. Indeed, the very existence of Christian rock and Christian themes in secular rock would seem to indicate a somewhat uneventful eliding of spheres. Furthermore, the necessity of now having to qualify rock as secular, which is precisely what it signified metonymically without qualification prior to evangelical appropriations of this genre of music, should not pass unnoticed. Given that the profane contamination of all things sacred by rock music and the concomitant decline of Western (Christian) culture have not occurred but, rather, rock has been co-opted by the Christian music industry (while "secular" radio stations now regularly play songs from self-identifying Christian rock bands), the early vitriol and antagonisms between rock and religion seem to have subsided to a large extent. Even if pockets of resistance remain, old axiological battles over the metaphysical evils of rock have moved on to other contemporary forms of "degenerate" music/noise, which remains symptomatic of that ancient religio-metaphysical ailment. Even the hyperbolic antagonisms that prompted the censorship of and legal proceedings against metal musicians in the 80s (headed up by the PMRC) have largely subsided—disorder has incorporated its other into a new order. Indeed, when Ozzy Osbourne/Black Sabbath, AC/DC, Judas Priest, and other denizens of the demonic from recent yesteryear can be co-opted—the commodification of one commodity for another—by an otherwise conservative advertising industry to sell cars, among other commodities, or can be heard at stadiums during football season (e.g., "Crazy Train"), it appears that the predicted apocalypse was not televised. What was once a disharmonious and discordant noise that threatened to pollute young and impressionable minds in order to bend them toward suicidal tendencies at the behest of Satan is now harmoniously incorporated into corporate business to generate sales from those same young and impressionable minds—now, much older and, paradoxically, much more susceptible to having their minds bent toward purchasing commodities or displaying camaraderie at sporting events.

Thus, the current relationship between rock and religion has become so established by religio-cultural convention that its commonplace status now provides an opportunity for rethinking the *religiosity of rock* music as a different sort of "evangelical" tool—one in which, ironically, the *evangel* is not found in a book or church doctrine so much as in an aesthetic experience combined with an ir/religious message of liberation from, rebellion against, or transcendence beyond organized religion, dogmatism, or clericalism. In so doing, religion returns the favor, if you will, of lending rock its *ethos* even as this religious *ethos* is used against itself—not unlike religion's appropriation of rock as a tool in its arsenal against the excesses and anarchism of rock in support of the Christian *evangel*.

Rock Idols/Religious Superstars and the Cult(us) of Personality

Another ironic "evangelical" twist occurs when a new ir/religious evangel was seen on full (Broadway) display with the release of the rock opera *Jesus Christ Superstar* in 1970. It is here that (Christian) religion in the person of Jesus is "reduced" to a cult of personality—a rock (idol) superstar—replete with screaming vocals. Just as rock was being appropriated by (Christian) religion during this period in and through the Jesus movement, so, too, was Jesus being appropriated by secular (rock) culture in the form of a rock superstar. In this musical, the cult of personality associated with "rock stars" is applied to Jesus through the critical eyes of the despised and denigrated other—Judas. In this case, *fandom is not interpreted as religion* but, rather, *religion is interpreted as fandom* and the etymologically religious *cultus* is ironically reinscribed against itself in a negative double gesture through its association with the "superstar" as the *cult(us)* of Jesus—the rock star fronting a (rock) band of holy rollers. This reversal of the *religious* god/idol as the *rock* star/idol comes full circle by folding back on itself yet again when the *rock* star/idol Marilyn Manson appropriates the title and provides yet another ironic twist in a critique of *religious* gods/idols in his *Antichrist Superstar* album. This critique of human propensities toward a fetishistic desire for the religious superstar or rock god, whether it is touching the hem of the cloth or the leather-studded garment, and regardless of the origin of this desire to worship, idolize, deify, or engage in a cult(us) of personality, is made possible by an ironic conjunction of an etymologically religious *cult(us)* and *cult* that calls both forms of worship and deification into question.

Consequently, the possibility of reading performers and prophets or music halls and houses of worship in contrary and substitutable ways depends to a large extent on this ironic structural economy for its condition of possibility. Another example would be the migration of the signifier "rock" across different contexts. In Christian rock, for instance, formulations such as "rock for the Rock" or the "Rock that makes us roll" are commonplace. Conversely, in *Authentic Fakes* Chidester provides some examples of "religious sites that sacralize the production of popular music, such as the Church of Rock, the First church of Holy Rock and Roll, and the Church of Rock and Roll Online Chapel" (204). It would appear that the difference between rock 'n' rollers and holy rollers depends largely on how one rolls. Although this play on "rock" and "roll" may be viewed as an accidental or anomalous feature of language, it is, perhaps, better theorized as an ironic structure that constitutes and generates these possibilities of reversal and conflation due to a binary semiotic or "digital" logic as a structural effect of language. These examples of ironic reversals and destabilizations seem to indicate that the longstanding historical relationship between (rock) music and religion is a function of a semiotic possibility of incorporating the other in a binary opposition into itself in an ironic reversal that is, perhaps, less metaphysical and spiritual than structural and semiotic, which neither precludes nor diminishes their effects. Indeed, I would suggest that these strategic ironies further enhance their effects by virtue of their counterintuitive, contradictory, and/or paradoxical speech acts that make them desirable formulations in the first place— irony confronts us as the site of a question by destabilizing "mutually exclusive" notions.

Digital and Analog "Recordings" of Rock and Religion

Since the marking or "recording" of religious and musical "identities" and their relationship to each other is the issue at hand, it is important to take into account how the various treatments addressed earlier have changed over time. One approach is to think about this in terms of two logics; namely, digital and analog(ical). Digital recordings or inscriptions function in terms of an either/or (on/off) binary opposition, while analog recordings or inscriptions allow for a continuous flow along a spectrum of possibilities (e.g., both/and). In the history of religions, what religion *is* (or is not) turns on some paradigmatic digital oppositions in the construction of the religious/ secular by way of slicing up the world/heaven into discrete and opposed binary units, which is evident in the essentialist approaches to religion theorized by Otto and Eliade, among others; for example, religion *is* the opposite of the secular; the sacred *is* the opposite of the profane. As an effect of the structure of language, however, this digital logic prefigures and makes possible ironic reversals, destabilizations, and conflations by bringing together these opposites that cannot be fully stabilized in any strict manner. Consequently, analogical possibilities are introduced by way of successive, though not necessarily linear, phases that can take the religion *or* secular digital opposition and yield *both/and* analogical formulations such as "secular religion" and "religious secularism." When these logics are applied to the relationship between the ostensibly discrete units rock/religion, we can trace its movement as follows: rock 'n' roll or religion → rock 'n' roll and religion → rock 'n' religion. This not-so-anomalous gesture opens up various possibilities by placing contraries (or opposites) in a *generative tension* that we have seen across other oppositions throughout the essay (e.g., music and/or noise; prophets and/or performers; gods and/or idols). Viewed from the perspective of a structural irony, Claire Colebrook, differentiating between Romantic irony and simple irony, states: "Irony was not just signalling the opposite of what was said; it was the expression of *both sides or viewpoints at once* in the form of contradiction or paradox" (*Irony* 53–4). Therein lies the difference between a digital logic of an either/or (simple irony: saying the opposite of what is meant) and an analogical logic, which, by bringing two poles together, opens itself up to the possibility of an analogical both/and (complex irony: holding contrary units or phenomena together in tension). Now, just as the audiophile's preference for digital or analog recordings of music depends on different considerations, so, too, how one utilizes these logics to conceptualize the relationship between rock and religion will depend on one's ideological predispositions, strategic purposes, and/or aesthetic preferences.

Nevertheless, one might simply view this as some arbitrary choice on the part of a subject who perceives and authorizes such reversals: one person's rock is another's religion; one person's performer is another's prophet; one person's music is another's noise; one person's idol is another's god, and so forth. This relativistic perspectivalism would be, ironically, true enough, except that the pervasive ironic formulations encountered seem to indicate more than just some completely arbitrary or unconstrained act of free-agency on the part of a subject. If one takes into account the very process of "subjection" to which we are subjected and through which one becomes a subject in the first place—through incorporation into a language that pre-exists and thereby constitutes a subject—it appears to be less an action of unconstrained free-agency and more, perhaps, a matter of exercising constrained "choices" of *contingently* arbitrary linguistic possibilities through a digital logic that may undergo an analogical expansion.

Thus, the very possibility of a relationship between rock and religion is governed by or generated through an ironic structure that both constructs each identity in relation to its other and introduces the structurally contingent possibility that one may take on characteristics of its other by virtue of this digital construction, which allows for the possibility of "religious rock" and "secular religiosity." Indeed, the very instability of this digital logic and the ever-present possibility of yielding an analogic reversal, destabilization, and conflation of opposing poles would help explain the perceived metaphysical threat that gives rise to policing such oppositions in the first place. If these were stable or self-evidently essentialist terms, such policing would not be required.

Following Jacques Derrida's deconstruction of a metaphysics of presence (with its privileging of the signified over the signifier) by means of the "trace" across unstable binary oppositions, what is present in each sign (signifier/signified) is the absent, excluded, and devalued other carried as a present-absent trace that both constitutes it as such and, ironically, destabilizes its essentialist identity by virtue of this trace of the other in the selfsame (62, 68, 70–3). Thus, rather than fully self-present identities in an opposition, where one is privileged over its other, there is a tenacious structural ineluctability for binary oppositions to enter into an ironic relationship whereby elements of the opposed other slip their "essential" identities and traverse the line, boundary, or limit by eliding contraries. As Colebrook notes regarding Derrida's reading of concepts, "There is an essential irony at the structural root of concepts; when we speak we use a system that precedes all use and that can therefore have effects that exceed all intent" (*Irony in the Work of Philosophy* 37).

Although some scholars make use of this structural instability in binary oppositions to rethink the religiosity of rock, in this formulation religion is still privileged. While some attribute religio-spiritual "impulses" "hidden" (viz., essences or *noumena*) within the depths of rock music and its cultures, they appear much less willing to attribute the *aesthetic* qualities of worship to the not-so-hidden visceral or psycho-physiological power of music (rock or otherwise). The former may be viewed as a transcendentalization, sacralization, or mystification of music that "elevates" it, while the latter is viewed as a reductionistic devalorization. One such example may be found in Sylvan's commentary on Otto's assertions regarding the power of music and religion. Sylvan explains that "Otto is saying that musical feeling is *analogous* to numinous feeling but is not *identical* with it.... In speaking of the analogy between music and the numinous, however, Otto goes on to say that 'the former may become a means of expression of the latter,' that music may become a means of expressing the numinous" (40). Thus, according to Sylvan, "the virtual world that music creates can be an analog of the heavenly world. When one hears music and it stirs the spiritual impulse within, one is reminded of the spiritual realm; one is given, as it were, a small taste of what the realm is like" (41). This analogical approach, not unlike Pythagoras' analogy of the unheard harmony of the spheres, substitutes the "unheard harmony" with the "hidden religious impulse" in its valorization of a numinous or spiritual experience at the expense of a musically aesthetic experience for Sylvan and Otto. Furthermore, one must "beware" of any reversal or equivalence in this process, according to Otto and Sylvan, where the experiential force of music and religion are equated or reversed (40). Thus, a certain ideological predisposition determines the outcome in advance of the proclamation—a metaphysical desire to still or police the fluid (linguistic and experiential) flux between rock and religion, where one sphere is treated as privileged at the expense of the other in this asymmetrical revalorization. Given my own ideological predisposition, the spheres of influence cannot be halted unidirectionally or asymmetrically.

Desiring the Other

Since the relationship between rock and religion turns on an appropriation of some crucial element associated with its other, we return to the questions with which we began. Why do musicians reach for the stars (i.e., the religio-spiritual sphere) when attempting to *articulate* the aesthetic power of music? Why do religions reach toward the worldly (i.e., the secular musical sphere) to *assist* in worship and edification? A "supplemental" possibility, in the Derridean sense (141–64), "presents" itself by way of an "absence" in each: Music seems to appropriate religion and its language by virtue of its "serious," "spiritual," and/or "transcendent" *telos* as a supplement to further its own aesthetic *telos*; religion seems to appropriate music and its viscerally aesthetic force in order to "elevate," "enervate," or "still the soul" as a supplement for its own religio-spiritual *telos*. In cases where this appropriation occurs, this underlying desire implicates each in its incompleteness. Given this general, but not universal, appropriation of some element of the other in both spheres, this absence or "incompleteness" appears, at the very least, to exhibit a strong desire for or gravitational pull toward the inclusion of its contrary other to fulfill or in some way elevate or empower its own teleology through an ironic structural process that constitutes and governs this relationship.

One might contest this by arguing that we have simply moved the goal posts in order to make our analysis seem conceptually adequate to the task, which may be the case. However, this argument would imply that the playing field and its goal posts are themselves uncontested, stable, or fixed, which belies the essentialist "pre-given" of such a position; namely, the essence of religion is fixed, the essence of music is fixed, and never the twain shall meet—

except in some linguistic, semiotic/semantic, classificatory/definitional, post-modernist, or poststructuralist gymnastics that would seek to efface and conflate their obvious (i.e., natural, self-evident, and non-constructed) differences. It is at this point that the foundationalism, realism, and essentialism of such a position shows itself and begs the question, since it is the epistemologically problematic notion and questionable assumption that such an essence of each sphere (i.e., term or experience) exists that has been put into question. Consequently, if one presupposes that religion is not an essence, and that rock is not an essence, then neither is experience—musical or religious—an essence that can be named in a direct relation between term and experience. As Mark C. Taylor notes in his Introduction to *Critical Terms for Religious Studies* regarding the relatively recent construction of the term religion and its relationship to "religious experience":

> Even if one were to admit that religion is not "a ubiquitous human phenomenon" but a recently constructed analytic category, surely it would seem that the experiences this second-order term designates are as old as humanity itself. But this conclusion is also problematic. The relation between term and experience is no less complex than the relation between category and object or phenomenon.... Experience, in other words, is no more prior to the terms designated to represent it than objects are antecedent to the concepts fabricated to grasp them. Historically and culturally specific practices constitute both the experiences of subjects and the objects of analysis [8].

This is not to say that these constructed terms and experiences do not have their effects; nor does it preclude a strategic deployment of such terms and experiences for one's theoretical purposes. It is simply to suggest there is an epistemological undecidability at work in different claims being made regarding the religiosity of rock (including my own claims regarding a governing structural irony) that constitutes such diversity. Nevertheless, regardless of one's position on the metaphysics of the relationship, the existence of Platonic essences, functions, family resemblances, or an ironic dis/harmony of the spheres, each contingent perspective attempts to do justice to a recognition of the historically interconnected and complex orbits of music and religion conjoined from antiquity to postmodernity.

Finally, the analogical language of dis/harmony, orbits, and apocalyptic collisions/fusions in this essay is not coincidental. It attempts to perform what it argues by means of an ironic and destabilizing gesture that analogizes an ancient metaphysical discourse on the relationship between music and the cosmos without commitment to its ancient metaphysical origins. Indeed, for those of us with no recourse to metaphysical or essentialist explanations for the consistently conjoined realms of (rock) music and religion (spirituality), we must look elsewhere. That elsewhere is language. As Colebrook suggests in the context of a Platonic notion of ideas or essences behind words,

"If, however, as the twentieth century has tended to do, we find the existence of real and eternal ideas or essences to be mystical, we will want to offer an explanation of meaning from within human language" (*Irony* 61). This approach has the value of allowing us to trace the history of the movement of the spheres of influence such that rock and religion have come to share a similar orbital space by means of a shared experiential quality mediated necessarily and structurally through an ironic linguistic field. The semiotic slippage that allows for reversals, displacements, and conflations of typically reified terms/spheres looks not to some *essential* religious feature, function, or even resemblance of rock music *as* religion but, rather, to an ironic structure between the signifiers.

In the case of rock, this structure gives voice to an analogical experience by means of another recognizable but more ostensibly "meaningful" or "serious" metaphysical discourse; namely, religion, religious, or spiritual. Appropriation of this metaphysical discourse lends the supposedly frivolous aesthetic experience of rock music, which is typically devalued as "mere entertainment," some *gravitas* that it would otherwise not have. And with this gesture, we return to a Pythagorean harmony of the spheres translated here as an ironic dis/harmony of the spheres. The powerful aesthetic experience of music by the musician/fan instigates an appeal to religion based on a desire to appropriate that which transcends itself in order to name its profundity or inspiration as a religio-spiritual experience beyond "mere entertainment." Similarly, religion appropriates the powerfully visceral experience of music in an attempt to mediate and achieve, at some level, an experience of the transcendence that is its "proper" and "serious" religious domain. In both cases, this desire for transcendence, which is a metaphysical desire, comes about through a supplemental relationship to its opposed other that is as ironic as it is necessary. Consequently, each lends to its other a different form of *gravitas* by way of a gravitational attraction that charts a new orbital trajectory—a dis/harmony of the spheres—rock 'n' religion.

Works Cited

Attali, Jacques. *Noise: The Political Economy of Music.* Translated by Brian Massumi, *Theory and History of Literature*, vol. 16, University of Minnesota Press, 1996.

Chidester, David. *Authentic Fakes: Religion and American Popular Culture.* University of California Press, 2005.

_____. "The Church of Baseball, the Fetish of Coca-Cola, and the Potlatch of Rock 'n' Roll." *Religion and Popular Culture in America*, edited by Bruce David Forbes and Jeffrey H. Mahan, revised edition, University of California Press, 2005, pp. 213–32.

Cole, Basil. *Music and Morals: A Theological Appraisal of the Moral and Psychological Effects of Music.* Alba House, 1993.

Colebrook, Claire. *Irony.* Routledge, 2004.

_____. *Irony in the Work of Philosophy.* University of Nebraska Press, 2002.

Derrida, Jacques. *Of Grammatology.* Translated by Gayatri Chakravorty Spivak, corrected edition. The Johns Hopkins Press, 1997.

Hendrix, Jimi. Interview by Dick Cavett. July, 1969. "Jimi Hendrix Interviewed." *Dailymotion,* uploaded by poetictouch, 31 December 2009. http://www.dailymotion.com/video/xbp9 z0_jimi-hendrix-interviewed_music.

Hutcheon, Linda. *Irony's Edge: The Theory and Politics of Irony.* Routledge, 1994.

Jesus Christ Superstar. Music by Andrew Lloyd Webber and lyrics by Tim Rice, 1970.

Marilyn Manson. *Antichrist Superstar.* Insomniac/Interscope Records, 1996.

Smith, Jonathan Z. "Religion, Religions, Religious." *Critical Terms for Religious Studies,* edited by Mark C. Taylor. University of Chicago Press, 1998.

Sylvan, Robin. *Traces of the Spirit: The Religious Dimensions of Popular Music.* New York University Press, 2004.

Taylor, Mark C. "Introduction." *Critical Terms for Religious Studies,* edited by Mark C. Taylor. University of Chicago Press, 1998.

Till, Rupert. *Pop Cult: Religion and Popular Music.* Continuum, 2010.

Turner, Steven. *Hungry for Heaven: Rock 'n' Roll and the Search for Redemption,* revised edition, InterVarsity, 1995.

Mystical Rock and Visionary Sounds

From the Sacramental Instructions of The Psychedelic Experience to Religious Ecstasy in The Beatles' "Tomorrow Never Knows"

MORGAN SHIPLEY

> "When that long-awaited at-one-ment shall have been con-summated, there will no longer be doubt, nor fallacious argumentation, nor unwise and unscientific Church-Council anathematizations directed against that paramount doctrine of pre-existence and re-birth.... And Western man will [then] awaken from that slumber of Ignorance which has been hypnotically induced by a mistaken Orthodoxy."
> —W.Y. Evans-Wentz, "Preface to the Third Edition," *The Tibetan Book of the Dead*

The Beatles song "Tomorrow Never Knows" holds that the "ego death" experienced under the influence of psychoactive substances unburdens the psychedelic voyager from instrumental reasoning. Taking their cue from *The Psychedelic Experience*, a manual of psychedelic exploration adapted from *The Tibetan Book of the Dead* by psychedelic pioneers Timothy Leary, Richard Alpert, and Ralph Metzner, "Tomorrow Never Knows" illustrates how psychedelics occasion a transcendent experience in which the dualisms that construct the modern moment give way to a sense of unitive oneness. By dispensing with chord changes and relying on cohesion through chance, The Beatles announced a sound that, in its very syncretism, recreated the esoteric wisdom highlighted within the pages of *The Psychedelic Experience*.

The song itself was an expression of what Leary, Alpert, and Metzner call psychedelic deconditioning. Backed by lyrics appropriated directly from *The Psychedelic Experience*, the structure of the song proposes how, in turning off the mind, we come to enter a world of pure, unmediated mindfulness (in Buddhism, this is known as *samādhi*, or a state of being totally aware of the present moment). Echoed in the effects of LSD, such pure awareness offered both the psychedelic voyager and song consumer a position freed from the conformist mentality of post–World War II western culture into one of absolute interdependence. By engaging "Tomorrow Never Knows" through the religious motifs and mystical understandings adapted from W.Y. Evans-Wentz's translation of *The Tibetan Book of the Dead* by Leary, Alpert, and Metzner in their now classic psychedelic manual, The Beatles offer listeners (both today and in the immediate postwar moment) a song that, through tape loops and modulations of a single chord (C), reflects the mystical notion of an eternal return. In his preface to *The Tibetan Book of the Dead*, Evans-Wentz describes the eternal return as "a potentially realizable consciousness, the memory of a forgotten past, in which each of us now incarnate shares" (viii). By encountering this collective past, the psychedelic voyager breaks free from the separative consciousness resulting from modern understandings based in antagonistic binaries (e.g., past vs. present, nature vs. human, sacred vs. profane, the haves and the have nots). The Beatles sought to map the nature of this awakening, creating a song, as Ian MacDonald details, whose mystical message represented a revolutionary and subversive rejoinder to the sterility of post–World War II culture: "'Tomorrow Never Knows' launched the till-then élite-preserved concept of mind-expansion into pop, simultaneously drawing attention to consciousness-enhancing drugs and the ancient religious philosophies of the Orient, utterly alien to Western thought in their anti-materialism, rapt passivity, and world-sceptical focus on visionary consciousness" (*Revolution in the Head*, 192).

Infused with the same Buddhist and perennial undertones that situated sixties-era mystical interpretations of psychedelic experimentation, the song highlights the aesthetic, appropriated, and numinous positionings of the psychedelic counterculture. When framed in relation to both *The Psychedelic Experience* and *The Tibetan Book of the Dead*, "Tomorrow Never Knows" embodies the visionary and ecstatic traditions that influenced 1960s music. More significantly, however, the song uncovers how these traditions, when placed within the frames of popular music, worked to destabilize postwar western culture in an effort to raise consciousness on both an individual and collective level. Just as *The Tibetan Book of the Dead* functions as "a key to the innermost recesses of the human mind ... a guide for initiates ... for those who are seeking the spiritual path to liberation," so too did *The Psychedelic Experience* seek to help psychonauts (a "sailor" or "voyager" of the soul) "jettison your ego program and float back to the radiant bliss of at-one-ness" (32). Through their own encounters with psychedelics, The Beatles sought to reflect this very dynamic, locating music and song as a means to breakdown the ego defense mechanisms that situate the modern individual as just another cog in the ever-widening neoliberal, capitalist machine. In the spaces of consciousness unburdened through religious ritual and psychedelic sacraments, "Tomorrow Never Knows" ultimately highlights the most significant value of engaging *The Tibetan Book of the Dead* from within the confines of western culture and vis-à-vis the frames of psychedelic consciousness. That is, the song helps us realize "that long-awaited at-one-ment," which, as Evans-Wentz details, helps "Western man ... awaken from that slumber of Ignorance which has been hypnotically induced by a mistaken Orthodoxy" (x).

More than a commercialized expression of the hippie counterculture, the song more broadly suggests how psychedelic rock reflects and expresses the height of psychedelic consciousness as a mechanism to transform the way we relate to each other, our planet, and ourselves. According to Colin Larkin, "Tomorrow Never Knows" represents "the most effective evocation of a LSD experience ever recorded" (*Encyclopedia of Popular Music*, 489). In directly mirroring Leary, Alpert, and Metzner's conclusion that psychedelic consciousness produces an unmediated experience of mystical ecstasy (from ex-stasis, "to be or stand outside oneself"), the spiritual perspective sacralized in "Tomorrow Never Knows" signals the sacred basis for the peace and love ethos of the sixties counterculture. The song illustrates how an experience of standing "outside oneself" results in a reality defined by unrestricted, reciprocal love. "The Sixties," as Lennon recalls, "saw a revolution among the youth ... a revolution in a whole way of thinking. The Beatles were part of the revolution, which is really an evolution" (*The Beatles Anthology*, 201). "Turned on" by Leary in 1961 at Harvard University, Michael Kahn connects the nature of this new way of thinking to a single perennial truth that emerges out of the evolutionary unfurling mapped by psychedelic exploration: "if we are to be saved there is only one way: *the rule of love must replace the rule of selfishness*" ("The Rule of Love," 114).

In identifying love as the mark that saves by freeing one from the inevitable suffering connected to selfishness, Kahn's description of psychedelic consciousness, as with "Tomorrow Never Knows," illustrates a consistent fact in the cultural history and scholarly study of mysticism. Mystics east and west often describe mysticism as an awakened state of interpenetration and interconnection (see, for instance, Frithjof Schuon or Alan Watts for comparative analysis). Likewise, from William James to Evelyn Underhill to W.T. Stace, scholars of mysticism often locate love and oneness as the essential perennial mark of mystical consciousness. As a cultural artifact, "Tomorrow

Never Knows" revives and celebrates the same sense of interdependent love that positions both the mystical state and the psychedelically inspired countercultural ethos that produced projects of political protest, social justice, and cultural alternatives. This was not merely about dropping out and escaping the moment, as many interpreted Leary's famous axiom ("turn on, tune in, drop out") to mean, but about tying into a consciousness, as "Tomorrow Never Knows" details, in which all is one. As George Harrison notes in his reflection on his and Lennon's first psychedelic encounter in 1965 (known as "The Dental Experience"), under the sway of LSD "suddenly I felt the most incredible feeling come over me. It was something like a very concentrated version of the best feeling I'd ever had in my whole life. It was fantastic," because, as Harrison stresses, "I *felt in love*, not with anything or anybody in particular, but with *everything*. Everything was perfect, in a perfect light" (*The Beatles Anthology*, 177). Yet as both recognized, the LSD experience could also overwhelm, thrusting the voyager into realms of consciousness that challenge the very coherency of their worldview by exposing the limitations of a "physical world … governed by duality" (*The Beatles Anthology*, 179). As Lennon stresses, "it was terrifying, but it was fantastic," a recognition also echoed by Harrison: "the down side of it can be that you go so far out in your mind that you think you've lost your grip and that you're never going to get back to the normal state of consciousness. And, in a way, you don't ever really return to how you were before" (*The Beatles Anthology*, 179).

Discerning early the "heaven and hell" potential of psychedelics (Aldous Huxley, in the follow-up to his classic psychedelic text, *The Doors of Perception*, relied on this very dynamic for his title), The Beatles locate how the ecstatic nature of psychedelic consciousness allows for an expansive awareness of one's place in the cosmos. Such an experience forever changes how one engages "ego identity" by helping the psychedelic voyager, as Harrison develops, to "see through the trees and see the roots of the trees … [to recognize how] I am not this body. I am pure energy soaring about everywhere, that happens to be in a body for a temporary period of time" (*The Beatles Anthology*, 179). Infused with both Hindu notions of *atman* (an undying, eternal self) and *samsara* (the cycle of birth-death-rebirth that tethers individual atman's to physical bodies), as well as Buddhist conceptions of *anatman* (the notion of non-self, a position beyond ego consciousness) and *pratitysamupada* (meaning dependent origination, or the idea that to exist is always already to be in a state of contingent co-existence), Harrison and Lennon's reflections speak to the nature, aim, and manifestation of psychedelic exploration. As with religious ecstasy, the sacramental use of psychedelics necessitatesd rituals, processes for helping one navigate through the "terrifying" moments in order to recover the sustained value of mystical understanding. The mystical encounter, as Harrison contends, saves the individual from "many years of indifference" by helping "you look at things differently." "It," as Ringo Starr continues, "makes you look at yourself and your feelings and emotions. And it brought me closer to nature, in a way—the force of nature and its beauty. You realize it's not just a tree; it's a living thing" (*The Beatles Anthology*, 180).

Through this lens, psychedelics emerge as sacramental devices that reveal how the end of existence is actually the beginning, and where knowing is not a rational, quantifiable process, but about a love that is everyone and everywhere. This circularity, in fact, situates the nature of *The Tibetan Book of the Dead*, the aim of *The Psychedelic Experience*, and both the musical structure and lyrical content of "Tomorrow Never Knows." In his now classic study of religious experiences, William James, writing at the turn of the 20th century, notes how "our normal waking consciousness, rational consciousness as we call it, is but one special type of consciousness, whilst all about it, parted from it by the filmiest of screens, there lie potential forms of consciousness entirely different" (*The Varieties of Religious Experience*, 388). In this sense, the song, as with the broader psychedelic counterculture, functions not simply as a reaction to, but as an alternative for, the post–World War II moment. In fact, as Lennon develops when thinking about the 1960s, the music of The Beatles, and specifically "Tomorrow Never Knows," function as a form of psychedelic contemplation, illustrating how "music reflects the state that the society is in. It doesn't *suggest* the state. I think the poets and musicians and artists are of the age—not only do they lead the age on, but they also reflect that age" (*The Beatles Anthology*, 201). Buried within the motifs, symbols, and sound of "Tomorrow Never Knows," we not only encounter guidance for disconnecting from a world gone mad, but also a reflection as to *how* and *why* postwar society lacked intrinsic values. Trapped by this reality, post–World War II American society failed to offer purposeful expressions of personal and interpersonal livelihood by cutting off experience from what R.M. Bucke labels the wisdom of "cosmic consciousness" (1–3).

A Response to Postwar Culture

A period of intense growth, post–World War II American society suffered from "the deadening of life," a condition resulting from what social theorist Erich Fromm described as "the automization of man" that occurred as a direct consequence of capitalist modernization and technological advancement ("Today's Spiritual Crisis and the Role of Psychoanalysis," 78). As evidenced further in the work of social theorists such as Herbert Marcuse, William Whyte, David Riesman, Paul Goodman, or Theodore Roszak, postwar success and capital growth led to a sense of alienation from one's self, from each other, and from nature. Although attended by progress and capital growth, postwar theorists lament the costs of postwar culture, highlighted by the dehumanization that results from the elevation of material wealth, the standardization and merit-orientation of the post-industrial society, and the resulting construction of a self defined by conformity, competition, and communal disconnect. This spiritual crisis of estrangement developed out of a postwar condition in which, as Fromm summarizes, "control by the intellect over nature, and the production of more and more things, became the paramount aims of life. In this process, man has transformed himself into a thing, life has become subordinated to property, '*to be*' is dominated by '*to have*'" ("Today's Spiritual Crisis and the Role of Psychoanalysis," 79). For both the sixties counterculture generally and The Beatles more specifically, psychedelics not only revealed the realness of this condition, but also offered a solution, a path to spiritual values and moral understandings antithetical to western religious and cultural constructs that operate through estrangement (e.g., human from the divine, humanity from nature).

Concurrent with economic growth, American society following World War II witnessed the emergence of Prosperity Gospels coupled with doomsday-centered Christian discourses that unveiled an entwining of capitalism and evangelical Christianity. Evangelical preachers, such as Charles E. Fuller (1887–1968) or Billy Graham (1918–2018), pointed to biblical end-times prophecies as explanations for the existential sickness consuming postwar culture. Drowning in an amoral mixture of liberal tolerance, Satanic secularism, and Cold War politics, Americans faced the wrathful side of God's final judgment—a judgment overcome, they argued, by resuscitating a vision of America (and Western culture) as a renewed Christendom. This politicization of evangelical Christianity was invigorated by the concurrent appearance of Christian Prosperity Gospels rooted in 1950s Healing Revivals of preachers including Oral Roberts (1918–2009) and A.A. Allen (1911–1970). Validating postwar consumer-competition orientations, prosperity theology affirms that God dictates financial and physical well-being, purchased through, among other self-interested strategies, one's own monetary payments to preachers and religious causes.

As a direct consequence, postwar consciousness, mired as it was in dual narratives of apocalyptic Christianity and meritocratic consumption, remained estranged from interpersonal responsibility and the interdependence of existence. This latter realization, as The Beatles develop in "Tomorrow Never Knows," connects directly to Buddhist-inspired readings of psychedelic consciousness, as well as Buddhist insight regarding the anxiety that develops when we individually and collectively ignore interconnection. Resulting in a lived reality of alienation and isolation, Alan Watts, a central voice who not only worked to expose western culture to eastern religious traditions, but also the value of psychedelics, stressed that "somehow th[ese] gap[s] must be closed, and among the varied means whereby the closure may be initiated or achieved are medicines which science itself has discovered, and which may prove to be the sacraments of its religion" (*The Joyous Cosmology*, xviii). Thus in addition to growing recognition regarding the therapeutic potential and medicalization of psychedelics over the past 20 years (for an effective outline of psychedelics, medicine, and therapy, see, for examples, Goldsmith's *Psychedelic Healing* or Shroder's *Acid Test*), returning to and highlighting the spiritual resonance of psychedelics, psychedelic manuals, and psychedelic rock holds distinct implications spiritually, politically, culturally, and socially. In fact, the song's defiant structure and appropriated lyrics only further a reading that contextualizes "Tomorrow Never Knows" as a radical and spiritualized counterpoint—a work of protest—against the capitalist structures and modern philosophies directing postwar culture. Aldous Huxley, in a 1962 letter to Timothy Leary, notes how the very personal encounter with psychedelic consciousness is always already impactful on the everyday waking consciousness we share with others. "The sacramentalizing of common life, so that every event may become a means whereby enlightenment can be realized, is therapy," Huxley stresses, "not merely for the abnormal, it is above all a Therapy for the much sickness of insensitiveness and ignorance we call 'normality.'" Given this backdrop of a sacramental therapy, "LSD and the mushrooms should be used," Huxley concludes, "in the context of this basic Tantrik idea of the yoga of total awareness, leading to enlightenment within the world of everyday experience—which of course becomes the world of miracle and beauty and divine mystery when experience is what it always ought to be" ("Letters: 2 February, 1962, Huxley to Leary," 109). Similarly, "Tomorrow Never Knows" presents a visionary narrative of disconnecting from a reality mired in difference and alienation in order to rescue how reality *ought* to be—that is, a "world of miracle and beauty and divine mystery."

As Leary, Alpert, and Metzner recognized early in their exploration with psychedelics, these substances, though able to propel "the subject through eight hours of unimagined experience," also "to use William James's phrase … 'open a region though they fail to give a map'" ("Rationale for the Mexican Psychedelic Training Center," 183). Within the frames of *The Tibetan Book of the Dead*, Leary, Alpert, and Metzner believed they located such a mapping. Although the text, on its surface, "treats of the intermediate state between life and death," Leary, Alpert, and Metzner ultimately locate and underscore "the esoteric aim of the book [which] was to instruct adepts in changing consciousness" (183). It is, in other words, not merely a text to help practicing Buddhists transition between the planes of physical and spiritual existence and death, but "a book of the living, a manual for recognizing and utilizing ecstatic states of altered consciousness and applying the ecstatic experience in the postsession life" (183). Once framed this way, *The Psychedelic Experience*, "because of its precise relevance to psychedelic sessions … 'translated' the manuscript" (183). Through this appropriation and translation, Leary, Alpert, and Metzner reveal how, more than the immediacy of the experience itself, the insights unveiled within psychedelic consciousness provided the means to actively reimagine and reengage the very structures of the post– World War II moment.

In turning to the manual as a source to uncover and direct their own LSD and spiritual explorations, The Beatles help realize the implications of psychedelic experimentation and the sacramental space *The Psychedelic Experience* sought to fill. The song, as with the manual and psychedelic substances themselves, helps one "to look inward" in order to "shield yourself from all the programmed stimuli of the political world and its controlled media, made for war and profits," to borrow from the reflections of Frank Barron, co-founder of the Harvard Psilocybin Project ("An Unfinished (R)Evolution," 29). Within this numinous space, what one ultimately encounters is "a commitment to fight for personal freedom, to oppose everywhere the war mentality, and the tyranny of dogmatic belief." The psychedelic evolution, as Barron thus emphasizes, "stands for equal rights for race and gender, and for ecological Earth-respecting ways of thinking and acting" (24). For The Beatles, "Tomorrow Never Knows" offered a means to both trace out this realization and enact a spiritualized vision of the world predicated on a sense of reciprocity and oneness.

From Psychedelic Manuals to the Sacred Instruction of Ecstatic Rock

As with the mystical state, Leary, Alpert, and Metzner recognized that the psychedelic experience provides access to "new realms of consciousness," leading to a "transcendence of verbal concepts, of space-time dimensions, and of the ego or identity" by releasing a "limitless range of awareness for which we now have no words" (*The Psychedelic Experience* 3, 5). As Lennon similarly grasps, "I got a message on acid that you should destroy your ego, and I did" (*The Beatles Anthology*, 180). Such an experience, however, necessitated reflection, a willingness to understand how, in the throes of ego death, value derives from what it produces relationally. It comes down, as Harrison pushes, "to what your greater consciousness is and if you can live in harmony with what's going on in creation" (*The Beatles Anthology*, 180). In fact, as the lyrics, structure, and sound of "Tomorrow Never Knows" makes clear, the "ecstatic state of non-ego" unveiled by psychedelic exploration leads one to what Leary, Alpert, and Metzner describe as "the realm of the Clear Light …

[where] the mentality of a person in the ego-transcendent state momentarily enjoys a condition of balance, a perfect equilibrium, and of oneness" (*The Psychedelic Experience*, 27).

Here, within the looping of sound and mirroring of *The Psychedelic Experience*, "Tomorrow Never Knows" helps us "remember the unity of all beings" (*The Psychedelic Experience*, 32). Echoing directly Ralph Metzner's reflections regarding his work with Leary and Alpert, "Tomorrow Never Knows" does so by offering a basic piece of advice: "remain detached and centered within yourself, don't become attracted to the pleasant visions or repelled by the painful ones. Remember,they are all in your mind. Accept them and float downstream" ("From Harvard to Zihuatanejo," 177). Within this notion to "float downstream," we ultimately locate not simply the direct referents and references used by Lennon and The Beatles, but also capture what the song—in its very structure and lyrics—seeks to do, which is to harness the ecstatic power of music to help evoke mystical experiences that make love a sacred imperative.

Bookending their 1966 album, *Revolver*, "Tomorrow Never Knows" highlights the broader experimentation directing the album. From the haunting beauty of "Eleanor Rigby" to the playfulness of "Yellow Submarine," The Beatles pushed the boundaries of their sound and lyrical orientation. Yet the album also captures The Beatles' broader awareness of the burgeoning counterculture and the avenues opened through psychedelic experimentation—while "Doctor Robert" outlines the broader drug culture, "Got to Get You into My Life" "was a song about pot." When juxtaposed to "I Want to Tell You," a song written by Harrison on the sitar to echo "the avalanche of thoughts that are so hard to write down or say or transmit" (*The Beatles Anthology*, 209), *Revolver* exemplifies a whole album dedicated to exploring the nature of reality, the consequences of death, and the potential to transcend material concerns for higher spiritual purpose.

This aim finds its apotheosis in "Tomorrow Never Knows." As McCartney reminisces, the song emerged directly after "John had got a hold of Timothy Leary's adaptation of *The Tibetan Book of the Dead*," leading The Beatles "for the first time" to the idea that, as with esoteric understandings of death, LSD opened the possibility to move beyond the phenomenal ego "for a huge voyage" into the noumenal world (*The Beatles Anthology*, 209). On a visit to London's Indica Bookstore in February 1966, co-owner Barry Miles recalls Lennon scanning the bookshelves when his "eyes soon alighted upon a copy of *The Psychedelic Experience*, Dr. Timothy Leary's psychedelic version of the *Tibetan Book of the Dead*. John was delighted and settled down on the settee with the book. Right away, on page 14 in Leary's introduction, he read, 'Whenever in doubt, turn off your mind, relax, float downstream.' He had found the first line of 'Tomorrow Never Knows,' one of the Beatles' most innovative songs" (*Paul McCartney: Many Years from Now*, 229; see also Goldman, *The Lives of John Lennon*, 195–6). In fact, as Lennon details directly, "we followed his [Leary] instructions in his 'how to take a trip' book. I did it just like he said in the book, and then I wrote 'Tomorrow Never Knows,' which was almost the first acid song: 'Lay down all thought, surrender to the void,' and all that shit which Leary had pinched from *The Tibetan Book of the Dead*" (*The Beatles Anthology*, 209). Stressing that he had "never seen it [*The Tibetan Book of the Dead*] in my life" (209), Lennon sought to recreate in song form the very dynamics of exploring LSD consciousness mapped in the pages of *The Psychedelic Experience*, illustrating for listeners how lyrics and musical structure could reveal, as Harrison develops, "the essence of Transcendentalism" (210). By this, Harrison not only invokes the radical, spiritual self-reliance of Transcendentalists such as Emerson, Thoreau, and Whitman, but also the very nature and aim of meditation, whose goal, like the mystical state, "is to go beyond (that is, transcend) waking, sleeping and dreaming … there is never a time from birth to death when the mind isn't always active with thoughts. But you can turn off your mind," Harrison advises (210).

The song, then, emerges as a type of psychedelic manual, a means to illustrate the Buddhist dynamic that "within sameness there is difference," meaning "both totality and differentiation" as Aldous Huxley underscores in his own psychedelic reflections (*The Doors of Perception*, 61). The song, as a result, becomes more than a pop culture relic—"the whole point," as Harrison details, "is that *we* are the song. The self is coming from a state of pure awareness, from the state of being. All the rest that comes about in the outward manifestation of the physical world (including all the fluctuations which end up as thoughts and actions) is just clutter." "The true nature of each soul," concludes Harrison, "is pure consciousness. So the song is really about transcending and about the quality of the transcendent" (*The Beatles Anthology*, 210). Beyond appropriating and adapting the language of *The Psychedelic Experience,* The Beatles formatted "Tomorrow Never Knows" to be dynamically present in an effort to capture and share the sacred narrative of total awareness made possible through psychedelics. The song, like Buddhism and *The Tibetan Book of the Dead*, thus illustrates the moral significance and ethical implications of being fully and contingently grounded in the ongoing moment.

Whereas modern American culture expects a type of rational output in which structure and narrative are predetermined and calculated, the heart of mysticism resides in awareness of an unmediated experience, unburdened by the confines of time or place. Situated fully in the eternal now, such an ecstatic sense allows the mystic to witness and experience oneness by overcoming the constructs that divide and differentiate. As Leary, Alpert, and Metzner importantly recognize, to overcome the ego is to realize the possibility for "both the mystic non-self and the mystic self experience" (*The Psychedelic Experience,* 32). This moment of sameness and difference, as the Buddha teaches, helps one realize the fleeting—though absolutely contingent—nature of the absolute present. Buddhist teachings stress *anitya* (impermanence), the notion that each moment is truly unique exactly because it is both constantly fleeting and always co-contingent. Revealing how reality is constructed relationally, Thich Nhat Hanh labels this state of co-existence as the truth of "interbeing," an understanding of reality in which every moment leads to the next, making experience immediate, co-determinative, and ephemeral. Importantly, realizing the interconnection of life leads one to approach each moment of existence with *mudita* (sympathetic or empathetic joy), the pleasure, in other words, that comes from delighting in other people's well-being (see Salzberg, chapter 8).

In order to trace this dynamic, "Tomorrow Never Knows" extends beyond lyrical appropriation by initiating, as producer and audio engineer George Martin stresses, "a great innovation" in sound. "John wanted," Martin continues, "a very spooky kind of track, a very ethereal sound" (*The Beatles Anthology,* 210). While Lennon originally "imagined in my head that in the background you would hear thousands of monks chanting" (211), it was through experimental "tape loops" and an aleatoric approach that ultimately produced the effects and affect of "Tomorrow Never Knows." Through the incorporation of chance into the process of musical creation, aleatoric music (from the Latin word *alea,* meaning dice) creates space for the performers to be actively dynamic in relation to some aspect of composition. As developed in a series of lectures by Werner Meyer-Eppler, "a process is said to be aleatoric … if its course is determined in general but depends on chance in detail" ("Statistic and Psychologic Problems of Sound," 55). Not incidental or improvisational, The Beatles turned to aleatoric composition in an effort to capture the sense of awareness produced by psychedelic consciousness. The tape loops, as Harrison recalls, pushed The Beatles to touch "on the Stockhausen kind of 'avant garde a clue' music" (*The Beatles Anthology,* 210). In referencing Karlheinz Stockhausen, an experimental German composer of the 20th/21st centuries, Harrison situates "Tomorrow Never Knows" as a visionary song. In addition to lyrical referents to spiritual ecstasy, its sound (re)produces the very mystical condition of psychedelic consciousness in order to fully realize the implications of dispatching with the rational instrumentality of the modern ego in favor of the contingent chance associated with living in the absolute present.

To achieve this dynamic, The Beatles combined traditional instrumentation with studio techniques that worked to expand the sound of their four-piece format. In addition to incorporating methods ranging from varispeeding to reversed tapes and closed audio miking, the manual construction of double tracking, so vital to the ethereal sound of "Tomorrow Never Knows," ultimately helped establish automatic double tracking (ADT). ADT describes an analogue recording technique designed to enhance the sound of voices or instruments during the mixing process by using tape delay to generate a delayed copy of an audio signal which then combines with the original. Although not used within the frames of "Tomorrow Never Knows," the development of such techniques—designed, as Martin notes, to create "a kind of 'in-and-out' effect" (*The Beatles Anthology*, 210–11)—not only captures the importance of chance, but also replicates the marks and experience often associated with psychedelic/mystical consciousness. Maybe most significantly then, The Beatles "Tomorrow Never Knows" offers a perspective beyond the confines of post–World War II's socio-cultural emphasis on rational order and bounded expression.

McCartney, who Martin describes as the most "avant-garde" of The Beatles, first "experimented with his tape machine at home, taking the erase-bead off and putting on loops, saturating the tape with weird sounds." He then "explained to the other boys," Martin continues, "how he had done this, and Ringo and George would do the same and bring me different loops of sounds, and I would listen to them at various speeds, backwards and forwards, and select some" (*The Beatles Anthology*, 210). In the studio, Martin ran these machines all the time, resulting in "a mix we did … [that] was a random thing that could never be done again. Nobody else," Martin stresses, "was doing records like that at the time" (210). The resulting aleatoric structure distinctly positioned the song as spontaneous, as grounded in the experiential through the experimental, a construct that reflects simultaneously the fleeting nature of reality as well as its co-dependence.

While always producing "a slightly different mix—a spontaneous thing" as Harrison recollects (*The Beatles Anthology*, 210), the song's format accords with what William James labels the four marks of mysticism (*The Varieties of Religious Experience*, 380–1):

- *ineffability*, or an experience that "defies expression … [and therefore] must be directly experienced" (this sense is expressed in a song title not found in the lyrics of "Tomorrow Never Knows");
- *noetic*, the recognition that "mystical states … [are] also states of knowledge … of insight into depths of truth unplumbed by the discursive intellect" (the heart of the song, as Harrison maintains, is found in its transcendent quality);
- *transiency*, accepting that mystical states "cannot be sustained for long" (such fleetingness is captured in the song's structure, in the fading in and out of tape loops); and
- *passivity*, which does not deny the role of "preliminary voluntary

operations," but stresses that the experience itself often includes a feeling of being "grasped and held by a superior power" (for The Beatles, the true value of psychedelic exploration begins by turning off our minds and letting it happen).

By echoing these conditions, "Tomorrow Never Knows" captures the most significant value James connects to mystical states of consciousness. Found not solely within the experience itself, true value is found in what "remains … they [mystical states] modify the inner life of the subject between the times of their recurrence … this overcoming of all the usual barriers between the individual and the Absolute is the great mystic achievement. In mystic states," James ultimately highlights, "we both become one with the Absolute and we become aware of our oneness" (381–2, 419).

The defiant nature of the song, its aleatoric backdrop, and its ethereal quality underscore this radical edge of mystical consciousness. By delineating a unitive experience beyond rational discourse, "Tomorrow Never Knows" connects mysticism to the radical potentialities found within the avant-garde. While often used to describe works of art that operate on the edge through experimental and unorthodox techniques and approaches, as originally applied, the avant-garde promotes radical social reform. It operates as both a critique of consumer culture and an affirmation that reality can be—because it already actually is—constantly changing yet always interconnected. In other words, the artist is not only a reflection of (or mirror for) a cultural moment, but can operate politically. As Olinde Rodrigues argues originally in his 1825 essay "The Artist, the Scientist and the Industrialist," artists can "serve as [the people's] avant-garde" exactly because "the power of the arts is indeed the most immediate and fastest way" to pursue radical change (cited in Calinescu, *The Five Faces of Modernity: Modernism, Avant-Garde, Decadence, Kitsch, Postmodernism*, 103). By addressing "ourselves to the imagination and feelings of people" (103), artists, according to Rodrigues, unveil the potential to break free from the rigidity and division of modernity by presenting a "utopian aim [which] is the equal sharing of all people of all the benefits of life" (104). In this sense, the song's structure replicates the challenge psychedelics and mysticism pose to the rational, the normal, and the modern by charting an understanding of "being" mired in a position of interconnection.

The song itself is dosed with this same recognition, mapping a space unburdened by the constructs that delineate and divide. From Harrison's use of the sitar to Lennon's vocals being recorded through a Leslie speaker in order to create a "kind of intermittent vibrato effect" (*The Beatles Anthology*, 211), to tape loops and a backward guitar solo, "Tomorrow Never Knows" directly imitates, in order to actualize, the most significant spiritual insight found within *The Tibetan Book of the Dead*. This message, as Lāma Anagarika

Govinda—a western convert to Buddhism who helped expose the west to Tibetan Buddhism and meditative practices—stresses in his introductory foreword, "is far more ... [than] religious speculation about death and a hypothetical after-death state ... it is a key to the innermost recesses of the human mind, and a guide for initiates, and for those who are seeking the spiritual path of liberation" (lix). For The Beatles, as with Leary, Alpert, and Metzner, the mystical height of psychedelic consciousness represented what Govinda, in reflecting on *The Tibetan Book of the Dead*, described as "the very consciousness that makes life possible in this universe" (Introductory Foreword to *The Tibetan Book of the Dead*, liii). When one awakens to this sense of consciousness, what remains, as both *The Psychedelic Experience* and "Tomorrow Never Knows" proposes, is a perennial notion of oneness, a sacred belief that mutuality and love describes the true nature of being.

Rather than dissonance, the aleatoric experimentation and lyrical narrative suggest a dependent unity below the various bizarre sound effects. As with psychedelic exploration, the song itself offers the necessary liminal space to escape modern "thought" in order to experience mystical transcendence. Mystics and psychonauts often describe this state of transcendence in terms of a void, which was actually the first title ("The Void") offered by Lennon for what became "Tomorrow Never Knows" (see Sheff, *All We Are Saying*, 174–5). The spiritual core of "Tomorrow Never Knows" echoes this lived experience of ego-death, of encountering "the void." Such an experience illustrates the circularity of life in which the end of the game of existence is the beginning, a notion that resides at the heart of mystical understanding. Scholar of religion Mircea Eliade labels this the "eternal return" (see *The Myth of the Eternal Return: Cosmos and History*), a mystical understanding found symbolically throughout global culture, including, for example, in the yin-yang or the esoteric symbol of the Ouroboros, which most commonly depicts a snake or dragon eating its own tail (every beginning is an end, and every end inflects a new beginning).

Although the song directly echoes and advances specific Buddhist philosophies of existence and reality, this notion of circularity—of a sacred reflection—ultimately positions "the void" and mystical transcendence as a perennial feeling of interconnection. Rather than nothingness, a term often used to describe transcendent states or the void, what one actually encounters is a sense of no-thing-ness, an overcoming of instrumental value in favor of intrinsic meaning. A moment, in other words, of "ecstatic unity" where, as Leary, Alpert, and Metzner conclude, "communication is unnecessary, since complete communion exists" (*The Psychedelic Experience*, 48–9). "Tomorrow Never Knows" thus grasps onto not only the Buddhist philosophy of *The Tibetan Book of the Dead*, but presents a perennial argument regarding the nature of being, a position in which the meaning found "within" is expressed as a perennial love between all beings. Through psychedelics, and as uniquely echoed in the structure and lyrics of "Tomorrow Never Knows," such meaning results in a "joyous discovery," to borrow from *The Psychedelic Experience* (73). A way, in other words, to "cut through the daze and doze of mindless existence and wake us up," as scholar of religion Huston Smith stresses in his reflections on Leary, psychedelics, and religious experiences ("Timothy Leary and the Psychedelic Movement," 242). Within this awakened state, the divides that propel peoples and cultures apart are seen as illusory, permitting moments of sacred interconnection in which, as Leary, Alpert, and Metzner conclude, "sincere love towards" others becomes the expressive motif of daily living (*The Psychedelic Experience*, 66). To reach such a state of transcendence, as *The Tibetan Book of the Dead, The Psychedelic Experience,* and "Tomorrow Never Knows" all outline, does not necessitate a dropping out of one's cultural moment or religious positioning. Rather, as John Beresford emphasizes when thinking of Leary and psychedelic exploration, it becomes a method to "dip into the reaches of the soul and face reality" ("To Tim from John," 32).

When viewed this way, "Tomorrow Never Knows" offers a response to an ever-maddening world by recalling a sacramental mechanism that ultimately replaces a sense of selfishness with imperatives of selflessness. The song articulates a mystical impulse to drop out from the restraints of post–World War II society, restoring ways of being defined in and through an always ready sense of interconnection. This foundational altruism emerges intuitively and responds directly to the mechanization of daily life and the routinization of interpersonal interactions. Psychedelics allow one to break-free from the false consciousness plaguing postwar culture, resulting in a prophetic vision, as Allen Ginsberg outlines in a 1966 article (the same year *Revolver* was released), where "we will all have seen some ray of glory or vastness beyond our conditioned social selves, beyond our government, beyond America even, that will unite us into a peaceable community" ("Public Solitude," 69). The song's resonance, then, extends beyond its structural innovation and psychedelically inspired experimentation—it resides in a capacity to offer listeners a way to look inward in order to act righteously in the here and now. Through the psychedelic narrative of "Tomorrow Never Knows," we encounter the archaic and the perennial, an encounter that helps revive the realization that the sacred precedes the secular. Within this heightened awareness, music becomes truly visionary, raising the consciousness of individual listeners to a cosmic level, one defined by collectivity and compassion. Such a revival, in the end, positions psychedelic rock and the sixties counterculture it mirrored not as projects of self-indulgent nihilism, but as agents of social, cultural, and political transformation by helping return the sacred and mystical to the consciousness of a generation.

Works Cited

Allison, Dale C., Jr. *The Love There That's Sleeping: The Art and Spirituality of George Harrison.* Bloomsbury Academic, 2006.

Barron, Frank. "An Unfinished (R)Evolution: A Memorial for Tim Leary." *Timothy Leary: Outside Looking In,* edited by Robert Forte. Park Street, 1999.

The Beatles. *The Beatles Anthology.* Chronicle, 2000.

_____. "Tomorrow Never Knows." *Revolver.* Parlophone, 1966, Record.

_____. *The Idea of the Avant Garde—and What It Means Today.* Edited by Marc James Léger. Manchester University Press, 2014.

Beresford, John. "To Tim from John." *Timothy Leary: Outside Looking In,* edited by Robert Forte. Park Street, 1999.

Blom, Jan Dirk. *A Dictionary of Hallucinations.* Springer, 2009.

Bowler, Kate. *Blessed: A History of the American Prosperity Gospel.* Oxford University Press, 2013.

Boyd, Jenny. *It's Not Only Rock 'n' Roll: Iconic Musicians Reveal the Source of Their Creativity.* John Blake, 2014.

Bucke, Richard Maurice. *Cosmic Consciousness: A Study in the Evolution of the Human Mind.* Dutton, 1969.

Bürger, Peter. *Theory of the Avant-Garde.* Translated by Michael Shaw. University of Minnesota Press, 1984.

Calinescu, Matei. *The Five Faces of Modernity: Modernism, Avant-Garde, Decadence, Kitsch, Postmodernism.* Duke University Press, 1987.

Eliade, Mircea. *The Myth of the Eternal Return: Cosmos and History.* Princeton University Press, 1971.

_____. *Shamanism: Archaic Techniques of Ecstasy.* Princeton University Press, 2004.

Evans-Wentz, W.Y. "Preface to the Third Edition." *The Tibetan Book of the Dead or the After-Death Experiences of the Bardo Plane, according to Lāma Kazi Dawa-Samdup's English Rendering,* compiled and edited by W.Y. Evans-Wentz. Oxford University Press, 2000.

Everett, Walter. *The Beatles as Musicians: Revolver through the Anthology.* Oxford University Press, 1999.

Feisst, Sabine. "Losing Control: Indeterminacy and Improvisation in Music Since 1950." *New Music Box: American Music Center Web Magazine,* 3/11, 2002.

Fromm, Erich. *To Have or to Be?* Bantam, 1976.

_____. "Today's Spiritual Crisis and the Role of Psychoanalysis." *Zen Buddhism and Psychoanalysis,* edited by Erich Fromm, D.T. Suzuki, and Richard DeMartino. Harper & Row, 1960.

Ginsberg, Allen. "Public Solitude." *Liberation,* April 1967. *Notes from the New Underground: Where It's At and What's Up,* edited by Jesse Kornbluth. Ace, 1968.

Goldman, Albert. *The Lives of John Lennon.* Chicago Review, 2001.

Goldsmith, Neal. *Psychedelic Healing: The Promise of Entheogens for Psychotherapy and Spiritual Development.* Healing Arts, 2011.

Goodman, Paul. *Growing Up Absurd: Problems of Youth in the Organized System.* Vintage, 1962.

Govinda, Lāma Anagarika. Introductory Foreword to *The Tibetan Book of the Dead or the After-Death Experiences of the Bardo Plane, according to Lāma Kazi Dawa-Samdup's English Rendering,* compiled and edited by W.Y. Evans-Wentz. Oxford University Press, 2000.

Hanh, Thich Nhat. "Interbeing." *Thich Nhat Hanh: Essential Writings,* edited by Robert Ellsberg. Orbis, 2001.

Harrell, David. *All Things Are Possible: The Healing and Charismatic Revivals in Modern America.* Indiana University Press, 1979.

Harris, Jonathan. "Introduction: Abstraction and Empathy—Psychedelic Distortion and the Meaning of the 1960s." *Summer of Love: Psychedelic Art, Social Crisis and Counterculture in the 1960s,* edited by Christoph Grunenberg and Jonathan Harris. Liverpool University Press, 2005.

Harrison, George. *I Me Mine: The Extended Edition*. Genesis, 2017.
Hertsgaard, Mark. "We All Want to Change the World: Drugs, Politics, and Spirituality." *A Day in the Life: The Music and Artistry of the Beatles*. Delta, 1996.
Huxley, Aldous. *The Doors of Perception; & Heaven and Hell*. Harper, 2009.
_____. "Letters: 2 February, 1962, Huxley to Leary." *Timothy Leary: Outside Looking In*, edited by Robert Forte. Park Street, 1999.
James, William. *The Varieties of Religious Experience: A Study of Human Nature; Being the Gifford Lectures on Natural Religion, delivered at Edinburgh in 1901–1902*. Dover, 1902.
Kahn, Michael. "The Rule of Love." *Timothy Leary: Outside Looking In*, edited by Robert Forte. Park Street, 1999.
Larkin, Colin. *Encyclopedia of Popular Music*, Volume 1. Oxford University Press, 2006.
Leary, Timothy, Richard Alpert and Ralph Metzner. *The Psychedelic Experience: A Manual Based on the Tibetan Book of the Dead*. Citadel, 2007.
_____. "Rationale for the Mexican Psychedelic Training Center." *Utopiates: The Use and Users of LSD-25*, edited by Richard Blum and Associates. Atherton, 1964.
Lewisohn, Mark. *The Complete Beatles Chronicle: The Definitive Day-by-Day Guide to the Beatles' Entire Career*. Chicago Review, 2010.
_____. *The Complete Beatles Recording Sessions*. Harmony, 1988.
MacDonald, Ian. *Revolution in the Head: The Beatles' Records and the Sixties*. Chicago Review, 2007.
Marcuse, Herbert. *One-Dimensional Man*. Beacon, 1964.
Metzner, Ralph. "From Harvard to Zihuatanejo." *Timothy Leary: Outside Looking In*, edited by Robert Forte. Park Street, 1999.
Meyer-Eppler, Werner. "Statistic and Psychologic Problems of Sound." Translated by Alexander Goehr, *Die Reihe* ("Electronic Music"), 1 (1957): 55–61.
Miles, Barry. *The Beatles: A Diary—An Intimate Day by Day History*. Omnibus, 1998.
_____. *Paul McCartney: Many Years from Now*. Holt, 1998.
Miller, Douglas T. *The Fifties: The Way We Really Were*. Doubleday, 1977.
Riesman, David. *The Lonely Crowd: A Study of the Changing American Character*. Yale University Press, 1950.
Roszak, Theodore. *The Making of a Counter Culture: Reflections on the Technocratic Society and Its Youthful Opposition*. Doubleday, 1969.
Salzberg, Sharon. *Loving-Kindness: The Revolutionary Art of Happiness*. Shambhala, 1995.
Schuon, Frithjof. *The Transcendent Unity of Religion*. Quest, 1984.
Sheff, David. *All We Are Saying: The Last Major Interview with John Lennon and Yoko Ono*. St. Martin's Griffin, 2000.
Shroder, Tom. *Acid Test: LSD, Ecstasy, and the Power to Heal*. Blue Rider, 2014.
Stace, W.T. *The Teachings of the Mystics*. Mentor, 1960.
Sutton, M. A. *American Apocalypse: A History of Modern Evangelicalism*. Harvard University Press, 2014.
Tillery, Gary. *Working Class Mystic: A Spiritual Biography of George Harrison*. Quest, 2011.
"Timothy Leary and the Psychedelic Movement: An Interview with Huston Smith." *Timothy Leary: Outside Looking In*, edited by Robert Forte. Park Street, 1999.
Turner, Steve. *A Hard Day's Write: The Stories Behind Every Beatles Song*. Harper, 2005.
Underhill, Evelyn. *Mysticism: A Study of the Nature and Development of Man's Spiritual Consciousness*. Dutton, 1961.
Watts, Alan. *The Joyous Cosmology*. Vintage, 1965.
_____. *The Two Hands of God: The Myths of Polarity*. Collier, 1963.
Whyte, William. *The Organization Man*. Doubleday, 1957.
Womack, Kenneth. *Long and Winding Roads: The Evolving Artistry of the Beatles*. Continuum, 2007.

Into the Slipstream

An Inquiry Concerning Inspiration and Creativity

ROBERT MCPARLAND

Van Morrison: Into the Slipstream

The first words on Van Morrison's solo album *Astral Weeks* (1968), focus on venturing into the slipstream in the midst of a dream. Here we will pursue an exploration of the slipstream. This will be a descriptive, speculative reflection utilizing an eclectic mix of literature, psychology, neuroscience, and religious references to suggest ways of thinking about musical experience, the creative arts, and religious experience. We will consider Van Morrison's *Astral Weeks* as an entry point for this reflection. In the second part, we will look further at inspiration, religious belief, and creativity in the work of George Harrison and Bob Dylan.

Much of rock music is quite extroverted. With an album like Van Morrison's *Astral Weeks* we encounter something introspective, more akin to the contemplative tradition: a kind of soul-play and dreaming. *Astral Weeks* addresses the mystery of music. It expresses an earthy mysticism—from the streets of Belfast to the mystery of love. Rudolph Otto, in *The Idea of the Holy*, once described the holy as a fascination: awful, powerful, yet compelling, an immediacy, not an abstraction. This is where wonder begins in surprise and our language and categories will not adequately describe this encounter. Rudolph Otto wrote: "The more I seek words to express this intimate intercourse, the more I feel the impossibility of describing it by any of the usual images."

Van Morrison: An Overview

Rolling Stone once described Van Morrison as "an enigma shrouded in Celtic garb." This is an artist who sings of how one sails into the mystic. His work includes many albums with decidedly religious/ spiritual titles which suggest a search into religious experience: *Astral Weeks* 1968 (I Believe I've Transcended); *St. Dominic's Preview* 1972; *Beautiful Vision* 1982; *A Sense of Wonder* 1985; *No Guru, No Method, No Teacher* 1986; *Enlightenment* 1990; *Hymns to the Silence* 1991; *The Philosopher's Stone* 1998.

Van Morrison is a performer who is an introvert. He is sometimes uncomfortable with the stage, but he is passionate and alive within the music. He is an Irish poet in touch with the blues and American music forms. In his work we might speak of an alliance between blues and spirituals. His band, Them, gave us "Here Comes the Night" and "Gloria" and "Mystic Eyes." With the emergence of Bang Records, Van Morrison was asked by Bert Berns to contribute to their recordings. Berns was the producer behind some of the Them work, but soon he died, leaving Van Morrison stuck in a contract quandary. Morrison created four singles for the company: one of them, "Brown Eyed Girl," went to #10 in 1967. Warner Bros. then signed him and he brought together a group of jazz musicians and jazz improvisation met with Irish romantic mysticism on *Astral Weeks*. A listener can hear flute, vibraphone, string bass, and Van Morrison's wailing vocals. Morrison called the songs "poetic stories."

There was next a shift in Morrison's life and music, as he lived at Woodstock for a time and brought together a horn section for *Moondance* (1970), his next album. He recorded "Into the Mystic" and so did Johnny Rivers, for whom the song became a hit. Morrison moved to California and *His Band and the Street Choir* followed with the single "Domino" and then "Tupelo Honey" and "Wild Night." Connie Kaye, a jazz drummer from Modern Jazz Quartet played on that record and had been involved with *Astral Weeks* in 1968. *St. Dominic's Preview*, which followed, opened up the improvisational landscape. By 1973 he had formed an 11 piece group that called themselves the Caledonia Soul Orchestra.

The Album: Astral Weeks

Astral Weeks has been looked at as a song cycle or a concept album and has been described as impressionistic. The impact of American blues on Van Morrison is clear and indisputable. At times he has quoted from Muddy Waters, Sonny Terry and Brownie McGhee, and many others. It is this black music pulse of blues and jazz that mixes it up with the improvisational orientation in much of his work. It meets with the Celtic spirituality that moves through his explorations.

Astral Weeks developed from three sessions between September and October of 1968 at Century Sound in New York. The musicians had not played together before. There were no lead sheets. The musicians were: John Payne, flute; Connie Kaye, drums;, Warren Smith, percussion; Richard Davis, bass; Jay Berliner, guitar; and Lewis Merenstein, producer. Van Morrison played acoustic guitar first and then engaged improvisations by all. Some overdubs were added later and edits were used to tighten the performances. While planned, the recording conveys a sense of improvisational openness.

This album is characterized by stream of consciousness: that is, a kind of free association of thought, allowing what comes to mind. This is akin to improvisation- and this album involves those deans of improv: jazz players. Morrison's lyrics evoke images and feeling in a non-discursive way with the symbolism of love and mysticism and they tend to look backward (except perhaps for the song "Sweet Thing").

On the opening cut, a flute sneaks in after the first line and the words speak of being born again. Later, we hear Van Morrison vamping that he is a stranger in this world and repeating that "we are going to heaven" in another time and place. This dissolves into strings- what would be called an obligato- and ends on an acoustic guitar run.

On "Beside You," Jay Berliner's guitar circles around with Van Morrison's vocal and there is an openness here. "Sweet Thing" follows with a descending circular progression. The lyrics evoke a hazy love, seeking some recovery of romance. We hear gentle acoustic guitar chords, an upright bass, a triangle, some work on the high hat. This brings to mind a description from of musical progressions from ethnomusicologist Curt Sachs, who has identified two melody types. One, we might call "tumbling," the other "horizontal." "Horizontal" moves to and from a prominent tone in relatively small steps. "Tumbling" has an initial leap to a high note followed by a step-wise descent. This tumbling can be heard here on this song and we hear this often in Van Morrison's music.

The fourth song on the album is one of the most interesting tunes on the record, "Cyprus Avenue": a three chord blues that begins on a street in Belfast and begins to musically explore realms beyond. The street was lined with trees and it was a place for reflection. "To me it was a very mystical place," he once told an interviewer. We hear the upright bass, distant strings, a bit of harpsichord, a violin. There is a dissolve of words into vocal improvisations, runs of words or just sound. The phrase "way upon" is repeated over and over as the tempo slides back into the same cadence. However structured the session may have been, one feels the sense that Van Morrison is creating on the spot. He is in the moment.

Turn the record over (we used to do that) and the second side begins with "The Way Young Lovers Do," which continues the theme of love. A vibraphone comes in. Then horns join the melody and we hear the drummer playing on the ride cymbal. This seems to be produced differently: more like the musicians are anticipating a single. There is a bit of scat and a horn solo and a repetition of lines. Greil Marcus didn't like this one. Other critics called it lounge jazz and said it felt out of place on this record.

"Madame George," which follows, is a different story. It engages the musicians in improvisation and runs almost ten minutes. We are given a character playing dominos in drag on a street corner. This is another stream of consciousness on Cypress Avenue: a montage of twilight, a kind of hypnogogic state. It is not rock or jazz or blues or folk exactly, but a kind of otherworldly melding of these in mystic poetry, spacious grooves, incantation, improvisation and moments of invention.

This is followed by "Ballerina," composed in 1966 while Morrison was still with Them. The song is given a bit of structure and comes to us via guitar, string bass, and vibraphone. "Slim Slow Slider," coming next, is a blues. We hear string bass and flute. There are no string overdubs. In the lyric the girl is fading away.

"*Astral Weeks* was like a religion to us," said Steve van Zandt of the E Street Band in 2008. He added that it influenced Bruce Springsteen's *Greetings from Asbury Park, N.J.* For Lester Bangs, in 1979, *Astral Weeks* was the rock record with the most significance for him "so far." He interpreted the lyrics as suggesting people "stunned ... overwhelmed by life." Greil Marcus also listened to it often, calling the album "adventurous."

It is said that Joel Brodsky's LP cover photo of Van Morrison and the squared circle is meant to suggest "the mystic symbol of the union of opposites, the sacred marrying of heaven and earth." Van Morrison had not yet read William Blake at this point, but Blake's *Marriage of Heaven and Hell*—a title derived from Emmanuel Swedenborg—like much of Blake's work, deals with "contraries," and the union of opposites (*Songs of Innocence/Songs of Experience*).

Music and Celtic Culture

To what extent is Van Morrison's musical spirit informed by his DNA, his heredity? Just how Celtic is he? Critics have pointed out that Van Morrison's music does not sound very Irish. Yet, the musical-poetic spirit of Van Morrison seems quite Irish and in line with the bardic qualities of Joyce, Beckett, and Yeats. Classical writers commented on the Celtic love of music and poetry. The Roman Diodorus Siculus wrote: "They have lyric poets whom they call bards. They sing to the accompaniment of instruments resembling lyres." Bards and Druids are distinguished in these classical sources. This is something like a priest, or shamanic figure. In Wales, Druids were musicians and poets. The Celtic Christian poets inherited this tradition and are distant sources for the art of Van Morrison, Bono (Paul Hewson) of U2, and others. Celtic mythology references music, musicians, and the other world. It speaks of keening and the revolving around three or four notes, as Van Morrison frequently does. There is in this vocal style a sense of incantation, or a theme and improvisation around the theme.

One might not call Van Morrison in his black hat and sunglasses a Druid, but one can call him a bard. The word Druid from the Gaelic *drui* connotes magician, or sorcerer, the magus. The Celtic bards were an order that included the druids, or priest-philosophers, the *vates*, or prophetic poets. Druids were the masters of invocation. Their teaching was conveyed orally: singing, as in a blessing over their students. The Welsh bards were learned poets. These Irish praise-poets became storytellers or entertainers, the *filidh*. The *vatis* or *fili* was a seer or a diviner. Julius Caesar states that Druids met in assembly in the tribal territory of the Carnutes, a center of Gaul.

The bards were conjurers of praise poems connected with ritual. Their priestly counterpart sang to God, or to the gods. This Celtic poet expressed magical powers as a shaman, or magician. The druids were in charge of ritual or chant. Celtic scholar J.G. McCullough points out: "Druidism was not a formal system outside Celtic religion. It covered the whole ground of Celtic religion; it was that religion itself." There is a very strong overlay of Christianity and Christian saints in Ireland. Brigid, despite pagan roots, was an agreeable and a popular saint. St. Columbae is also among the earliest. Are such roots hereditary: a cultural sense embedded in the psyche?

Into the Slipstream

The first line of Van Morrison's song "Astral Weeks," like many other qualities of his album and his search into mystery and broadly religious themes in his later albums, beckon to us to inquire into improvisation—those moments when a musician opens into a kind of uncertainty and spontaneously invents within a groove and harmonic pattern. Contrary to the ancient philosopher Heraclitus, who said you can't step into the same changing stream twice, music listeners and players can dip into the same slipstream. At best this is a flow or fluency, a pattern which eventually, gradually, *may* move into an altered state of consciousness.

A musician who is performing without a score or lead sheet is working from memory. That musician retrieves the music from memory. An improviser can carry on well-learned routines, or may stretch past these. Musicians learn the devices that express different musical ideas and venture out from them. In a group, as social creators we engage in emotional exchange, picking up signals, responding. In our uniqueness—musically and personaly—we then link, combine, or bind our differences. The motif, or riff, creates the possibility of associating ideas in music. This is a repeating figure. One can vary this pattern in simple ways, or in novel ways- maybe moving it up a pitch, inverting it, combining variations. You might consider Beethoven's Fifth Symphony as an example. Yet, in the collective dynamics of music making some mysterious things seem to sometimes happen.

In this synchrony, it is as if the music plays itself. There is a communication, a sharing, a dynamic at work. It is like as the poet T.S. Eliot put it in "Dry Salvages": "you are the music while the music lasts." The musicians are temporarily integrated, attentive, even rhythmically entrained. Music becomes an exploration of mystery. This appears to have been part of Van Morrison's approach to *Astral Weeks*.

This is the slipstream—social, neurological, a kind of collective dreaming. Might this move toward what we call the spiritual? One lets go of left-brain logic and enters sensuous right brain design. Musical memory is repeating itself in the groove stream and might bring an almost out of body experience—call it astral, if you will—that may accompany some music performances, if one is in the moment. The jam is cooperative; we are coinciding, supported by the music- which is a vehicle for a kind of collective intentionality beneath the individual selves contributing to this. The music is a means of sharing with trust in group synchrony. It takes you somewhere. One's subjectivity enters into the slipstream with the others. Coupled in musicking, our emotions are transmitted to each other; we adjust to one another. Those islands of Cartesian subjectivity dissolve. We connect and are conditioned and regulated by the song and by each other. The body is involved. The mind is involved. The nervous system is involved. We are always listening to each other and to the sound. How are we to understand this?

The interesting thing about the Van Morrison sessions for *Astral Weeks* is that the musicians had not played together before. They could rely upon their musical learning, of course, but they could not know or anticipate another player's typical moves, as one might in a band that has played together for a long time. They were, in fact, creating on the spot, in the moment.

Maybe it is not "spiritual" but it can be rather mysterious. Yes, there are improvisatory strategies that musicians may use. But what if something different "happens"? There are some particular notes, a riff, an inspiration that flashes out with unexpected spontaneity. This is felt and this may be social. One musician may be challenged to continue with a lead by the others in the band- and where does one go? A focus is found, a shift of attention. One feels not anxiety but a movement toward coherence. One may even go into over-drive. What emerges musically from this exchange between the members of the group?

In *Astral Weeks*, Van Morrison is inventive and he leans on blues structures with jazz players. Most listeners can recognize some of these patterns, based upon their previous listening. One does not have to be musically trained for this. As Leonard Meyer once said in *Emotion and Music* (1956), musical phrases create expectations in a listener. Sometimes a listener is expecting a resolution of a pattern and is surprised by where the music goes—and one is maybe delighted. Listeners may be interested in the surprising, the unexpected, the sense of wonder that Van Morrison refers to in his songs.

Rock Poetry

Van Morrison is one of the poet laureates of rock. Rock critic Lester Bangs observed Morrison's repetitions of single words or phrases. Bill Friskics Warren asked if Van Morrison seeks a personal relationship with the God of Judaism and Christianity, or a transpersonal state of enlightenment (25). Dave Marsh asserted that neither Bruce Springsteen, Bob Seger, nor Gram Parsons "has yet taken the spiritual basis of rock and rhythm and blues and the blues so far into an almost religious concept" as Van Morrison (25).

Van Morrison is a rock performer who explores mystery. Mystery is where any division of subject and object breaks down. To a religious believer, the immanent, indwelling God is a mystery beyond all comprehension. So too is love. If we think of Self as incarnate spirit, a person who believes may be said to be working out the "music" of his or her life in faith, love, and hope to be a beneficial presence in the world—to heal, enlighten, and transform. The bard-poet/shaman priest is engaged in this work.

Van Morrison once told an interviewer: "I am an inspirational writer" (10). By this he seems to mean that he regards his music as a medium that is inspired and through which he may inspire others. Morrison's music resists categorization as rock and owes much to the blues and gospel. From these traditions he draws inspiration and transforms his work into an inspiration.

Yet, what are we to make of this word "inspiration" that we use so casually? Inspiration has a long history, one that has been recorded in Biblical passages and in other sacred texts, as well as in the records of psychological studies and in the accounts of creative artists. Inspiration comes from the Greek concept of mind (*nous*) which they believed fills the universe. The word shares etymological connections with breath, as in the Greek *pneuma* and the Hebrew *ruah*, or our English word respiration. To free word and emotion by one's breath as a vocalist seems to be a way for the artist to tap into inspiration. Van Morrison told his interviewer: "I release the words into singing syllables ... signs and phrases" (Miles, Introduction). He begins to enter the flood, as Billy Harrison of Them put it: to "throw words at it." Greil Marcus suggests that Van Morrison is on "a kind of quest: for the moment when the magic word, riff, note, or chord is found and everything is transformed." He engages in an art in which fragments appear, broken and remade, a dissolving of words into music (Marcus, Introduction). So the adventure begins.

George Harrison: Living in the Material World

George Harrison was the quiet one: the Beatle most devoted to the guitar, to a gentler, wry sense of humor, and to the wonder of what he believed must be a divine source that had somehow set his life amid the whirlwind of Beatlemania. He sought his voice alongside two of the finest songwriters of the age, John Lennon and Paul McCartney. He sought oneness and wholeness, and he sought privacy. George Harrison, turning East, opened an Eastern path for many seekers. He wrote songs with titles like "The Inner Light" and "Within You Without You": songs flavored with the sound of sitar that introduced the music and mysticism of the East to Western listeners. His distinctive guitar lines and slide guitar sound went far beyond The Beatles into a solo career of songs that were sometimes sketchy, sometimes profound, and always thoughtful. He was a man deeply attached to the intricacies of his guitar who could not help but be influenced by the context he worked within alongside the talents of Lennon, McCartney, and Ringo Starr, or the many artists, from Eric Clapton and Klaus Voorman to Jeff Lynne, with whom he worked afterward. Yet, his deepest influences arose from the deepening of his spirit, his search and the experience of inspiration he found in the Vedas, the *Bhagavad Gita*, and in meditation, prayer, and the work of setting aside his ego to be open to the heart and to mystery.

For George Harrison, to meditate was "a means to an end." It was a way "to infuse energy." he commented to Jenny Boyd: "To be really in touch with creative energy, you will find that it lies within the stillness" (Boyd 254). The song "I Me Mine" referred to a dissolving of the ego in his LSD experiences. Through these experiences Harrison came to an understanding of his personal self as an expression of a greater transpersonal collective force, a universal consciousness. "LSD did unlock something for me," Harrison told Boyd. However, feeling that he needed to be clearer in writing songs, he learned to separate the intake of substances from when he was working (Boyd 206). His experience also urged him to transcend ego and in "I Me Mine" he was critical of his own and others' selfish behavior. Harrison wrote in his autobiography that he had come to dislike his ego: "it was a flash of everything false and impermanent" (158). Harrison reflected that despite the depths of mind, spirit, and consciousness, people in the West often fixed their attention upon mundane realties and to live like this was to be like "beggars in a gold-mine" (242). The *Bhagavad Gita* says: They are forever free who renounce all selfish desires and break away from the ego-cage of I-me-mine, to be united with the Lord. Attain to this and pass from death to immortality" (2:71–72, ctd. in *Beatles Encyclopedia*, 420).

Some of Harrison's most memorable songs seem to have emerged naturally, to have been suggested in a moment of inspiration. "Here Comes the Sun" came to mind while he was strolling with his acoustic guitar through Eric Clapton's garden. "While My Guitar Gently Weeps" began when he was reading the *I Ching, Book of Changes*, which encourages randomness. Following the Eastern concept that all changes and whatever happens is meant to be, the *I Ching* teaches that there is no coincidence. Harrison's eyes fell upon the words "gently weeps" and his beautiful song often covered by other artists began to unfold (Beatles Anthology 306). Of course, the song itself is well-structured around its A minor, G, F chord pattern and smooth melodic line. It arose in Harrison's imagination through his familiarity with his instrument and the music of others that he had heard for a long time. The song came from his spirit but it also came from a context. It did not suddenly appear like the sunshine through the clouds.

Was it simply chance that the lives and music of The Beatles converged in Liverpool? Was it coincidental that things came together as they did in the *zeitgeist* of that time to bring us their music and make their songs such an enduring part of our culture? With The Beatles, George Harrison was caught up within a world-wide phenomenon. "It made me nervous, the whole magnitude of our fame," Harrison once said (Huntley 10).

All Things Must Pass was a fitting title for a time when the members of The Beatles went their own ways. Of course, the multi-sided album was a creative milestone for George Harrison and his phrase offers his recognition of the evanescent quality of the process of life. In *Rolling Stone* (January 21, 1971) Ben Gerson wrote that Harrison's music for this record came "pouring out…. It is both an intensely personal statement and a grandiose gesture, a triumph over artistic modesty, even frustration." Gerson called the album an "extravagant expression" of "piety and sacrifice and joy." On that album, "What Is Life?" asks a perennial question and adds the lover's realization— who am I without you? —which may be addressed to a beloved friend, a lover, or the divinity regarded gratefully by the singer.

"My Sweet Lord," a staple of radio airplay in the early 1970s, is George Harrison's best known post–Beatles song. The lyric to "My Sweet Lord" evokes seeking. The musical pattern may owe much to many other songs besides Ronald Mack's "He's So Fine." Despite Harrison's distinctive guitar lines and apparently earnest intention, he was charged with "unconscious plagiarism" of the Chiffon's "He's So Fine." The song actually owes more to "Oh, Happy Day" by the Edwin Hawkins Singers which inspired Harrison while he was on tour in Europe with Eric Clapton and Delaney and Bonnie in December 1969. The repetition of the chorus with layered vocals suggests community and harmony. The Hallelujahs became linked with the Maha Mantra and Sanskrit prayer (Gururbrahmaa Guru Vishnu,/Gururdeeoo Mahesvarah/ Gurussaakshaat Param Brahma/ Tasmai Shri Garav Namhah).

Several songs from *All Things Must Pass* were performed at The Concert for Bangladesh, which included two concerts on the afternoon and evening of August 1, 1971, at Madison Square Garden in New York City. The first of rock's benefit concerts, the show was intended to bring attention to the plight of the people of Bangladesh following the Bhola cyclone of 1970 and civil strife and poverty in the country. With the support of Ravi Shankar and a host of well-known popular musicians the concert and subsequent album and film raised $12 million in aid. The album won the 1973 Grammy Album of the Year Award.

In the preface to Harrison's autobiography *I Me Mine*, his wife, Olivia Harrison comments on George Harrison's desire to shed attachment and identification with the ego, to arrive at a point of realization that there is no "I Me Mine" and that creativity is a "bestowed" and "divine gift" (1). In her preface, Olivia Harrison says that she often asked him what his songs were about and his answers seldom satisfied her questions (4). George Harrison appreciated the lyrics of Bob Dylan but he did not explain his own lyrics. Olivia Harrison says that she believes that his lyrics were "the most spiritually conscious of our time" (3).

In his autobiography, George Harrison says that he has been inspired by "all kinds of mystics and ex-mystics" (184). *Living in the Material World* owes something to the teaching of A.C. Bhaktivedanta Swami: "we are not our bodies." Harrison's "Give Me Love (Give Me Peace on Earth) is perhaps the most memorable song on George Harrison's *Living in the Material World* (1973). It is a prayer that rises with his familiar slide guitar lead. Harrison recalled the spontaneity of the song's creation: "Sometimes you open up your mouth and you don't know what you are going to say and whatever comes out is the starting point" (*Beatles Encyclopedia* 321) There is an approach to songwriting in this: an idea emerges while one is playing, or a word or phrase comes to mind, and the songwriter follows it.

Creativity

One of the Webster dictionary's definitions for the word "inspire" is "to animate by supernatural infusion." The Greek "*entheous*" means "in God," that is, inspired by the divine. Enthusiasm is an ecstasy of mind, (*ec-stasis*, or standing out from) possessed by a spiritual influence or presence, or by an ardent love for a subject. In this sense, making art is like making love: the creator is one with her lover. Enthusiasm is about being "fired up." We call a former love affair "an old flame." The word inspiration is related to the word "spiritual." Religious examples of a fiery inspiration abound: Moses was startled by a burning bush. The apostles of Jesus in the Upper Room experienced tongues of fire. The mystic Richard Rolle observed what he believed was divine presence an experience of "warmth," a "silent fire." The mystic Jakob Boehme claimed, "Art has not wrote here—But all was ordered in the direction of the Spirit." Such experience attributes to inspiration a metaphysical source. For one who turns to the Hindu meditation like George Harrison a person is grounded in the pervading energy of consciousness and the energy of *prana* flows through one's being.

Of course, there are a variety of approaches to examining artistic creativity besides making reference to mystical explanations. Graham Wallas, in his 1926 book *The Art of Thought*, posited a four step process for creative discovery:

1. Preparation (Study, research, think, ask questions, dialogue)
2. Incubation (Gestation, the idea is in the subconscious just below the surface.)
3. Illumination (A-ha!, solution, the little lightbulb over the cartoon character's head.)
4. Verification (Review, proof, validation)

In *The Creative Process* (1952), the poet Brewster Ghiselin indicated the following factors:

1. Oceanic consciousness (A yearning, an intimation, a hunch leading to a sense of religious experience, or of a self that is greater than the ego-self.)
2. Authenticity (Like riding a bicycle, after much practice art comes naturally.)
3. The creator feels restless and innovates from this restlessness.
4. The creator is emotion-driven, feels a passion, or a response to beauty. The musician hears a musical phrase which he or she loves. The painter notices a pattern in the visual world.
5. Organic unconscious processes are at work.

6. Concentration (The artist has a conscious focus or goes into a sort of creative trance)

7. The artist consciously works.

George Harrison was aware that a rapid paced, distraction filled society may keep us away from the silence, from dreamwork, affirmation, relaxation and focus. He recognized that altered states, meditation, resting in his belief and openness to his sense of the divine, and taking the mind off-line have some creative benefits.

Creativity has something to do with our sense of wonder, our curiosity, our instincts for discovery, our capacity to tune in to and to feel music. This creativity enriches our lives. Psychologist Frank Barron, who studied creativity across several decades, recognized that with respect to religion creative people tend to "combine skepticism about fundamentalist dogmas with an often passionate search for symbolic meanings" (Maps 112). He wrote, "Creative individuals are persons whose dedication is nothing less than a quest for ultimate meanings" (Boyd 18). These individuals are flexible, drawn toward paradoxes like "the one and the many, unity and variety, determinism and freedom, mechanism and vitalism, good and evil, time and eternity..." (Maps 112). Such creativity grows and develops in connection with others, not only in isolation. Rock artists entertain us, yet are also engaged in a process in which symbols are made newly relevant and transformed. Religion, like rock, responds to the communal as well as to the individual. Rock bands and rock audiences are communal.

There are many factors involved in creativity and there are a variety of approaches involved in attempts to understand this complex human talent. Psychologists speak of divergent thinking. Whereas convergent thinkers assemble date and use logic to determine a correct and often conventional response, divergent thinkers draw out a variety of associations (Gardner 20). Freud brought attention to instinctual, sexual factors, to the idea that artistic creation involves libidinal energies, or sublimation into music, writing, dance and other creative forms. Freud wrote: "Might we not say that every child at play behaves like a creative writer.... The creative writer does the same as the child at play" (ctd. By Gardner 24). A more pragmatic approach perhaps is that of the behaviorist who considers the connection between motivation and reward. For B.F. Skinner positive reinforcement is the key: a previous background of reward produces the expectation of future reward. However, most artists appear to be intrinsically motivated. They create music because they love music. They create because the work of originality brings its own rewards, including a sense of being "in flow," fully alive, actualizing or realizing the spirit in and about oneself, or experiencing the high of peak experience. One tolerates the effort or pain of the discipline for these satisfactions.

We are all creative, the cognitive scientist Steven Pinker points out (360). However, an intensively developed skill is central to accomplished creativity. Psychologist Howard Gardner points to continual focus on a domain of work and the regular expression of creativity as preparation for any kind of breakthrough (36). Steven Pinker observes that the creative individual, immersed in a genre, "pays dues for at least ten years before contributing anything of lasting value" (361). Gardner refers to the idea that creative individuals enter a Faustian bargain in which they "pay some price to sustain that gift" (386). The artist works in a discipline and a symbol system in relation to predecessors and to those who work in this field. They engage in risk, draw upon and transform previous models, are sorely tested, and develop relationships with the context in which they work. In the case of popular music, this context includes musicians, lyricists, critics, agents, producers, and people connected with the band.

[Note: Howard Gardner writes: "These arrangements are typically not described as pacts with anyone, but at least to me, they resemble that kind of semimagical, semimystical arrangement in the West we have come to associate with Dr. Faustus and Mephistopheles. Equally, they have a religious flavor, as if each creator had, so to speak, struck a deal with a personal god" (386).]

What is inspiration and how does it help a lyricist, an artist, or a scientist to reach beyond the limits of logic, reason, and sensory experience or to combine these in new and insightful ways? Is there some native and radical power which the poetic sensibility possesses?

Studies from psychology and brain physiology shed some light on this process. But they are frequently reductive and they do not quite explain "poetry." Sigmund Freud wrote that "the poets and philosophers before me discovered the unconscious, what I discovered was the scientific method by which the unconscious can be studied." Freud's study of the symbols of the unconscious in *Interpretation of Dreams* and his method of free association opened a path to acknowledgment of the unconscious. Yet, we are left with the question as to whether there is any religious or spiritual aspect to the unconscious, as psychologists like Victor Frankl or Gerald May have suggested.

Humans, from earliest times, have long sought a relationship to supernatural powers or divinity. The convictions of religious believers tend to not rest upon rational proofs but rather upon personal encounters, intuition, emotion, choices, and faith. Religions point to extraordinary personal experiences. Buddah received enlightenment under the bodhi tree. Mohammed (Peace Be Upon Him) experienced a revelation and heard a call. Paul of Tarsus on the road to Damascus was blinded by the light. Myths of light and ascent suggest escape or transcendence from one mode of being to another, the crossing of boundaries or thresholds. Inspiration may seem like an extraordinary experience: a peak experience, or a gift of grace. Someone with a religious perspective may turn toward mysticism for an explanation. Mysticism suggests a spiritual dimension that is experiential. Those who have referred to mystical experience have described a sense of oneness, an encounter with the ground of being, a quality of God/divinity, a cosmic consciousness, or revelation.

The great psychologists have ventured different approaches to these religious accounts. Sigmund Freud, wrote of the "oceanic" experience from an atheistic standpoint in which he viewed religion as an illusion. Carl Jung explored the mysteries of the archetypal collective unconscious. In *Varieties of Religious Experience*, William James attempted to gather the extraordinary experiences of 'ordinary' people. He recorded these accounts carefully, while acknowledging his lack of mystical consciousness. "Yet, there is something in me that responds when I hear others talk about it," he wrote. James called this "ineffability." In *The Varieties of Religious Experience*, he writes, "Although so similar to states of feeling, mystical state seem to those who experience them to also be states of knowledge. They are states of insight into depths of truth unplumbed by the discursive intellect." That is, the experience "defies expression … no adequate report of its content can be given in words."

Victor Frankl wrote of the spiritual unconscious. This was an expanded view of the unconscious. Frankl held that when Freud focused only upon instinct, the id, "he denigrated the unconscious, in that he saw in it only the instinctual and overlooked the spiritual" (27). How do we regard the person and mind, he asked. He pointed to a model from Max Scheler in which the mind appears something like an onion, or a series of concentric circles. Then he insisted that depth psychology, following Freud, "has followed man into the depth of his instincts, but too little into the depth of his spirit" (30).

Frankl, a Jewish psychoanalyst who survived camp incarceration in the Holocaust, is attentive to "man's search for meaning." He suggests that the modern Western world has lost sight of the ontological level of existence. Individual conscience, love, and art suggest the spiritual, he says. "In fact, in his creative work the artist is dependent on sources and resources deriving from the spiritual unconscious" (37) Art may grow in unconscious depths, in an "intentional feeling" rather than mere emotion in "an emotional state." He adds that such "feeling can be much more sensitive than reason can ever be sensible" (39). Frankl continues: "existential analysis has uncovered— within the spiritual unconscious- unconscious religiousness" understood as "a latent relation to transcendence inherent in man" (61). This relation is "profoundly personal" (63).

For George Harrison the experience was no doubt profoundly personal. He was responsible for "bringing Indian musical influences to the attention of the Western world," notes Eliot Huntley (10), and for "the resurgence of

Indian mysticism," as biographer Marc Shapiro points out (xiii). The front-piece to an edition of his autobiography, a passage from the *Bhagavad Gita*, suggests the path of his spiritual journey:

> Among thousands of men perhaps one strives for spiritual attainment; and, among the blessed true seekers, that assiduously try to reach Me. Perhaps one perceives me as I am [*Bhagavad Gita*, Chapter 7, verse 3].

This became George Harrison's goal and intention: the ultimate source of his inspiration and creativity.

Bob Dylan: Tracing the Muse

For centuries artists have employed religious imagery and symbols as a means of expressing and inspiring insight, wonder, or devotion. Many thinkers have tried to understand the states of consciousness, or religious sensibility, that have inspired such artistic creation. Rudolph Otto writes: "According to our scale of values" we will consider the mystic's vision "either a strange fantasy or a glimpse into the eternal relationships of things" (Mysticism East and West, p. 42). What might be said about that enigmatic song-poet Bob Dylan: his songs of social justice, his drug enhanced reveries, and his overt "theology" of 1979–1981?

Bob Dylan picked up an acoustic guitar and traveled to New York's Greenwich Village, into the heart of a folk revival. With a mind filled with folk songs, the blues, and the voice of Woody Guthrie, he fell into a context that nurtured his particular vision and style. The folk revival of the early 1960s intersected with the Civil Rights movement and this called forth Dylan's prophetic voice in songs like "Blowing in the Wind," "The Times They Are A-Changin'," and "Masters of War." One might connect this voice with the call of the Old Testament prophets, like Isaiah and Ezekiel, to their society and find in Bob Dylan's work a direct line to his Jewish origins. Or, one might trace his relationship to dozens of folksingers, bluesmen, and poets, or wonder at his Christian turn in albums like *Slow Train Coming*. In his song "Every Grain of Sand" Bob Dylan refers to a vision of spirit in the tiniest grains of life and nature that animated the perception of the poet William Blake. To follow the phases of Dylan's career is to raise questions about what moved and inspired him. More broadly, it raises questions about material context, individual talent, artistic process, and inspiration.

Critics have long sought Bob Dylan's influences—Woody, first wife Sarah, Joan Baez, Ramblin' Jack Elliott, his Tambourine Man, Rimbaud, Jesus, the Bible, obscure poets and old blues players. They have turned over his biography, his inscrutable interviews, and his wordplay. Dylan, they have shown, has been open to surrealism, blues improvisation, rock, folk, and blues influences, Christianity, and the Jewish justice tradition. Yet, there are only hints in Dylan's memoir *Chronicles* (2004) and interviews of his artistic and spiritual life journey.

Two books on Bob Dylan published in the past decade may be of interest in this respect. In *The Gospel According to Bob Dylan* (2011), Michael J. Gilman observes that "Religious content is ubiquitous in popular music" and recalls how Dylan's *Slow Train Coming* affected him personally in what he calls his "newfound faith" (xvi). The author adds that "matters of faith and opinions about organized religion are as private, idiosyncratic, and deeply felt as our experiences of music" and notes the difficulty in arriving at ways to "articulate the emotional content" of our experiences (Gilman xiv).

Seth Rogovny ventures what he calls a Jewish biography of Bob Dylan in *Bob Dylan: Prophet, Mystic, Poet* (2009). He discusses Dylan's "engagement with Jewish themes" (11) and draws our attention to a poetic mind involved in Biblical texts. Rogovny names the chapters of his book after the books of the Hebrew Bible, from the Torah (or Tanakh, the Books of Moses) through the Books of the Prophets and the Psalms. He cites Dylan songs that are rich in Biblical references. "Highway 61 Revisited," with its reference to Abraham's son, a road that extends from Minnesota to New Orleans, represents Bob Dylan's own journey from Dinkytown in Minneapolis to the Delta blues. "Love Minus Zero/No Limit" draws upon the Book of Daniel. The lyrics of "Forever Young" are enriched by the Bible and Kabbalah. Dylan's "I Pity the Poor Immigrant" are traced by Rogovny to Chapter 26 of Leviticus. If Bob Dylan's song-poetry "comes from an ancient place," as U2's Bono suggests, what is this place? (Rogovny 10) Since songs are not poems and lyrics always live within the context of music and performance, in what sense is Bob Dylan a poet? In what respect might he be *Bob Dylan: Prophet, Mystic, Poet*?

The Creative Mind

The creative mind appears to be one of receptivity. For all of the conscious striving efforts one makes at construction, there are times when the artist seems to receive an idea, an emotion, or a tune. The experience of having a word or phrase simply pop up from the unconscious has often been remarked upon by writers and poets. Lewis Carroll spoke of his *Alice in Wonderland*: "I was walking on a hillside, alone, one bright summer day, when suddenly there came into my head one line of verse, one solitary line: "For the Snark was a Boojum, you see." I know not what it meant then. I know not what it means now. But I wrote it down."

Music creators have awakened from dreams with melodies in their minds, as did Paul McCartney with the tune for "Yesterday." Of his song "Every Breath You Take" Sting remarked: "I woke up in the middle of the night [...] and went straight to the piano and the song came out in ten minutes." Giuseppe Tartini dreamed that he handed the devil his violin. The devil played a stunning sonata of extraordinary beauty. Upon awakening, Tartini set down a trace of what he had heard and called his piece *The Devil's Sonata*. Oscar Hammerstein, who carefully worked at his lyrics, wondered at the origin of some of them: "Jerome Kern played a melody for me; in the middle of it, I got some words—the words were "couldn't you, couldn't I, couldn't we." At the moment I thought of them, I had no idea what you and I couldn't do. It just seemed to sing." In her book *Musicians in Tune* (1992), Jenny Boyd, the psychologist sister of Patti Boyd who married George Harrison and then Eric Clapton, considers the power of archetypes and records musicians' comments about their experiences of creative discovery. In her interview with The Eagles' Don Henley, we read his observation that in some rare moments there is an experience "where you feel like something is being given to you from somewhere else, or its coming through you" (82). Jackson Browne, also interviewed calls it "something like a current" (84) and Graham Nash calls it "a void" or "a suspension" (85). In those interviews, Joni Mitchell recognizes that there are "scary things" in the subconscious mind but that a person can learn much from facing this and can come to greater self-knowledge (86).

What is this phenomenon of creative epiphany that rock music artists appear to be able to sometimes access? Sigmund Freud called dreams "the gateway to the unconscious." William James wrote that the subconscious is like "a river flowing through a man's (or woman's) conscious waking hours." C.G. Jung spoke of moments of "synchronicity" as expressions of a unified cosmos and the collective unconscious.

Mysteries of Art

Creative artists have addressed their experience of wonder, insight, illumination, or epiphany:

George Eliot told J.W. Cross that something not herself seemed to possess her so that she felt that she was "merely the instrument through which this spirit, as it were, was acting" (G.N.M. Tyrell, *The Personality of Man*. London, 1946, 35).

"I have been surprised at the observations made by some of my characters," said William Makepeace Thackeray. "It seems as if an occult power was moving the pen."

Robert Louis Stevenson, in "A Chapter on Dreams," discussed how he arrived at the idea for *The Strange Case of Dr. Jekyll and Mr. Hyde*. Robert

Louis Stevenson said that at night his "brownies" came to him. *The Strange Tale of Dr. Jekyll and Mr. Hyde* came to Stevenson in a dream (*Complete Works*, Vol. 12. New York: Charles Scribner's Sons, 1921).

Richard Wagner commented on a dreary day in Spezia in northern Italy during which he was tired and lay down for a nap. Upon doing this he heard a "rushing noise" like water and an E flat major chord that was followed by an enchanting melody. This became his inspiration for the prelude to *Das Rheingold*.

Poets continue to respect the mysteries of their art. Goethe spoke of poetry as a foreign land: "Who wants to understand the poem/Must go to the land of poetry/Who wishes to understand the poet/Must go to the poet's land." Perhaps more humorously, one poet, the Russian Vladimir Mayakovski, made an appeal to this mystery for practical ends. When discussing his travelling expenses with the tax collector, he said: "Consider my travelling expenses, Poetry—all of it—is a journey into the unknown" (*Selected Poems*, 130).

"Poetry is a search for the inexplicable," said Wallace Stevens. Robert Frost wrote: "A poem begins as a lump in the throat, a sense of wrong, a homesickness, a lovesickness. It finds the thought and the thought finds the words." In his Preface to the *Lyrical Ballads*, William Wordsworth wrote: "Poetry is the spontaneous overflow of powerful feelings; it takes its origins from emotion recollected in tranquility." Poe called it "the rhythmical creation of beauty." William Butler Yeats claimed that in the poet's purification of himself of all "irrelevant analysis" the ritual of one's verse comes to "resemble the great ritual of nature, and become mysterious and inscrutable." The poet, said Yeats, "becomes, as all the great mystics have believed, a vessel of the creative power of God." These poets knew the wonder of poetic discovery. They experienced that "yes!," that "a-ha!" that echoes in a poet when his or her voice says something that rings true, when what one is passionate about lifts into life.

In a sense, each night we are all moviemakers or pictorial artists as our images and signs or symbols emerge within our dreaming minds. Is this dreaming process similar to the waking dream of the artist in the creative process? What is the role of dream, intuition, insight, and perhaps divinity in the experience and process of creation?

The German Romantics were particularly attuned to the ineffable qualities of music. "It is the most romantic of the arts," wrote E.T.A. Hoffman, "for its sole subject is the infinite" (Strunk, Source Readings, 75). "How can one say Mozart has composed Don Juan?" Goethe once said. "Composition! As if it were a piece of cake or biscuit…. It is a spiritual creation, in which the details, as well as the whole, are pervaded by one spirit, and by the breath of one life" (June 20, 1831, John Oxenford, 553, *Conversations of Goethe with Eckermann and Soret*. London: G. Bell and Sons, 1874).

It has sometimes been suggested that rock's attitude of rebellion and its emphasis on passionate emotion and authenticity reflects a relationship with Romanticism. The English Romantic poets were attentive to emotion, awe, and the sublime. John Keats wrote of "negative capability": the capacity of the poet to dwell in ambiguity and uncertainty until an idea took shape. Samuel Taylor Coleridge fell into an opium induced sleep while reading tales of China and awoke to write: "In Xanadu did Kublai Kahn a stately pleasure dome decree," a poem-dream he then had to work to recall after being interrupted by a messenger, the man from Porlock. William Blake (1757–1827) claimed that he saw angels and expressed his visions in iconography, as well as in poetry. ("You have the same faculty as I," William Blake told his friends, "only you do not trust or cultivate it. You can see what I do, if you choose.") Percy Bysshe Shelley's companion Mary Godwin imagined a creation from which our moviemakers have made a monster. Mary Godwin Shelley, on those rainy days at the Villa Diodati in 1816, listened to the horror tales of Percy Bysshe Shelley, Lord Byron, and John Polidori's vampire story. The air was charged by a reading of Coleridge's "Christabel" and discussions on galvanism. For three days Mary Shelley struggled for a story and none would come. Then as she rested by the fire she rose in a trance: there had come to her the frightening birth-myth of *Frankenstein.*

Experiences like this suggest that the poem, the story, the song is somehow waiting beneath the surface and the artist has to open his or her skill to working it out. "If the soil is ready," said Tchaikovsky, "that is to say, if the disposition for work is there- it takes root with extraordinary force and rapidity, shoots up through the earth, leaves, and finally blossoms. I cannot define the creative process in any other way."

Tchaikovsky observed the need for the artist to live in ordinary realities, free from the demands of inspiration. "If that condition of mind and soul we call inspiration lasted long without intermission no artist could survive it," he said (Tchaikovsky Journals).

Mysteries of Mind

For centuries artists have employed religious imagery and symbols as a means of expressing and inspiring insight, wonder, or devotion. Many thinkers have tried to understand the states of consciousness, or religious sensibility, that has inspired such artistic creation. Rudolph Otto writes: "According to our scale of values" we will consider the mystic's vision "either a strange fantasy or a glimpse into the eternal relationships of things" (Mysticism East and West, p. 42). What are we to make of the testimonies of Sufis, or swamis, the interior castle of St. Theresa of Avila, or the dark night of the soul of St. John of the Cross? What are the boundaries of the human mind? The ancient Greeks once held that our universe was filled with a conscious force. They used words like *nous* (mind) and *apeiron* (unlimited, boundless, infinite) to describe this. In the twentieth century, the Jesuit paleontologist Teilhard de Chardin interpreted what he viewed as the consciousness within life, what he called the noosphere, as ever enriching the divine milieu. What are we to make of the mysteries of sudden inspiration? What can be said about Ramanujan's untrained mathematical equations, or the insight of August Kekule von Stadonitz, who stared into a fireplace and visualized carbon rings, or the testimony of dozens of creative artists concerning their "a-ha" moments of inspiration? Creativity researcher Frank Barron once wrote: "The creative individual not only respects the irrational in himself, but courts the most promising source of novelty in his own thought" (ctd. by Willis Harman and Harold Rheingold in *Higher Creativity*).

When the Renaissance aesthete Marsilio Ficino discussed the divine inspiration of poets, the prevailing belief was that the fantastic constructions of the poets came from some enigmatic source beyond them. In this neo-Platonic view, human consciousness taps into a greater sphere of consciousness, mind, or world-soul. Ficino recognized that inspiration is something which requires a poet's receptivity and the ability to mediate inspiration. The ideas which come to the poet, Ficino asserted, have a higher origin (*De Furore Divino passim*, Problemata XXX, 954 a). In *The Anatomy of Melancholy* (1621), Robert Burton wrote of melancholy individuals as "of a deep reach, excellent apprehension, judicious, wise, and witty" (Oxford Mind 468).

When the human psyche, in its complexity, encounters music and poetry the experience may generate questions for religion and for science. (Alfred Russel Wallace, one of the proponents of evolutionary theory, wondered why we need music and why we possess the facility of language. Unable to answer this from an evolutionary perspective, he eventually turned toward spiritualism.) Since we are each aware of our own consciousness, can we suggest the idea of a consciousness not limited to this world of objects? Might one's own experience of subjectivity suggest a broader intelligent consciousness? What is the source of our drive to know, our spirit of inquiry, and our desire for intelligibility? This is not limited to instrumental reason and calculating but includes intuition, feeling, a freedom, a restless yearning. One may feel love or sublimity or feel awe, humility, and appreciation. When an artist attempts to speak of this in language he or she is gesturing toward a sense of presence or the ineffable. There is a non-verbal, non-propositional truth that is not merely emotive. There is, as theologian Bernard Lonergan observed in *Insight*, an "unrestricted drive to know" (4, 9, 74). Or, to follow the thought of the Danish philosopher Søren Kierkegaard, this is not a belief by conditioning or convention, or complacent acquiescence. Rather, this is a radical leap of faith to what may break in upon consciousness like sunshine through clouds.

Our perspective may be formed by what we think of the capacities and reach of the human mind. In *The Critique of Pure Reason*, the philosopher Immanuel Kant held that the human mind has limits. For Kant, what can be thought and named is the phenomenal (in distinction from what he called the noumenal): space, time, quantity, causality. The mystic, in contrast, suggests that consciousness extends beyond these limits and that one's consciousness has access to the presence of the divine, or can be available to the universal force. The mystic believes that that this force, sometimes described as light or as presence, can flow through one's spirit into one's awareness. Such a view rests uneasily in a Cartesian-Newtonian view of the world. However, Romanticism asserted that feeling is surely as important as reason. In the view of Romantic poets and artists, intense emotion and intuition can supersede rationalism and empiricism. Later, in response to the positivism and materialism of his age, the philosopher Henri Bergson asserted that knowledge involves, on the one hand, reason and empiricism, and creative intuition on the other (Bergson, *The Two Sources of Morality and Religion*). Psychologist William James, who studied the phenomenon of religious experience from the standpoint of empirical observation, wrote: "Although so similar to states of feeling, mystical states seem to those who experience them to also be states of knowledge. They are states of insight into depths of truth unplumbed by the discursive intellect." One need not associate artistic inspiration with religious experience—which may be of a different order. However, many artists have been aware of moments of what we might call 'inspiration.' The notion of the Muse has ancient origins: the nine Muses of Greek mythology were associated with the various arts. The lives of the saints and hagiography will show that the saints have demonstrated unique subjectivity. The convergence of mysticism and poetry is particularly interesting in the Canticle of St. Francis of Assisi, or the poetry of the Spanish mystic St. John of the Cross, or in the works of the Mideast poet Rumi.

The artist may work like a man possessed. Jack Kerouac worked continuously for days when writing *On the Road*. Eugene O'Neill noted that his wife brought him dinners which were left uneaten as he worked feverishly on his play *Long Day's Journey into Night*. Joseph Conrad likened his work with the Biblical Jacob's spiritual struggle: "All I know is that for twenty months, neglecting the common joys of life that fall to the lot of the humblest of this earth, I had, like the prophet of old, wrestled with the Lord for my creation."

Other writers affirm the careful conscious attention and discipline which goes into the creation of a literary work. Gustav Flaubert noted: "We do not live in inspiration. Pegasus walks more often than he gallops." George Sand wrote of Frederic Chopin: "Following his inspiration, coming to his piano suddenly, singing in his head during a walk, [Chopin] began the most heart-rending labor I ever saw. It was a series of efforts and irresolutions, of frettings to seize again certain details of the theme he had heard. He would shut himself up in his room for whole days, weeping, walking, breaking his pens, repeating and altering a bar a hundred times."

This type of sheer effort reminds us that all creation is a labor as well as a hope. Inspiration is fickle. It is a grace. Tchaikovsky observed that unless we are prepared "to meet it halfway we easily become indolent and apathetic." He wrote: "This guest (inspiration) does not always respond to the first invitation. We must always work[....] We must be patient and believe that inspiration will come to those who can master their disinclinations" (Letter of February 17, 1878, Vernon).

For the artist, the work of creation is as inevitable as breathing. The psychologist Abraham Maslow, who was so interested in peak experiences, put it this way: "A musician must make music, an artist must paint, a poet must write if he is to be ultimately at peace with himself. What a man must be, he must be."

The Perspective of Science

In any study of creativity we must also listen to the perspectives of cognitive science and evolutionary biology. Neuroscientist-trumpeter, Bill Benzon, in his book *Beethoven's Anvil*, writes of "feeling subcortical impulses go into action." As a jazz musician, Benzon knows the wonder of these moments. As a scientist, he seeks an empirical explanation. He observes that aminergic processes are at a low level, below that of ordinary waking consciousness but input-output gating is different from that of the dreamer. The right cortical hemisphere of the brain tends to play more of a role in emotion than the left, mediating intonation patterns, conveying emotional shading, suggesting musical form regulated in the right brain, following the tonal flow of a piece.

Cognitive neuroscience holds that our information processing relies upon our internal representations as we respond to stimuli. Scientists study the mental processing that undergirds performance. The computer is a metaphor for this. In considering how our brains and bodies process information, scientists refer to the molecular and cellular basis of cognition and how neuronal signaling and synaptic transmission occurs.

Neuroscience explores "feeling" with respect to mind-body: neurons, hormones, neurotransmitters. The nervous system of the artist can be explored at "different levels of organization." Antonio Damasio points out: "If anything in our existence can be revelatory of our simultaneous smallness and greatness, feelings are" (Damasio, *Looking for Spinoza*, 7). Daniel Dennett recognizes that human beings are quite good at imitation (or what are called replicator memes). This may include songs, stories, habits, and skills.

A cognitive psychologist like Edward De Bono would seek to demystify creative thought by describing lateral thinking. Studies of the brain have shown hemispheric specialization, or laterality. The cerebral cortices are connected by the corpus callosum. Early studies by Broca and Wernicke linked the left hemisphere of the brain with the language function. Early on, scientists began to hypothesize that the left hemisphere was verbal and analytical and the right was spatial and holistic. The overall tendency of the left hemisphere was to decipher language into its component parts, whereas the style of the right hemisphere was more often inclined toward flow and patterns. De Bono describes lateral thinking as "timeless, diffuse, holistic, visuo-spatial, intuitive, and simultaneous" whereas the left hemisphere is "sequential, rational, propositional, and time oriented" (Maps 110–111). Even given these findings from split brain studies, scientists point out that the brain is interactive and left and right work together.

Even with the many scientific inquiries into brain functioning, into neurology, or from the standpoint of evolutionary biology, many people continue to approach the notion of inspiration as if there is some sort of mysterious, divine communication involved in the "a-ha" experience.

Rock Music and Religion

The work of Van Morrison, George Harrison, and Bob Dylan are points in a kaleidoscope of possibilities from which we might we think of religion as both a very personal and individual journey and as a collective quest for meaning. An anthropologist would understand the sacred realm as one entered by a ritual process, a collective state of social consciousness. A theologian would call this a soul's encounter with the divine. From the perspective of sociology, religion may be understood from a functionalist perspective as a socio-cultural system that binds people (*religare*) in a set of social identifications, values, and beliefs. This provides people with communal structures for daily life, a belief system they might adhere to, doctrines they may subscribe to. Sociology, from Emile Durkheim and Max Weber, has shown a fascination with religious forms.

A sociologist might point out that performing artists are often inspired by their audiences, which create energy, or push them toward a new level of accomplishment. There is the synchrony of certain audiences which Durkheim calls by the name of "collective consciousness": a fascinating linking of energy. The scholar of comparative religion Mircea Eilade brings our attention to the notion of ritual, mythic structures, and hierophanies. He says that theophany, or encounter with the holy, offers an organizational principle for life around which personal identity and a community's self-understanding may be structured. Psychologist Abraham Maslow urges us to think about peak experiences and a host of transpersonal psychologists and gurus have us thinking about expanded consciousness. Music critics like Robert Walser and Deena Weinstein have brought us accounts of religious themes in the heavy metal of the 1970s and 1980s and Weinstein has described the metal concert as parallel with celebrations, festivals, ceremonies that characterize religions. Along these lines, we might see the musician-performer in a shamanic, or priest-like role. There is also a sense that young adults, in a media saturated environment, are working out their spirituality through popular culture. Call it a kind of displacement, or call it networking or hooking up, if you want.

Religious Emotion

Van Morrison and Bob Dylan have repeatedly drawn inspiration from gospel music and the blues. The blues taps into emotion. B.B. King once commented that there was "a thin line" between the blues and gospel (Boyd 121). That may, in part, be because religion tends to be related to human emotional life. Of course, believers will insist that none of this is 'merely emotional.' Musicians "feel" their music and they are known to imitate other artists. Working together they may enter synchrony with each other. In an interview with Jenny Boyd, Ringo Starr commented: "It's magic actually. It's pure magic. Everyone who is playing at that time knows where everybody's going. We all feel like one. Where you go, everyone feels that's where we should go" (Boyd, 176).

The dream, the waking dream, or trancelike concentration in relation to art has been noted throughout the ages. Dreams, oracles, prophecies appear in the religious writings of all cultures. Mohammad (Peace Be Upon Him) had a dream vision. Biblically, dreams were frequently viewed as prophetic. The second part of the *Book of Daniel* consists of four units of dreams and visions in which future world events are revealed to Daniel. These dreams have an apocalyptic character to them. Poetry entertains connections with the prophetic voices of Ezechial, Isaiah, Jeremiah, Hosea, and Daniel of the Hebrew Bible. In the vatic tradition of poetry we might place poets of prophetic voice like Blake or like Whitman. Shelley was perhaps self-serving when he called poets "the unacknowledged legislators of the world," but his statement suggests the prophetic dimensions of art.

The creative work of Van Morrison and George Harrison each reveal a sensibility that has been open to a profoundly personal journey. When Van Morrison sings "Hymns to the Silence," or George Harrison sings "My Sweet Lord," we may ask what these expressions about God mean and what they may say to each of us. How does the poet-lyricist name the whirlwind? Surely, these artists express in poetic-musical gestures a sensibility and a longing that is otherwise incommunicable. These musicians do not believe because philosophers and theologians have told them that it is reasonable to do so. For Van Morrison, George Harrison, Bob Dylan, or others of our "saints and sinners" the argument from experience is more vivid and vital.

So, where are we now? In Europe, the rationalism of the Enlightenment placed value in common sense but tended to overlook subjectivity. The religious tradition of Augustine or Francis of Assisi and Bonaventure embraced it. In the Twenty-First Century we continue to recognize that no person is an object. A person seeks meaning, awareness, self-actualization, and desires to be loved, to understand, to welcome the good, and may embrace humanism, or a spiritual path that says yes to creativity, to love, to wonder. Kierkegaard and Nietzsche saw a death of God in their society's complacency. Artists like Van Morrison, or George Harrison, stand before the silence, listen for the song, and try to reanimate it.

WORKS CITED

Barron, Frank. *Creativity and Personal Freedom*. New York: D. Van Nostrand, 1968; Princeton: Princeton University Press, 1968.

Benzon, William. *Beethoven's Anvil: Music in Mind and Culture*. New York: Basic, 2002.

Boyd, Jenny, and Holly George-Warren, *Musicians in Tune*. New York: Fireside, Simon & Schuster, 1992.

Bucke, R.M. *Cosmic Consciousness*. 1901. New York: Penguin, 1991.

Burwick, Frederick. *Cultural Interactions in the Romantic Age*. Ed. Gregory Maertz. Albany: State University of New York Press, 1996.

Campbell, Joseph, with Bill Moyers. *The Power of Myth*. New York: Doubleday, 1988.

Collis, John. *Van Morrison: Inarticulate Speech of the Heart*. London: Da Capo; Boston: Little, Brown, 2010.

Conrad, Joseph. *A Personal Record*. London, 1912.

De Bono, Edward. *Lateral Thinking: Creativity Step by Step*. New York: Harper and Row, 1970.

Ducioux, Walter. "Das Rheingold," *San Francisco Opera Magazine* (October 1972).

Dylan, Bob. *Chronicles*, Vol. 1. New York: Simon & Schuster, 2004.

_____. *Slow Train Coming*. Columbia Records, 1979.

_____. *Writings and Drawings*. New York: Random House, 1973.

Eliade, Mircea. *The Sacred and Profane*. New York: Harper and Row, 1957.

Eliot. T.S. "Dry Salvages" *The Complete Poetry and Plays of T.S. Eliot*. New York: Harcourt Brace, 1971.

Ficino, Marsilio. *De furore dinivo passim*. (*The Divine Fury*). Problemato XXX. *Marsilio Ficino: Collected Writings*, ed. Angela Voss. Berkeley: University of California Press, 2006.

Frankl, Victor. *Psychotherapy and Existentialism: Selected Papers on Logotherapy*. New York: Washington Square Press, 1967. Rpt. New York: Touchstone, 1968.

_____. *The Unconscious God* (1946). New York: Simon & Schuster, 1975.

Freud, Sigmund. *The Future of an Illusion*. Trans. James Strachey. New York: W.W. Norton.

Friskics-Warren, Bill. *I'll Take You There: Pop Music and the Urge for Transcendence*. London: A&C Black, 2006.

Gardner, Howard. *Creating Minds: An Anatomy of Creativity Seen Through the Lives of Freud, Einstein, Picasso, Stravinsky, Eliot, Graham, and Gandhi*. New York: Basic, 1993.

Gates, David. "Dylan Revisited." *Newsweek* (October 5, 1997).

Gerson, Ben. "George Harrison: All Things Must Pass," *Rolling Stone* (January 21, 1971).

Ghiselin, Brewster. *The Creative Process* (1952). Berkeley: University of California Press, 1985.

Gilman, Michael J. *The Gospel According to Bob Dylan*. Louisville: Westminster John Knox Press, 2011.

Greene, Joshua M. *Here Comes the Sun: The Spiritual and Musical Journey of George Harrison*. Wiley, 2010.

Gregory, Richard L., ed. *The Oxford Companion to the Mind*. New York and Oxford: Oxford University Press, 2004.

Hampden-Turner, Charles. *Maps of the Mind*. New York: Macmillan, 1981.

Harding, Rosamond E.M. *Anatomy of Inspiration*. New York: Frank Cass, 2012.

Harman, Willis, and Howard Rheingold. *Higher Creativity: Liberating the Unconscious for Breakthrough Insights*. New York: Tarcher, 1984.

Harrison, George. *All Things Must Pass*. 1970.

_____. *The Concert for Bangladesh*. 1971.

_____. *I Me Mine*. San Francisco: Chronicle, 1980.

_____. *Living in the Material World*. 1973.

Harrison, Olivia, and Mark Holborn. *George Harrison: Living in the Material World*. New York: Abrams, 2011.

Hillman, James. *The Soul's Code*. New York: Random House, 1997.

Huntley, Eliot J. *Mystical One: George Harrison After the Breakup of the Beatles*. Tonawanda: Guernica, 2004.

Inglis, Ian. *The Words and Music of George Harrison*. Santa Barbara: Praeger, 2010.

James, William. *Varieties of Religious Experience*. London: Longmans Green, 1902. Rpt. New York: Collier, Macmillan, 1961.

Jaynes, Julian. *The Origins of Consciousness in the Breakdown of the Bicameral Mind*. Boston: Houghton Mifflin, 1976.

Jung, C.G. *Collected Works*. Bollingen. Princeton: Princeton University Press, 1956–1970.

_____. *Memories, Dreams, Reflections*. ed. Anelia Jaffe. Trans. Richard and Clara Winston. New York: Vintage, 1989.

_____. *The Portable Jung*. Ed. Joseph Campbell. New York: Viking, 1976.

Kant, Immanuel. *The Critique of Pure Reason* (1781). Indianapolis: Hackett, 1996.

Laing, R.D. *The Divided Self*. New York: Penguin, 1965.

Lane, J. *Life and Letters of Peter Ilyich Tchaikovsky*. London, 1906, 274–312.

Marcus, Greil. *When That Rough God Goes Riding*. New York: Public Affairs, 2011.

Maslow, Abraham. *Religions, Values, and Peak Experiences*. New York: Viking Penguin, 1987.

May, Rollo. *The Courage to Create*. New York: Bantam, 1985.

Mayakovsky, Vladimir. *Selected Poems*. Trans. James McGavran III. Evanston: Northwestern University Press, 2013.

Mills, Peter. *Hymns to the Silence: Inside the Words and Music of Van Morrison*. New York: Continuum/Bloomsbury, 2010.

Morrison, Van (George Ivan). *Astral Weeks*. Warner, 1968.

Ornstein, Robert. *The Psychology of Consciousness*. San Francisco: W.H. Freeman, and Harmondsworth: Penguin/Pelican, 1975.

Otto, Rudolph. *The Idea of the Holy*. (1917) Oxford and New York: Oxford University Press, 1968.

Oxenford, John. *Conversations of Goethe with Eckermann and Soret*. (Goethe, June 20, 1831.) London: G. Bell and Sons, 1874.

Pinker, Steven. *How the Mind Works*. Scientific American Modern Classics. New York: W.W. Norton, 1997.

Poe, Edgar Allan. "The Poetic Principle," 1850.

Ricks, Christopher. *Dylan's Visions of Sin*. New York: Ecco, 2004.

Rogovny, Seth. *Bob Dylan: Prophet, Mystic, Poet.* New York: Scribner's, 2009.

Shapiro, Marc. *Behind Sad Eyes: The Life of George Harrison.* New York: St. Martin's Griffin, 2003.

Stevens, Wallace. "Aphorisms," Sur Plusieres Beaux Sujects. *Opus Posthumous: Poems, Plays, Prose.* Ed. Milton J. Bates. New York: Vintage, Random House, 1989.

Stevenson, Robert Louis. "A Chapter on Dreams," *The Collected Works of Robert Louis Stevenson.* Vol. 12. New York: Charles Scribner's Sons, 1921.

Tart, Charles T. "Transpersonal Realities or Neurophysiological Illusions? Toward an Empirically Testable Dualism." In *The Metaphors of Consciousness.* Ed. Ronald S. Valle and Rolf von Eckartsberg. New York and London: Plenum, 1981.

Tarver, John Charles. *Gustave Flaubert as Seen in His Works and Correspondence.* London: Constable, 1895.

Tchaikovsky, Peter Ilyich. Letter of February 17, 1878, from Vernon. See *Higher Creativity*, ed. Willis Harman, 1970.

Teilhard de Chardin, Pierre. *The Divine Milieu.* New York: Harper, 2004.

Tillery, Gary. *Working Class Mystic: A Spiritual Biography of George Harrison.* Wheaton, IL: Quest, 2011.

Tyrell, G.N.M. *The Personality of Man.* London, 1946.

Underhill, Evelyn. *Mysticism.* London: Methuen, 1911.

Valle, Ronald S., and Rolf von Eckartsberg. *The Metaphors of Consciousness.* New York and London: Plenum, 1981.

Von Eckartsberg, Elsa. "God Consciousness and the Poetry of Madness." In *The Metaphors of Consciousness*, ed. Ronald S. Valle and Rolf von Eckartsberg. New York and London: Plenum, 1981.

Wallas, Graham. *The Art of Thought.* New York: Harcourt Brace, 1926.

Weinstein, Deena. *Heavy Metal: The Music and Its Culture.* New York: Da Capo, 2000.

Appendix: Discography of Works Discussed (by artist)

Bad Religion

"Voice of God Is Government" (*How Could Hell Be Any Worse?*, Epitaph, 1982)

The Beatles

"Tomorrow Never Knows" (*Revolver*, Parlophone, 1966)
"Within You, Without You" (*Sgt. Pepper's Lonely Hearts Club Band*, Parlophone, 1967)
"The Inner Light" (single, Parlophone, 1968)
"While My Guitar Gently Weeps" (*The Beatles*, Apple, 1968)
"Here Comes the Sun" (*Abbey Road*, Apple, 1969)
"I Me Mine" (*Let It Be*, Apple, 1970)

Black Sabbath

Black Sabbath (Vertigo, 1970)
Paranoid (Vertigo/Warner Bros., 1970)
Master of Reality (Vertigo, 1971)
Vol. 4 (Vertigo, 1972)
13 (Vertigo/Universal, 2013)

The Crucified

Take Up Your Cross (cassette, 1986)
Nailed (cassette, 1987)
The Crucified (Narrowpath, 1989)

Bob Dylan

"Blowin' in the Wind," "Masters of War" (*The Freewheelin' Bob Dylan*, Columbia, 1963)
"The Times They Are a-Changin'" (*The Times They Are a-Changin'*, Columbia, 1964)
"Love Minus Zero/No Limit" (*Bringing It All Back Home*, Columbia, 1965)
"Highway 61 Revisited" (*Highway 61 Revisited*, Columbia, 1965)
"I Pity the Poor Immigrant" (*John Wesley Harding*, Columbia, 1967)
"Forever Young" (*Planet Waves*, Asylum, 1974)
Slow Train Coming (Columbia, 1979)

The Feederz

"Jesus Entering from the Rear" (*Let Them Eat Jellybeans: 17 Extracts from America's Dark Side*, Alternative Tentacles, 1981)

Freedom Call

Eternity (Steamhammer, 2002)
Master of Light (Steamhammer, 2016)

Heart Attack

God Is Dead (EP, Damaged Goods, 1981)

The Jimi Hendrix Experience

"Are You Experienced?" (*Are You Experienced*, Track, 1967)

Manowar

Into Glory Ride (Megaforce, 1983)
Sign of the Hammer (Megaforce, 1984)
Fighting the World (Atco, 1987)
Louder Than Hell (Geffen, 1996)

Matisyahu

Shake Off the Dust...Arise (JDub, 2004)
Live at Stubb's (JDub, 2005)
Youth (JDub/Epic, 2006)
Shattered (EP, Epic, 2008)
Light (JDub/Epic, 2009)
Live at Stubb's, Vol. 2 (Fallen Sparks, 2011)

Spark Seeker (Fallen Sparks, 2012)
Akeda (Akeda/Elm City, 2014)

Van Morrison

Astral Weeks (Warner Bros., 1968)
St. Dominic's Preview (Warner Bros., 1972)
Beautiful Vision (Mercury/Warner Bros., 1982)
A Sense of Wonder (Mercury, 1985)
No Guru, No Method, No Teacher (Mercury, 1986)
Enlightenment (Polydor, 1990)
Hymns to the Silence (Polydor, 1991)
The Philosopher's Stone (Polydor, 1998)

Nine Inch Nails

"Terrible Lie" (*Pretty Hate Machine*, TVT, 1989)
"Hurt" (*The Downward Spiral*, Nothing/TVT/Interscope, 1994)
"The Big Come Down," "The Day the World Went Away," "Underneath It
   All" (*The Fragile*, Nothing/Interscope, 1999)
"Suck" (*All That Could Have Been*, Nothing, 2002)
"Every Day Is Exactly the Same," "Getting Smaller," "The Hand That
   Feeds," "Only," "Right Where It Belongs" (*With Teeth*, Nothing/
   Interscope, 2005)
"In This Twilight," "My Violent Heart" (*Year Zero*, Interscope, 2007)
"All Time Low," "In Two," "Various Methods of Escape" (*Hesitation Marks*,
   Columbia, 2013)

Officer Negative

Dead to the World (Screaming Giant, 1997)

One Bad Pig

Smash (Pure Metal, 1989)

Powerwolf

Lupus Dei (Metal Blade, 2007)
Bible of the Beast (Metal Blade, 2009)
Blood of the Saints (Metal Blade, 2011)
Preachers of the Night (Napalm, 2013)
Blessed & Possessed (Napalm, 2015)

The Sex Pistols

"God Save the Queen," "Anarchy in the UK" (*Never Mind the Bollocks, Here's the Sex Pistols*, Virgin, 1977)

Duncan Sheik

Duncan Sheik (Atlantic, 1996)
Humming (Atlantic, 1998)
Phantom Moon (Nonesuch, 2001)
Spring Awakening (Universal, 2006)
Whisper House (RCA Victor, 2009)
Legerdemain (Sony, 2015)
American Psycho (Original London Cast Recording) (Concord, 2016)

Patti Smith

"Gloria" (*Horses*, Arista, 1975)

Pete Townshend

Who Came First (Track/Polydor, 1972)
"(Let My Love) Open the Door" (*Empty Glass*, Atco, 1980)

Undercover

God Rules (A&S, 1983)

The Who

The Who Sell Out (Track, 1967)
Tommy (Decca, 1969)
"The Seeker" (single, Track, 1970)
Live at Leeds (Decca/MCA, 1970)
Who's Next (Track/Decca, 1971)
Who Are You (Polydor/MCA, 1978)

About the Contributors

Erin E. **Bauer** is an assistant professor of musicology at the University of Wisconsin-Whitewater. She holds a Ph.D. in musicology from Claremont Graduate University and was formerly director of instrumental music at Laramie County Community College in Cheyenne, Wyoming.

Sabatino **DiBernardo** is an associate lecturer in religion, philosophy, and humanities in the Philosophy Department at the University of Central Florida. He holds a Ph.D. in religion and is the director of the Religion and Cultural Studies Program, which emphasizes critical and cultural theory in relation to religion and popular culture.

Alex **DiBlasi** is a writer and social worker based in Oregon. He has two BAs from Indiana University, in cultural studies and in rock history. He earned his master's in musicology from Brooklyn College and is an ordained interfaith minister.

Karen **Fournier** holds a Ph.D. in music theory from the University of Western Ontario and teaches in the School of Music, Theater and Dance at the University of Michigan. She is the author of *The Words and Music of Alanis Morrisette* and *Punk and Disorderly*.

Candace Ursala **Grissom** has a Ph.D. from Middle Tennessee State University and a masters' degree in film and music from Sewanee University of the South. She holds a J.D. from the Cumberland School of Law in Alabama and has worked as an attorney for EMI Music Publishing and as an attorney in private practice.

Gavin F. **Hurley** has a Ph.D. from the University of Rhode Island and teaches there. His academic background is in philosophy and theology and his specialization is rhetoric. He studies rhetorical transcendence and mystical speech and has written essays on rethinking Anselm's Ontology, Kierkegaard's Rhetoric, and other topics.

Robert **McParland**, Ph.D., is a professor in the Department of English at Felician University in New Jersey. He is a professional songwriter member of the American Society of Composers, Authors, and Publishers and a performing musician.

Erika M. Nelson **Mukherjee** holds a Ph.D. in German studies from the University of Texas in Austin and she teaches at Union College in Schenectady. She is the author of *Reading Rilke's Orphic Identity* and has published on comparative literature, poetics, myth, and media. She speaks and reads Spanish and French and has near native fluency in German.

Morgan **Shipley** holds a Ph.D. in religious studies and teaches in the Department of Religious Studies at Michigan State, where he is also the director of Philosophy in American Studies. With Michael Blouin, he is the author of *The Silence of Fallout* and articles on communal utopianism and religious community and American culture.

James E. **Willis** III holds a Ph.D. in comparative religion from King's College, London, with a focus on Buddhist Sunyata and Christian apophaticism. He teaches at Indiana University, after several years at Purdue University. His articles focus upon digital humanities, ethics, and technologies, while his book reviews have reflected upon topics in religion and philosophy.

Index